SPIDER-MAN SPIDER-GWEN

SITTING IN A TREE

SPIDER-MAN #12-14

BRIAN MICHAEL BENDIS
WRITER

SARA PICHELLI
ARTIST

GAETANO CARLUCCI
INKING ASSIST, #12-13

JUSTIN PONSOR
COLOR ARTIST

VC'S CORY PETIT
LETTERER

SARA PICHELLI & JASON KEITH
COVER ART

SPIDER-GWEN #16-18

JASON LATOUR
WRITER

ROBBI RODRIGUEZ
ARTIST

RICO RENZI
COLOR ARTIST

VC'S CLAYTON COWLES
WITH TRAVIS LANHAM (#16)
LETTERERS

ROBBI RODRIGUEZ
COVER ART

ALLISON STOCK
ASSISTANT EDITOR

DEVIN LEWIS
ASSOCIATE EDITOR

NICK LOWE
EDITOR

SPIDER-MAN CREATED BY STAN LEE & STEVE DITKO

COLLECTION EDITOR JENNIFER GRÜNWALD
ASSISTANT EDITOR CAITLIN O'CONNELL
ASSOCIATE MANAGING EDITOR KATERI WOODY
EDITOR, SPECIAL PROJECTS MARK D. BEAZLEY
VP PRODUCTION & SPECIAL PROJECTS JEFF YOUNGQUIST
SVP PRINT, SALES & MARKETING DAVID GABRIEL

EDITOR IN CHIEF AXEL ALONSO
CHIEF CREATIVE OFFICER JOE QUESADA
PRESIDENT DAN BUCKLEY
EXECUTIVE PRODUCER ALAN FINE

SPIDER-MAN/SPIDER-GWEN: SITTING IN A TREE. Contains material originally published in magazine form as SPIDER-MAN #12-14 and SPIDER-GWEN #16-18. First printing 2017. ISBN# 978-1-302-90762-4. Published by MARVEL WORLDWIDE, INC., a subsidiary of MARVEL ENTERTAINMENT, LLC. OFFICE OF PUBLICATION: 135 West 50th Street, New York, NY 10020. **Printed in Canada.** DAN BUCKLEY, President, Marvel Entertainment; JOE QUESADA, Chief Creative Officer; TOM BREVOORT, SVP of Publishing; DAVID BOGART, SVP of Business Affairs & Operations, Publishing & Partnership; C.B. CEBULSKI, VP of Brand Management & Development, Asia; DAVID GABRIEL, SVP of Sales & Marketing, Publishing; JEFF YOUNGQUIST, VP of Production & Special Projects; DAN CARR, Executive Director of Publishing Technology; ALEX MORALES, Director of Publishing Operations; SUSAN CRESPI, Production Manager; STAN LEE, Chairman Emeritus. For information regarding advertising in Marvel Comics or on Marvel.com, please contact Vit DeBellis, Integrated Sales Manager, at vdebellis@marvel.com. For Marvel subscription inquiries, please call 888-511-5480. **Manufactured between 3/24/2017 and 4/25/2017 by SOLISCO PRINTERS, SCOTT, QC, CANADA.**

10 9 8 7 6 5 4 3 2 1

PREVIOUSLY

High-schooler Miles Morales was bitten by a stolen, genetically altered spider that granted him incredible arachnid-like powers. This is a secret he has shared only with his best friend Ganke and his father, Jefferson.

Concerned for his son's well-being, Jefferson approached his old employers at the intelligence agency S.H.I.E.L.D., offering to return to active duty in exchange for protection for his son. This is a secret he has shared with no one.

And now, following his training for a dangerous mission, Jefferson has disappeared.

Meanwhile, in an alternate universe, teenager Gwen Stacy was bitten by a mutated spider. The bite transformed her, granting her amazing powers. However, she recently lost her powers and now relies on radioactive isotopes — "power-ups" — to continue fighting crime as Spider-Woman.

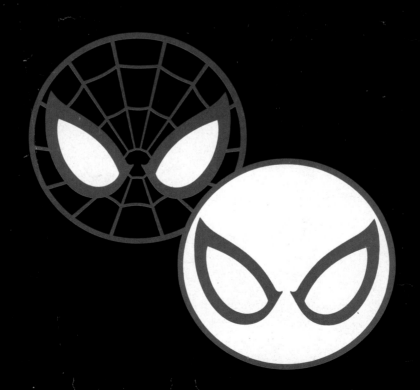

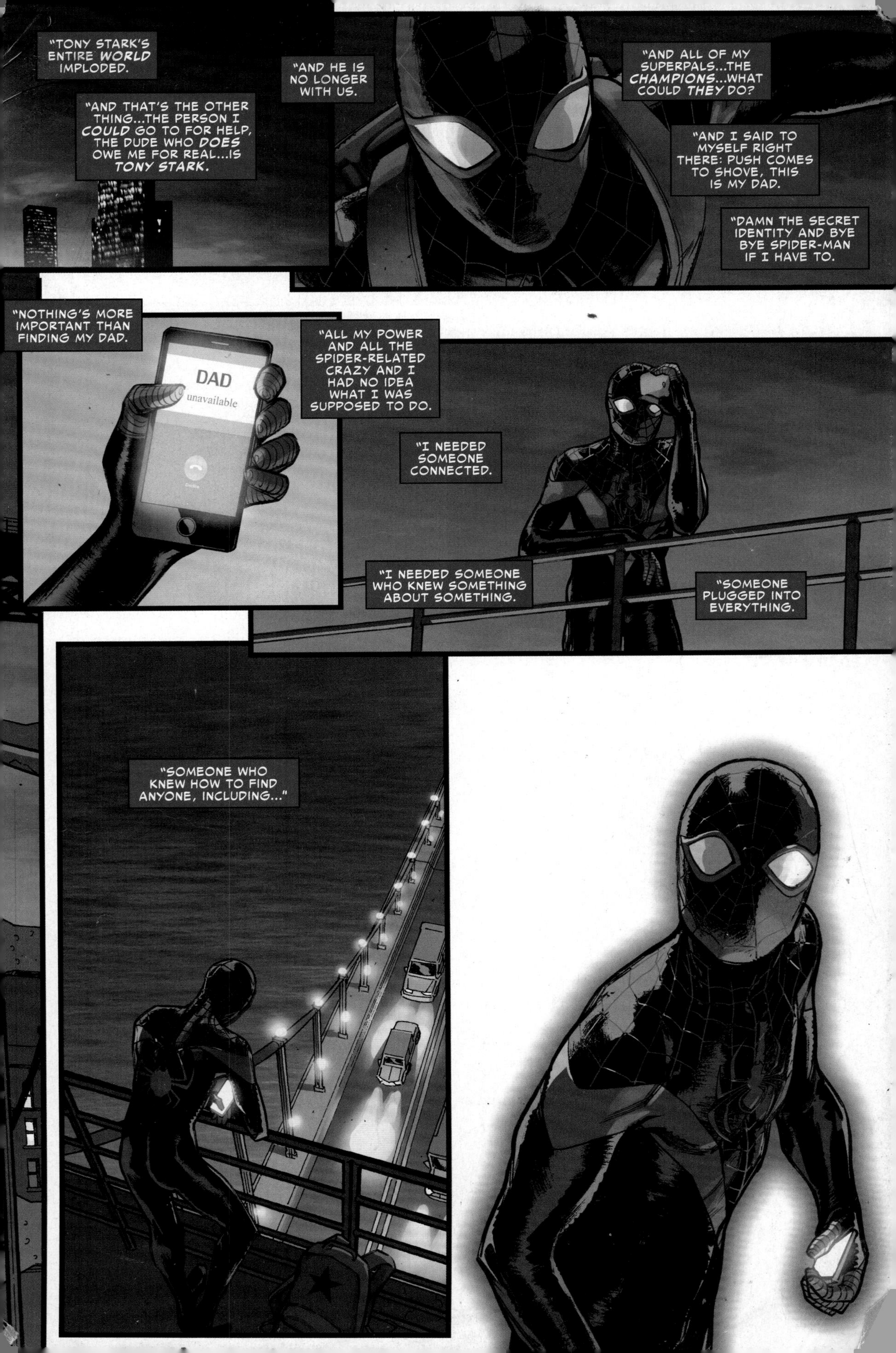
"TONY STARK'S ENTIRE *WORLD* IMPLODED.
"AND THAT'S THE OTHER THING...THE PERSON I *COULD* GO TO FOR HELP, THE DUDE WHO *DOES* OWE ME FOR REAL...IS *TONY STARK.*
"AND HE IS NO LONGER WITH US.
"AND ALL OF MY SUPERPALS...THE *CHAMPIONS*...WHAT COULD *THEY* DO?
"AND I SAID TO MYSELF RIGHT THERE: PUSH COMES TO SHOVE, THIS IS MY DAD.
"DAMN THE SECRET IDENTITY AND BYE BYE SPIDER-MAN IF I HAVE TO.
"NOTHING'S MORE IMPORTANT THAN FINDING MY DAD.
DAD
unavailable
"ALL MY POWER AND ALL THE SPIDER-RELATED CRAZY AND I HAD NO IDEA WHAT I WAS SUPPOSED TO DO.
"I NEEDED SOMEONE CONNECTED.
"I NEEDED SOMEONE WHO KNEW SOMETHING ABOUT SOMETHING.
"SOMEONE PLUGGED INTO EVERYTHING.
"SOMEONE WHO KNEW HOW TO FIND ANYONE, INCLUDING..."

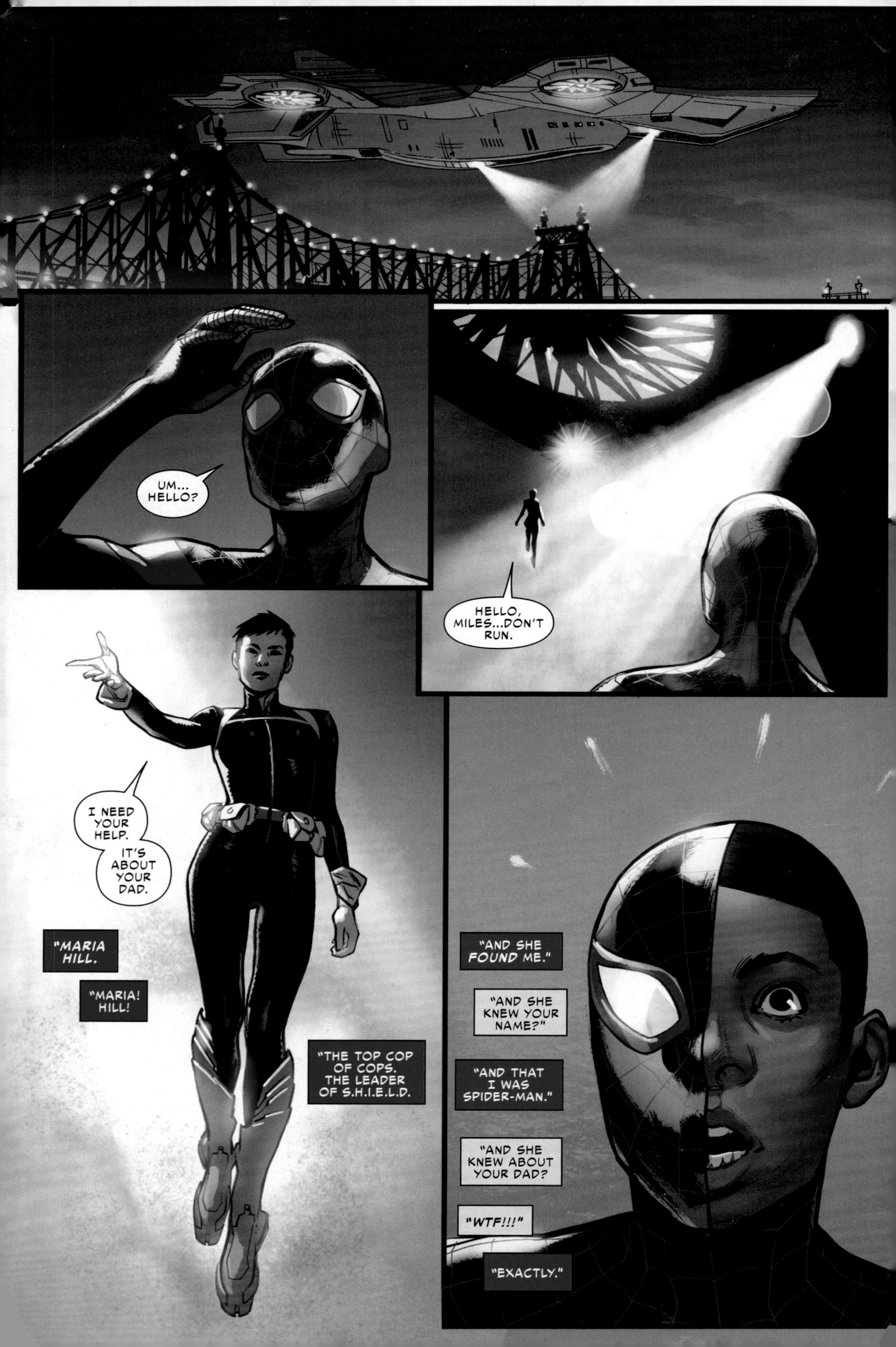
UM... HELLO?
HELLO, MILES...DON'T RUN.
I NEED YOUR HELP.
IT'S ABOUT YOUR DAD.
"MARIA HILL.
"MARIA! HILL!
"THE TOP COP OF COPS. THE LEADER OF S.H.I.E.L.D.
"AND SHE FOUND ME."
"AND SHE KNEW YOUR NAME?"
"AND THAT I WAS SPIDER-MAN."
"AND SHE KNEW ABOUT YOUR DAD?
"WTF!!!"
"EXACTLY."

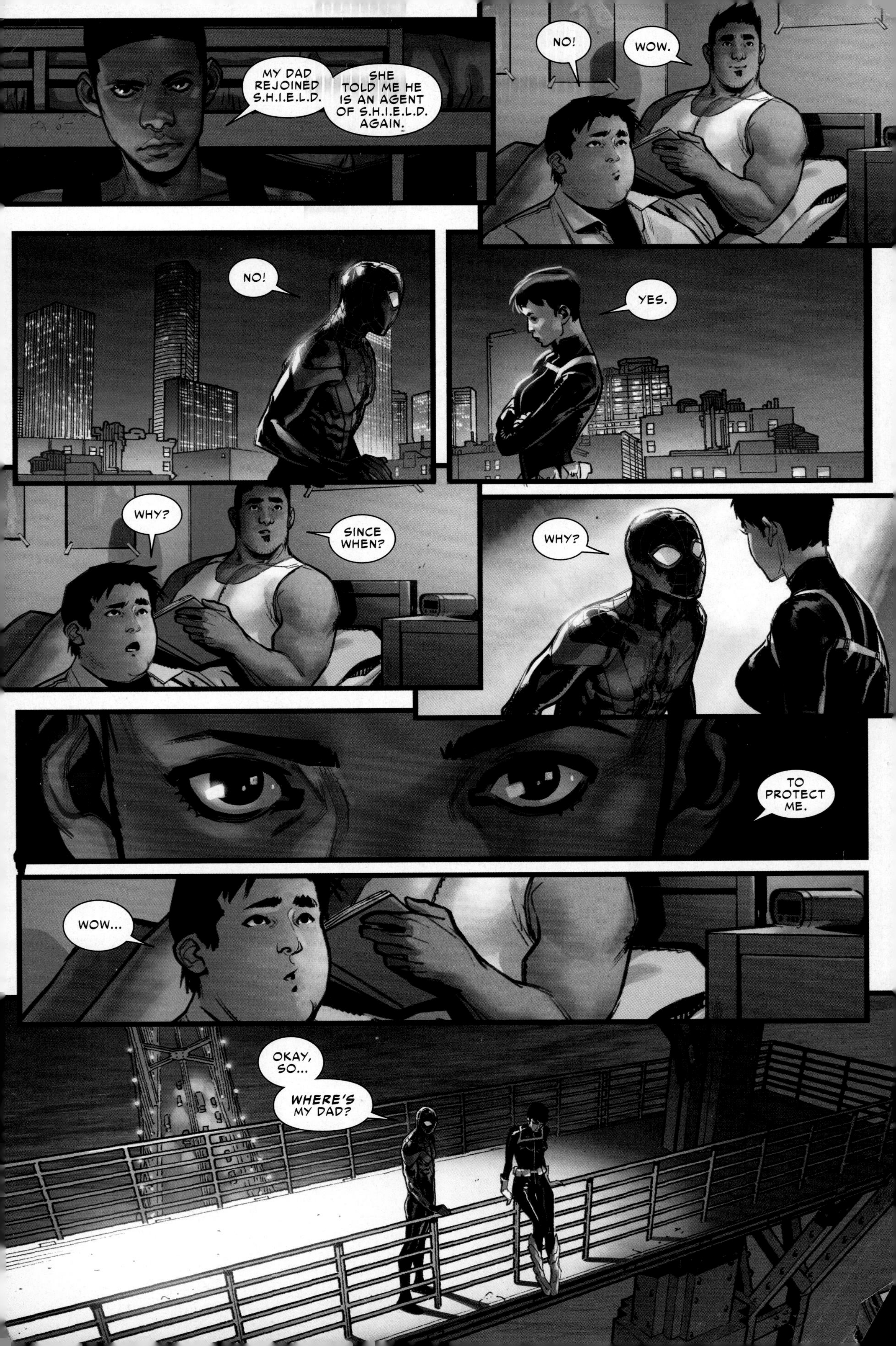
MY DAD REJOINED S.H.I.E.L.D.
SHE TOLD ME HE IS AN AGENT OF S.H.I.E.L.D. AGAIN.
NO!
WOW.
NO!
YES.
WHY?
SINCE WHEN?
WHY?
TO PROTECT ME.
WOW...
OKAY, SO...
WHERE'S MY DAD?

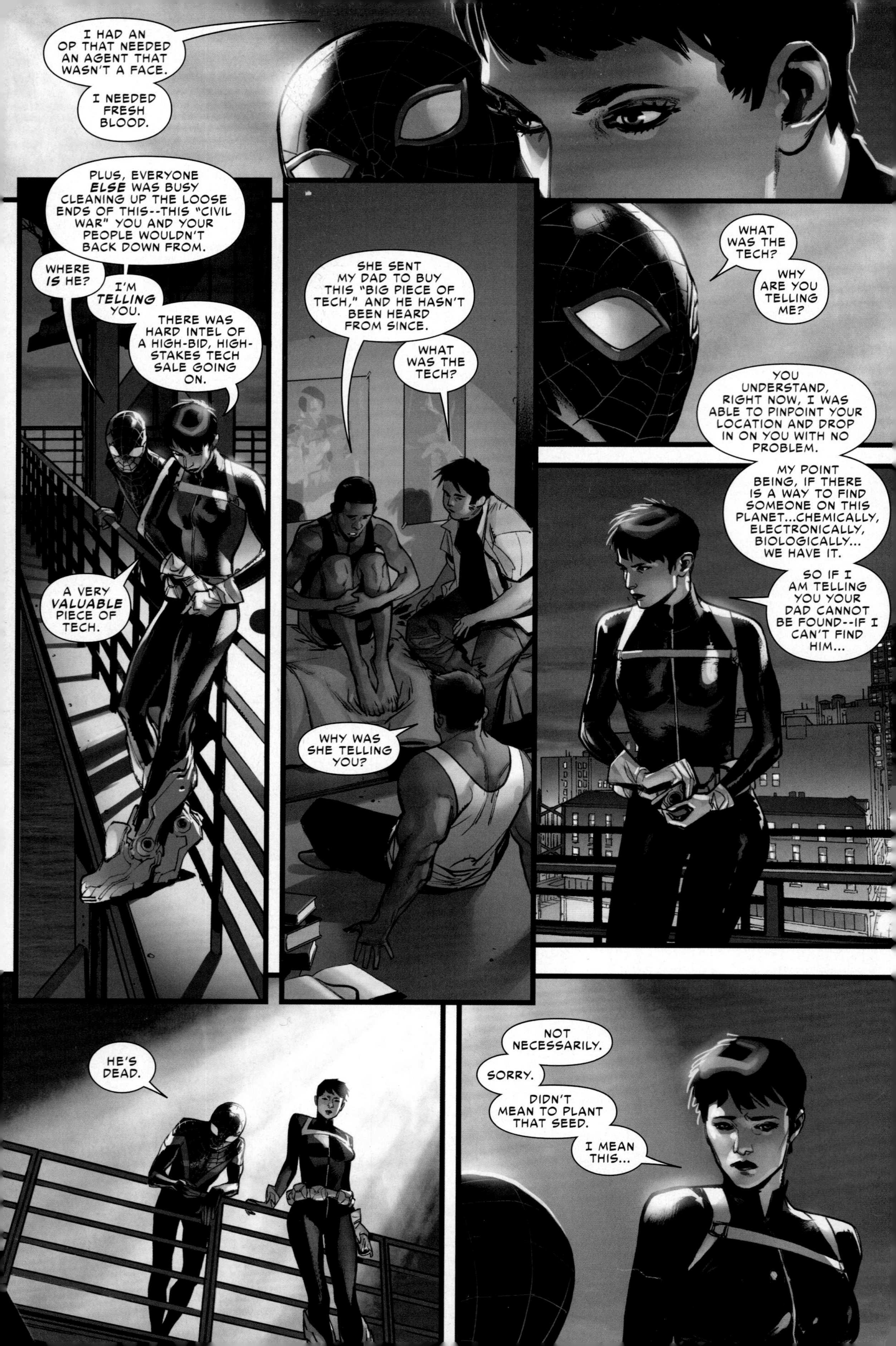
I HAD AN OP THAT NEEDED AN AGENT THAT WASN'T A FACE.
I NEEDED FRESH BLOOD.
PLUS, EVERYONE *ELSE* WAS BUSY CLEANING UP THE LOOSE ENDS OF THIS--THIS "CIVIL WAR" YOU AND YOUR PEOPLE WOULDN'T BACK DOWN FROM.
WHERE *IS* HE?
I'M *TELLING* YOU.
THERE WAS HARD INTEL OF A HIGH-BID, HIGH-STAKES TECH SALE GOING ON.
A VERY *VALUABLE* PIECE OF TECH.
SHE SENT MY DAD TO BUY THIS "BIG PIECE OF TECH," AND HE HASN'T BEEN HEARD FROM SINCE.
WHAT WAS THE TECH?
WHY WAS SHE TELLING YOU?
WHAT WAS THE TECH?
WHY ARE YOU TELLING ME?
YOU UNDERSTAND, RIGHT NOW, I WAS ABLE TO PINPOINT YOUR LOCATION AND DROP IN ON YOU WITH NO PROBLEM.
MY POINT BEING, IF THERE IS A WAY TO FIND SOMEONE ON THIS PLANET...CHEMICALLY, ELECTRONICALLY, BIOLOGICALLY... WE HAVE IT.
SO IF I AM TELLING YOU YOUR DAD CANNOT BE FOUND--IF I CAN'T FIND HIM...
HE'S DEAD.
NOT NECESSARILY.
SORRY.
DIDN'T MEAN TO PLANT THAT SEED.
I MEAN THIS...

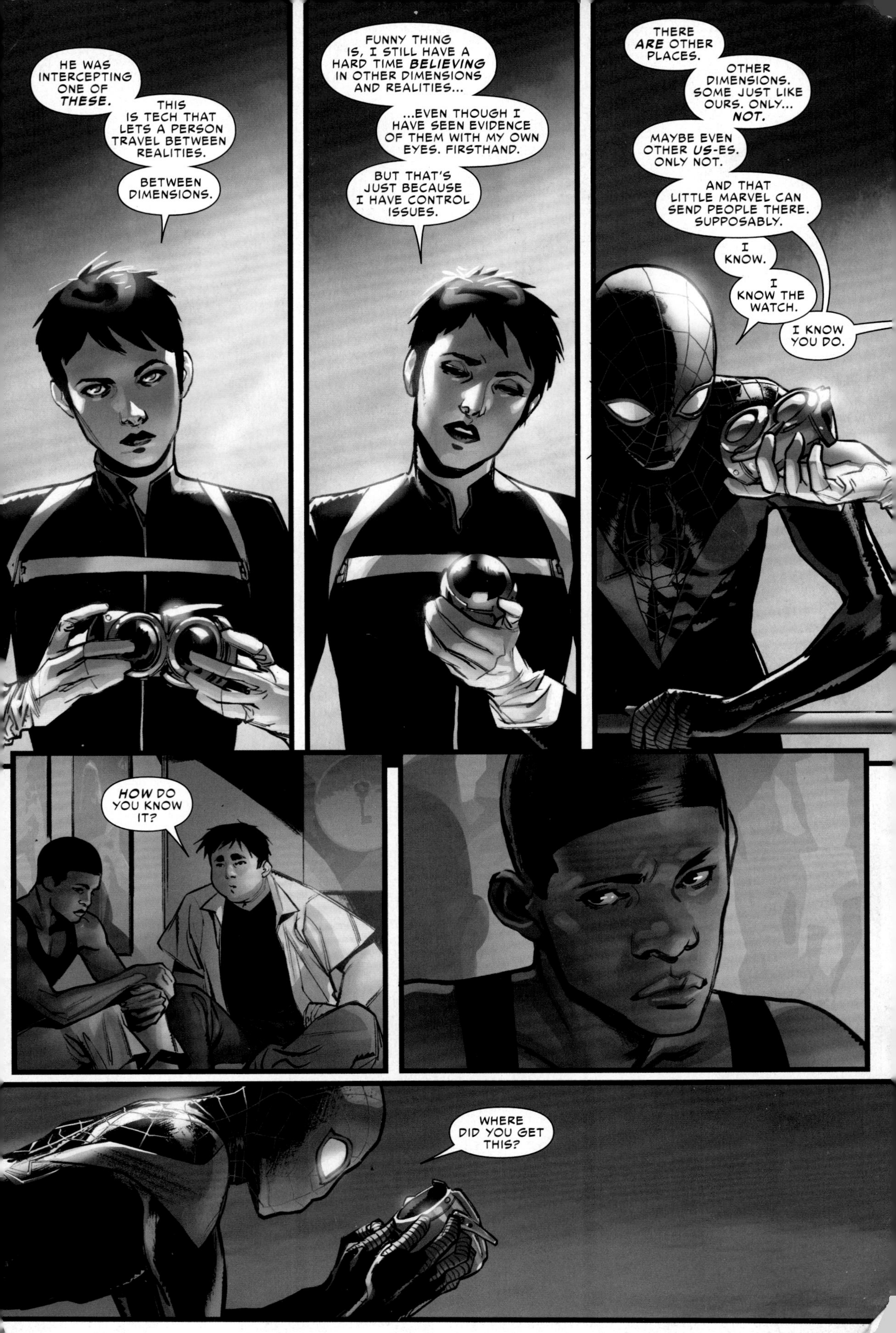
HE WAS INTERCEPTING ONE OF *THESE.*
THIS IS TECH THAT LETS A PERSON TRAVEL BETWEEN REALITIES.
BETWEEN DIMENSIONS.
FUNNY THING IS, I STILL HAVE A HARD TIME *BELIEVING* IN OTHER DIMENSIONS AND REALITIES...
...EVEN THOUGH I HAVE SEEN EVIDENCE OF THEM WITH MY OWN EYES. FIRSTHAND.
BUT THAT'S JUST BECAUSE I HAVE CONTROL ISSUES.
THERE *ARE* OTHER PLACES.
OTHER DIMENSIONS. SOME JUST LIKE OURS. ONLY... *NOT.*
MAYBE EVEN OTHER *US*-ES. ONLY NOT.
AND THAT LITTLE MARVEL CAN SEND PEOPLE THERE. SUPPOSABLY.
I KNOW.
I KNOW THE WATCH.
I KNOW YOU DO.
HOW DO YOU KNOW IT?
WHERE DID YOU GET THIS?

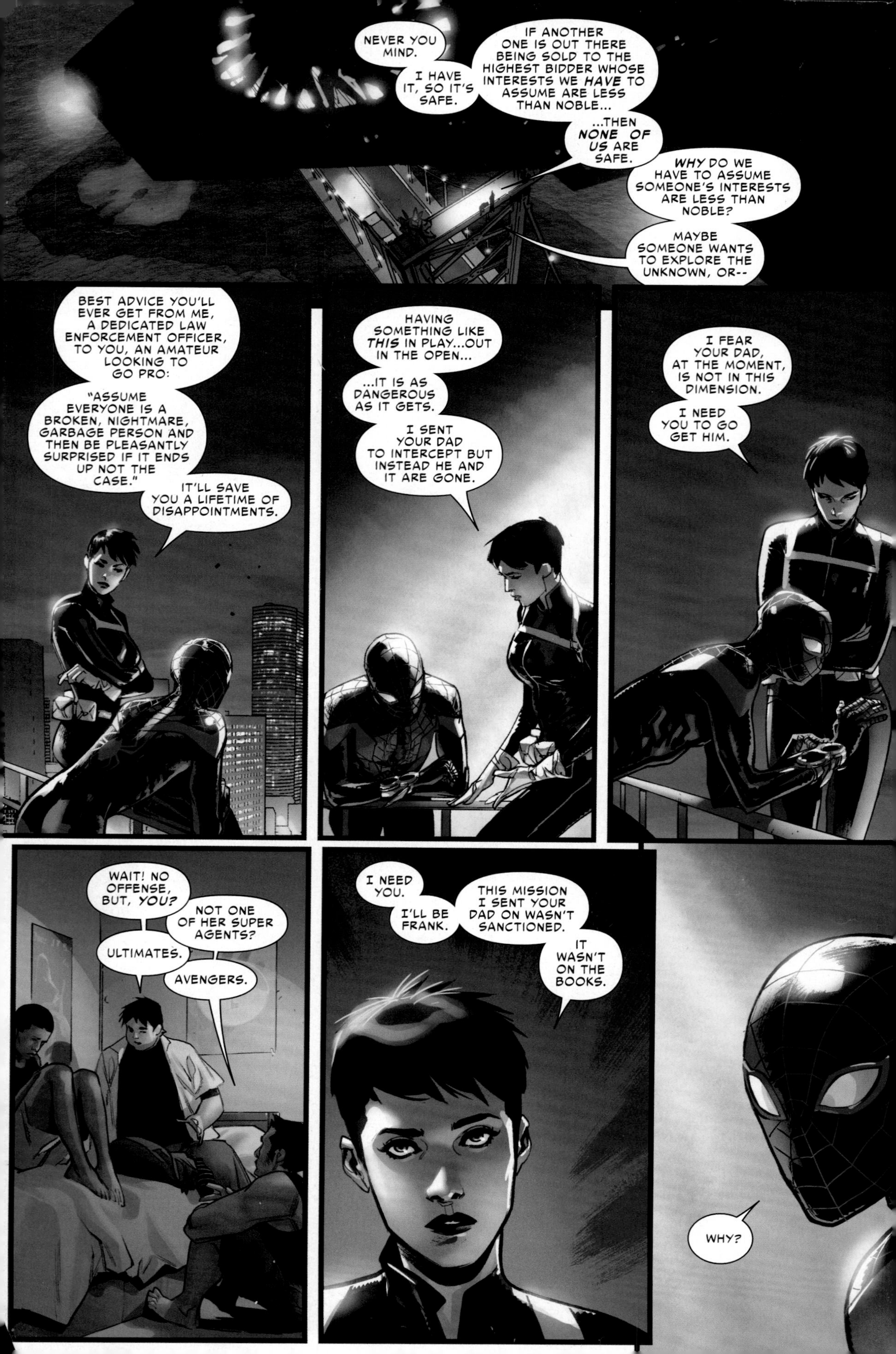
NEVER YOU MIND.
I HAVE IT, SO IT'S SAFE.
IF ANOTHER ONE IS OUT THERE BEING SOLD TO THE HIGHEST BIDDER WHOSE INTERESTS WE *HAVE* TO ASSUME ARE LESS THAN NOBLE...
...THEN *NONE OF US* ARE SAFE.
WHY DO WE HAVE TO ASSUME SOMEONE'S INTERESTS ARE LESS THAN NOBLE?
MAYBE SOMEONE WANTS TO EXPLORE THE UNKNOWN, OR--
BEST ADVICE YOU'LL EVER GET FROM ME, A DEDICATED LAW ENFORCEMENT OFFICER, TO YOU, AN AMATEUR LOOKING TO GO PRO:
"ASSUME EVERYONE IS A BROKEN, NIGHTMARE, GARBAGE PERSON AND THEN BE PLEASANTLY SURPRISED IF IT ENDS UP NOT THE CASE."
IT'LL SAVE YOU A LIFETIME OF DISAPPOINTMENTS.
HAVING SOMETHING LIKE *THIS* IN PLAY...OUT IN THE OPEN...
...IT IS AS DANGEROUS AS IT GETS.
I SENT YOUR DAD TO INTERCEPT BUT INSTEAD HE AND IT ARE GONE.
I FEAR YOUR DAD, AT THE MOMENT, IS NOT IN THIS DIMENSION.
I NEED YOU TO GO GET HIM.
WAIT! NO OFFENSE, BUT, *YOU?*
NOT ONE OF HER SUPER AGENTS?
ULTIMATES.
AVENGERS.
I NEED YOU.
I'LL BE FRANK.
THIS MISSION I SENT YOUR DAD ON WASN'T SANCTIONED.
IT WASN'T ON THE BOOKS.
WHY?

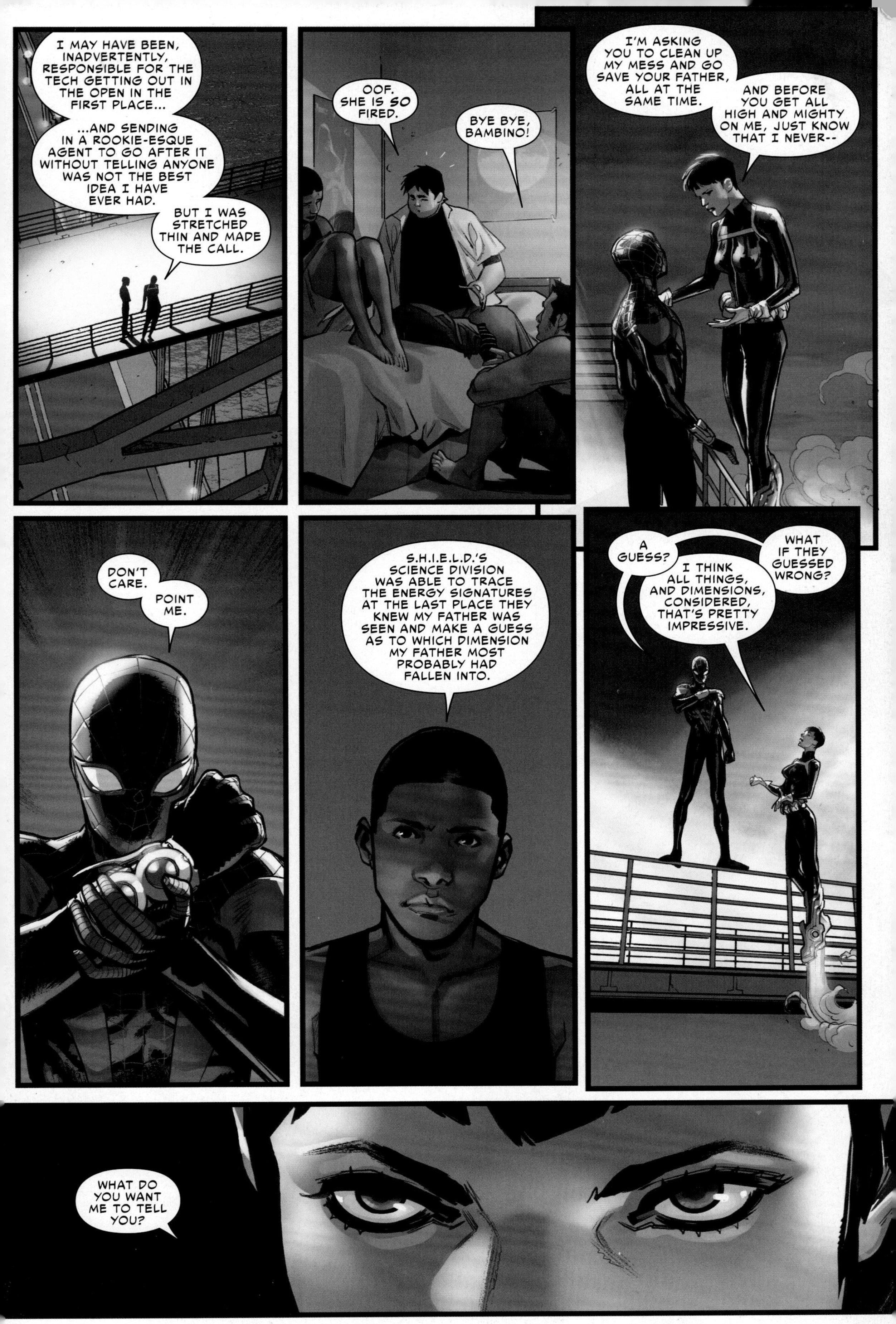
I MAY HAVE BEEN, INADVERTENTLY, RESPONSIBLE FOR THE TECH GETTING OUT IN THE OPEN IN THE FIRST PLACE...
...AND SENDING IN A ROOKIE-ESQUE AGENT TO GO AFTER IT WITHOUT TELLING ANYONE WAS NOT THE BEST IDEA I HAVE EVER HAD.
BUT I WAS STRETCHED THIN AND MADE THE CALL.
OOF. SHE IS SO FIRED.
BYE BYE, BAMBINO!
I'M ASKING YOU TO CLEAN UP MY MESS AND GO SAVE YOUR FATHER, ALL AT THE SAME TIME.
AND BEFORE YOU GET ALL HIGH AND MIGHTY ON ME, JUST KNOW THAT I NEVER--
DON'T CARE.
POINT ME.
S.H.I.E.L.D.'S SCIENCE DIVISION WAS ABLE TO TRACE THE ENERGY SIGNATURES AT THE LAST PLACE THEY KNEW MY FATHER WAS SEEN AND MAKE A GUESS AS TO WHICH DIMENSION MY FATHER MOST PROBABLY HAD FALLEN INTO.
A GUESS?
WHAT IF THEY GUESSED WRONG?
I THINK ALL THINGS, AND DIMENSIONS, CONSIDERED, THAT'S PRETTY IMPRESSIVE.
WHAT DO YOU WANT ME TO TELL YOU?

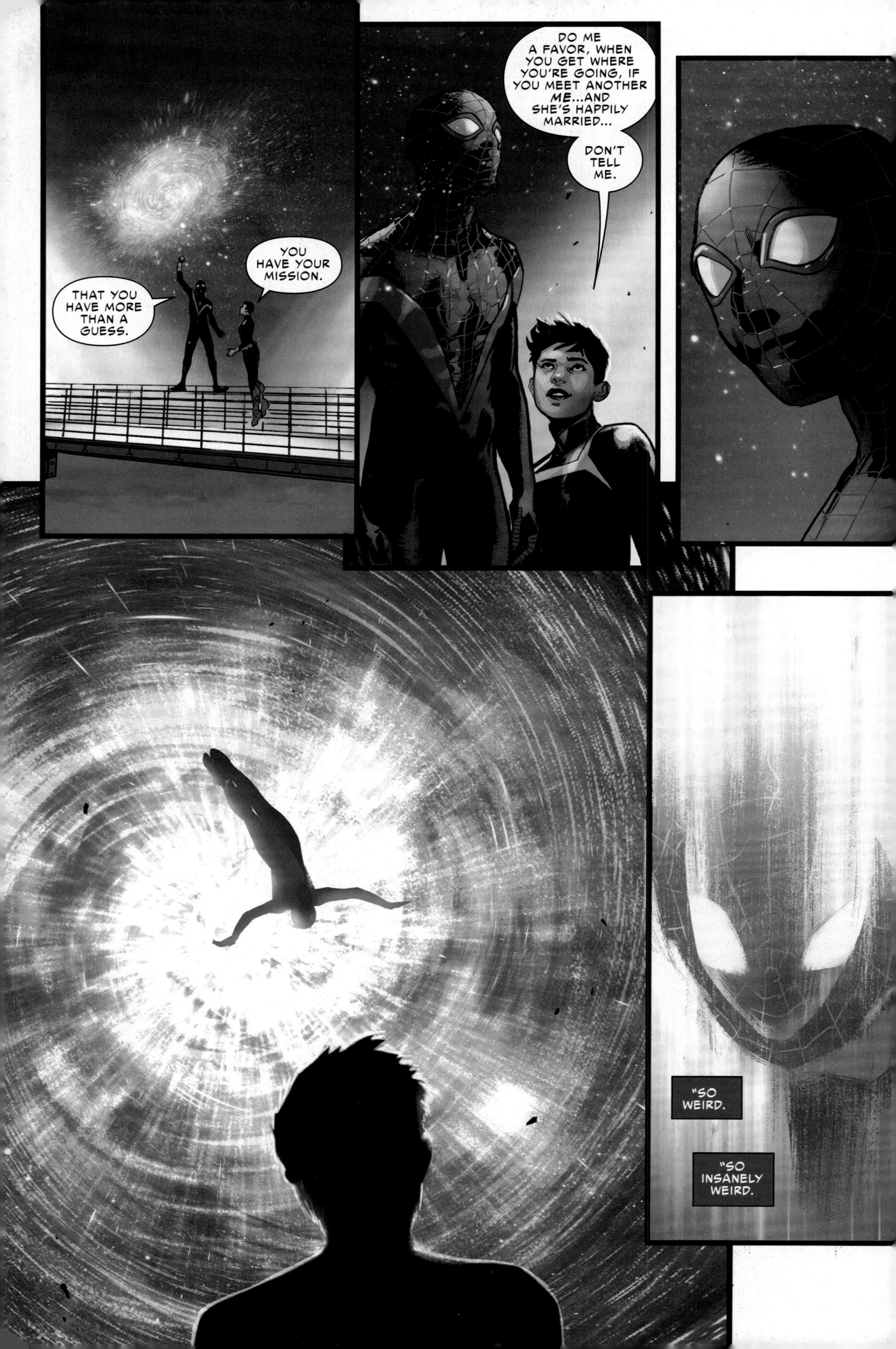
YOU HAVE YOUR MISSION.
THAT YOU HAVE MORE THAN A GUESS.
DO ME A FAVOR, WHEN YOU GET WHERE YOU'RE GOING, IF YOU MEET ANOTHER *ME*...AND SHE'S HAPPILY MARRIED...
DON'T TELL ME.
"SO WEIRD.
"SO INSANELY WEIRD.

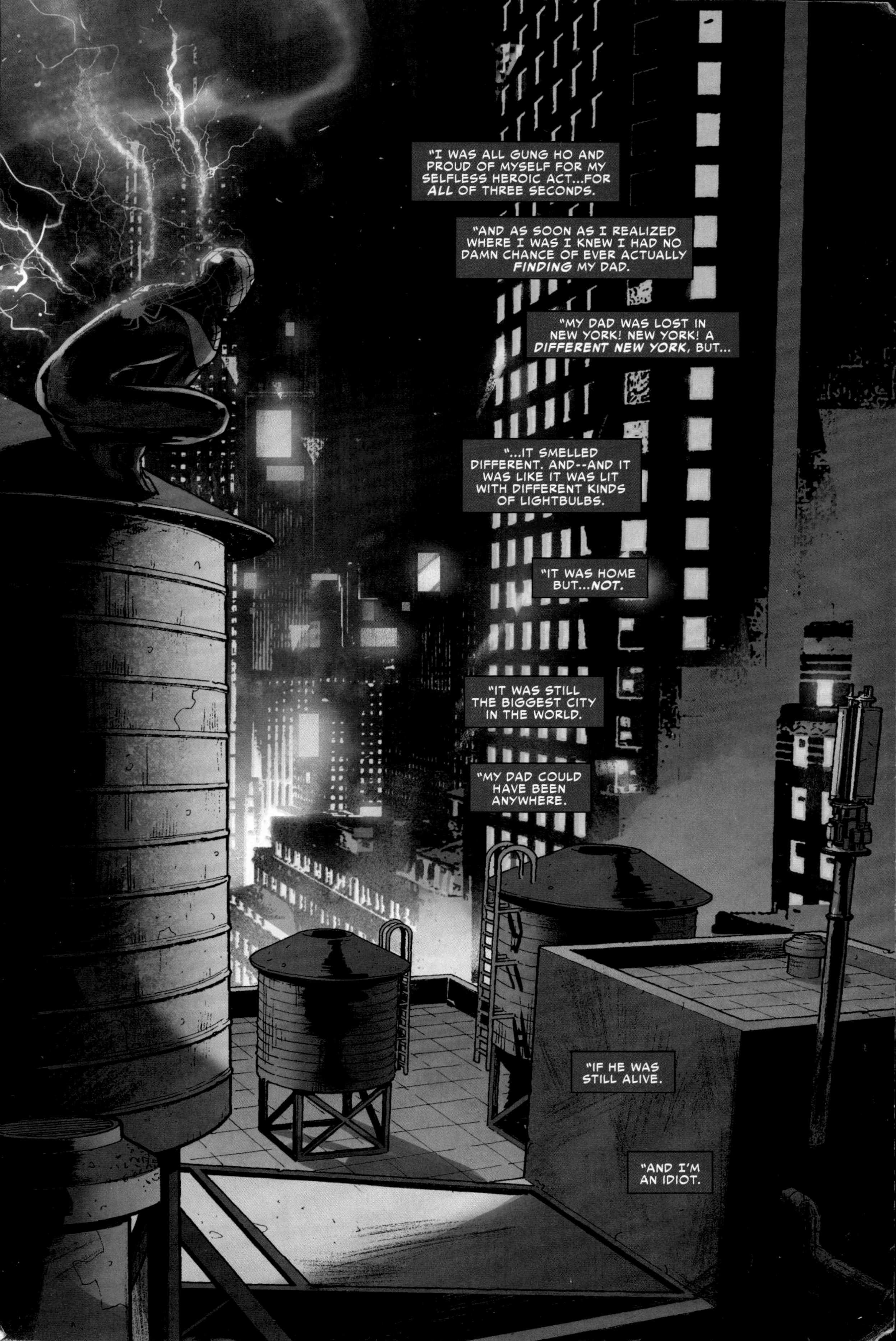
"I WAS ALL GUNG HO AND PROUD OF MYSELF FOR MY SELFLESS HEROIC ACT...FOR *ALL* OF THREE SECONDS.
"AND AS SOON AS I REALIZED WHERE I WAS I KNEW I HAD NO DAMN CHANCE OF EVER ACTUALLY *FINDING* MY DAD.
"MY DAD WAS LOST IN NEW YORK! NEW YORK! A *DIFFERENT NEW YORK*, BUT...
"...IT SMELLED DIFFERENT. AND--AND IT WAS LIKE IT WAS LIT WITH DIFFERENT KINDS OF LIGHTBULBS.
"IT WAS HOME BUT...*NOT.*
"IT WAS STILL THE BIGGEST CITY IN THE WORLD.
"MY DAD COULD HAVE BEEN ANYWHERE.
"IF HE WAS STILL ALIVE.
"AND I'M AN IDIOT.

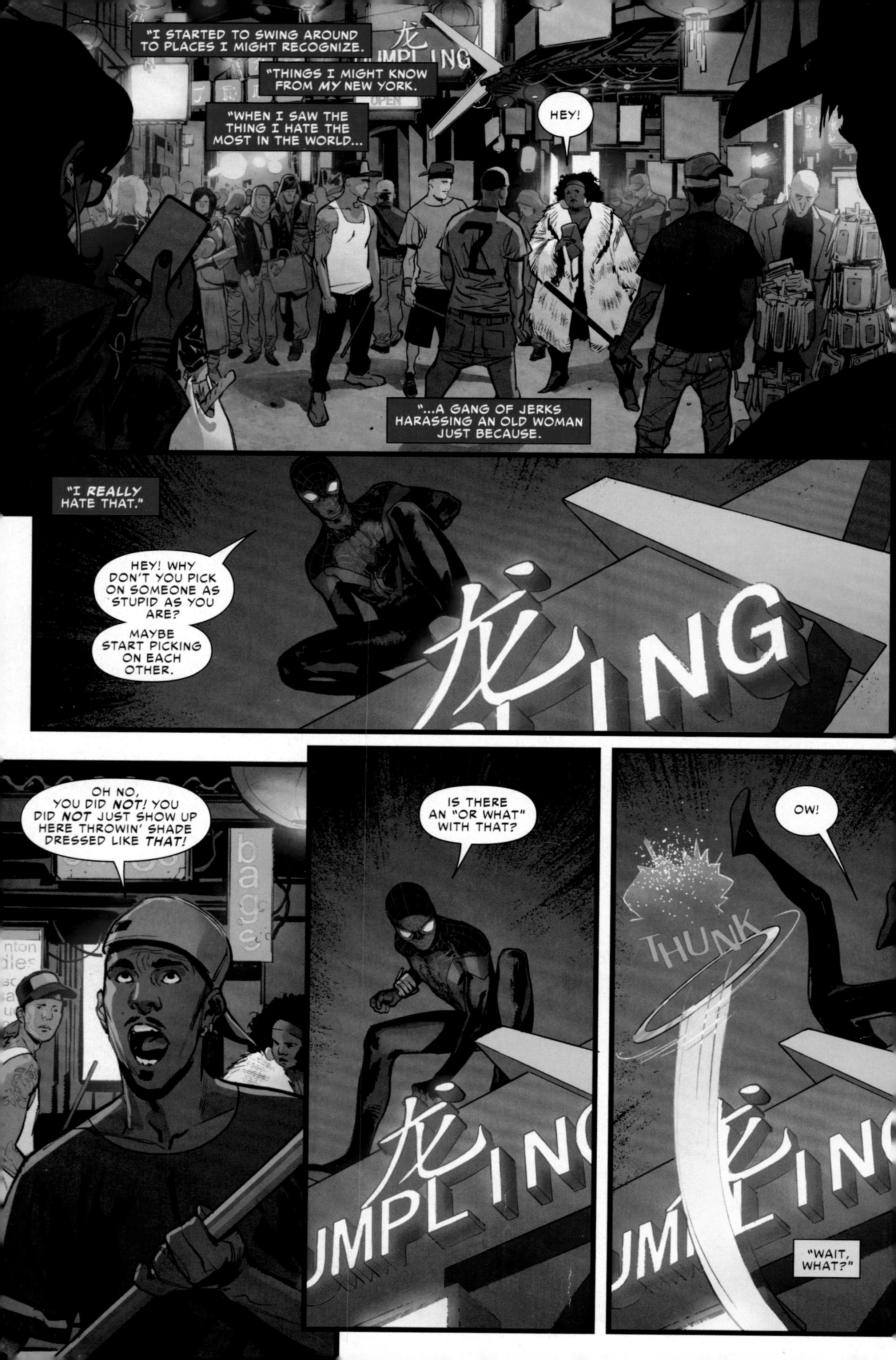
"I STARTED TO SWING AROUND TO PLACES I MIGHT RECOGNIZE.
"THINGS I MIGHT KNOW FROM MY NEW YORK.
"WHEN I SAW THE THING I HATE THE MOST IN THE WORLD...
HEY!
"...A GANG OF JERKS HARASSING AN OLD WOMAN JUST BECAUSE.
"I REALLY HATE THAT."
HEY! WHY DON'T YOU PICK ON SOMEONE AS STUPID AS YOU ARE?
MAYBE START PICKING ON EACH OTHER.
OH NO, YOU DID NOT! YOU DID NOT JUST SHOW UP HERE THROWIN' SHADE DRESSED LIKE THAT!
IS THERE AN "OR WHAT" WITH THAT?
THUNK
OW!
"WAIT, WHAT?"

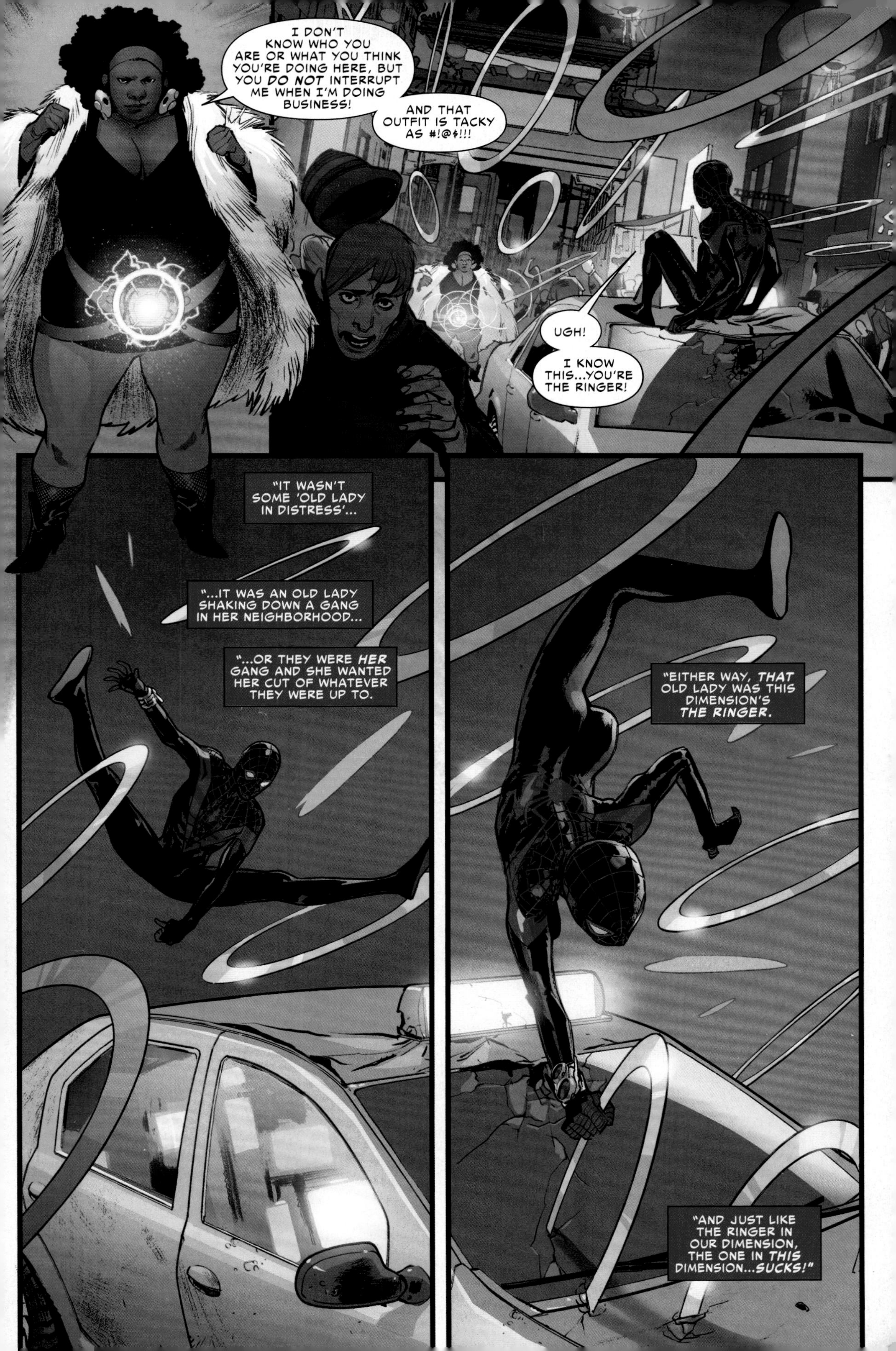
I DON'T KNOW WHO YOU ARE OR WHAT YOU THINK YOU'RE DOING HERE, BUT YOU DO NOT INTERRUPT ME WHEN I'M DOING BUSINESS!
AND THAT OUTFIT IS TACKY AS #!@$!!!
UGH!
I KNOW THIS...YOU'RE THE RINGER!
"IT WASN'T SOME 'OLD LADY IN DISTRESS'...
"...IT WAS AN OLD LADY SHAKING DOWN A GANG IN HER NEIGHBORHOOD...
"...OR THEY WERE HER GANG AND SHE WANTED HER CUT OF WHATEVER THEY WERE UP TO.
"EITHER WAY, THAT OLD LADY WAS THIS DIMENSION'S THE RINGER.
"AND JUST LIKE THE RINGER IN OUR DIMENSION, THE ONE IN THIS DIMENSION...SUCKS!"

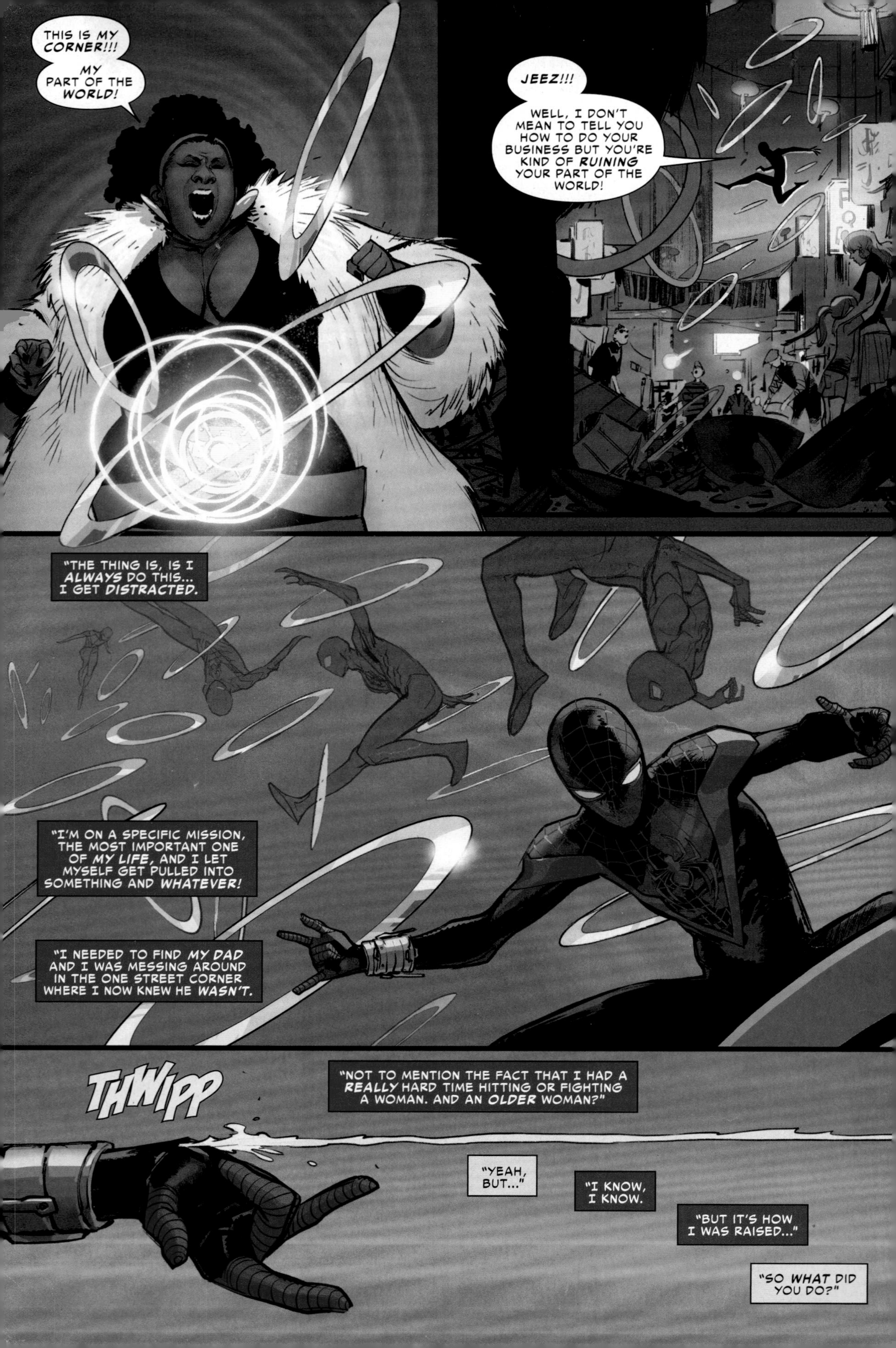
THIS IS MY CORNER!!! MY PART OF THE WORLD!
JEEZ!!!
WELL, I DON'T MEAN TO TELL YOU HOW TO DO YOUR BUSINESS BUT YOU'RE KIND OF RUINING YOUR PART OF THE WORLD!
"THE THING IS, IS I ALWAYS DO THIS... I GET DISTRACTED.
"I'M ON A SPECIFIC MISSION, THE MOST IMPORTANT ONE OF MY LIFE, AND I LET MYSELF GET PULLED INTO SOMETHING AND WHATEVER!
"I NEEDED TO FIND MY DAD AND I WAS MESSING AROUND IN THE ONE STREET CORNER WHERE I NOW KNEW HE WASN'T.
THWIPP
"NOT TO MENTION THE FACT THAT I HAD A REALLY HARD TIME HITTING OR FIGHTING A WOMAN. AND AN OLDER WOMAN?"
"YEAH, BUT..."
"I KNOW, I KNOW.
"BUT IT'S HOW I WAS RAISED..."
"SO WHAT DID YOU DO?"

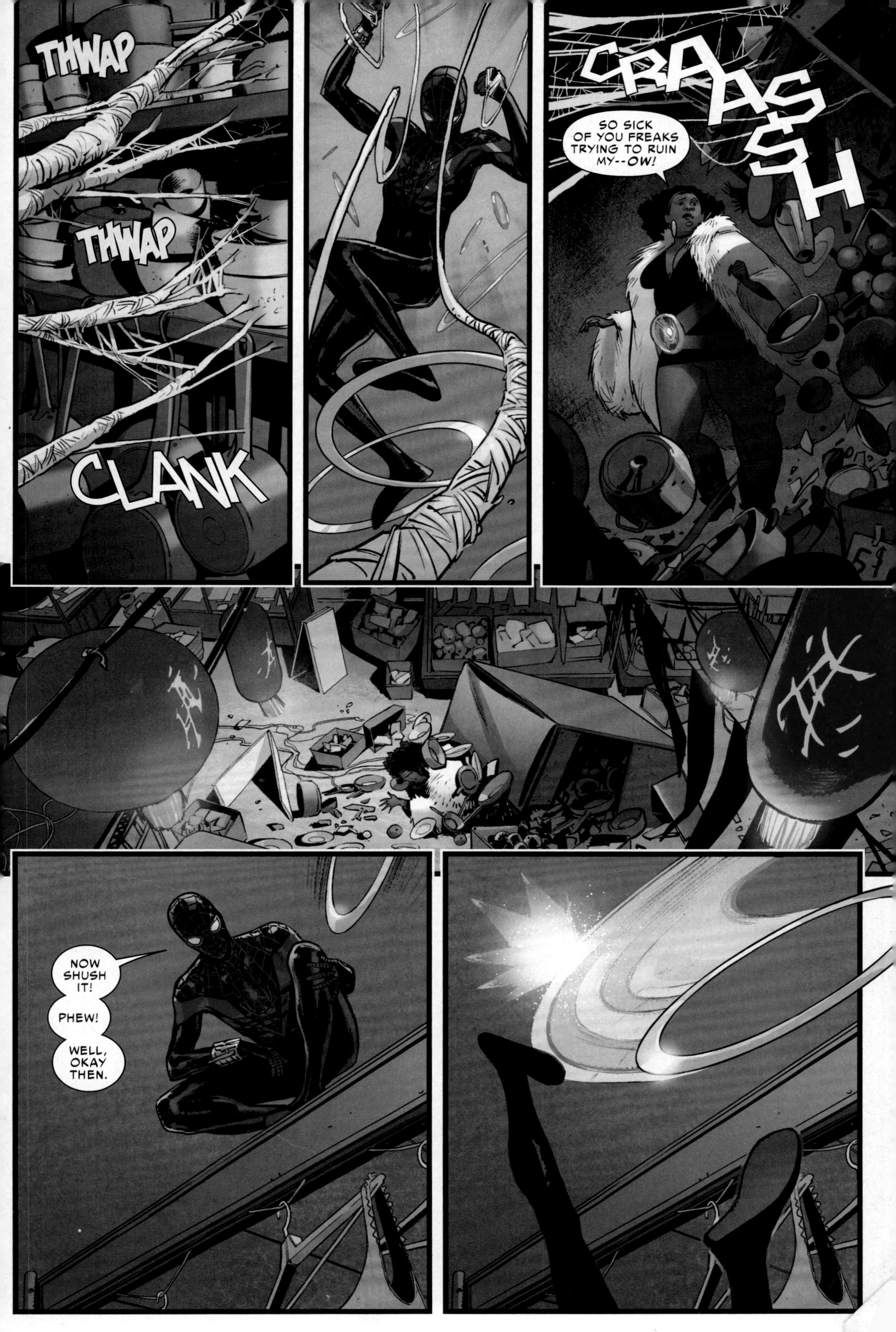
THWAP
THWAP
CLANK
CRAASH
SO SICK OF YOU FREAKS TRYING TO RUIN MY--OW!
NOW SHUSH IT!
PHEW!
WELL, OKAY THEN.

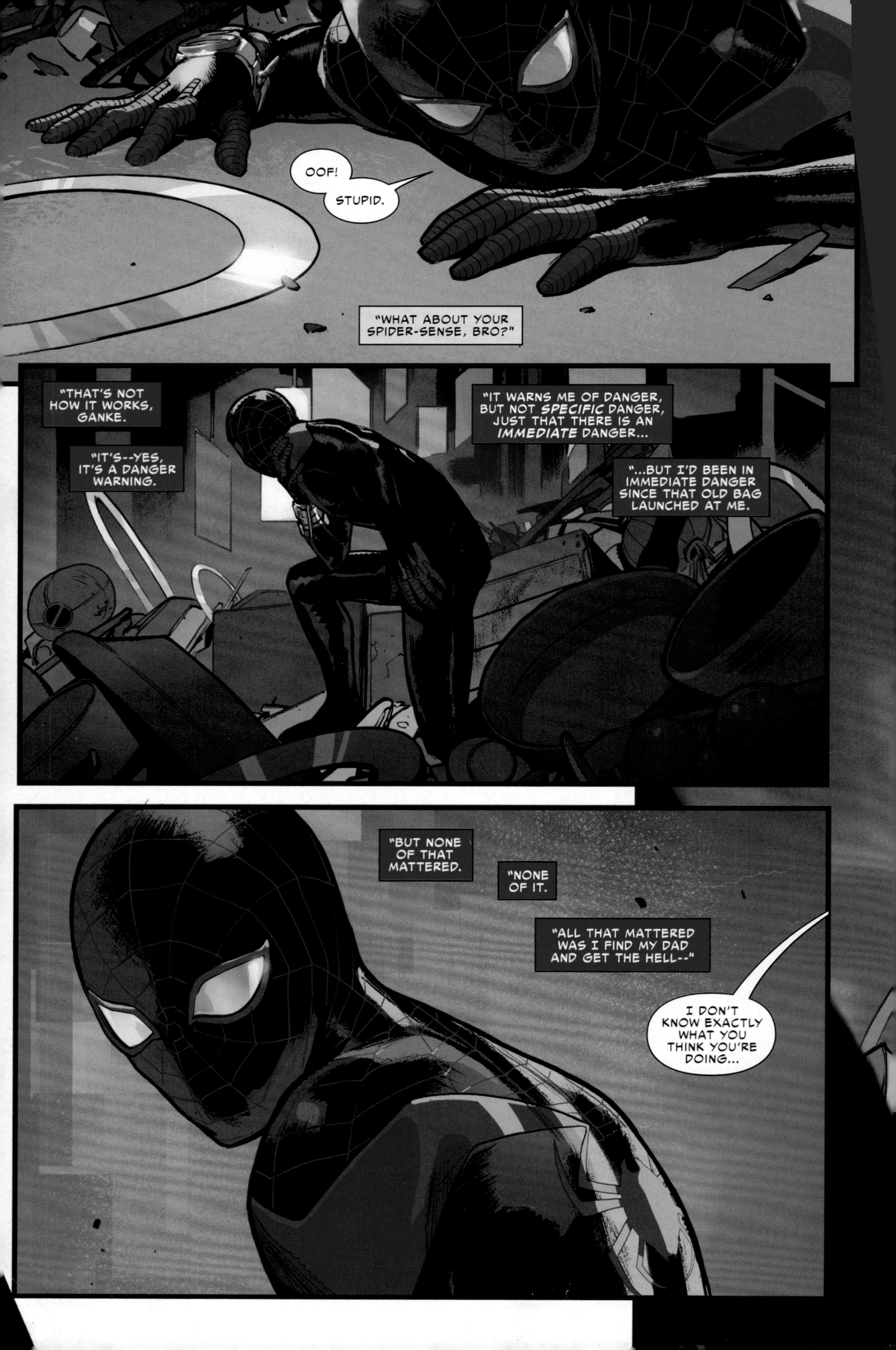
OOF!
STUPID.
"WHAT ABOUT YOUR SPIDER-SENSE, BRO?"
"THAT'S NOT HOW IT WORKS, GANKE.
"IT'S--YES, IT'S A DANGER WARNING.
"IT WARNS ME OF DANGER, BUT NOT *SPECIFIC* DANGER, JUST THAT THERE IS AN *IMMEDIATE* DANGER...
"...BUT I'D BEEN IN IMMEDIATE DANGER SINCE THAT OLD BAG LAUNCHED AT ME.
"BUT NONE OF THAT MATTERED.
"NONE OF IT.
"ALL THAT MATTERED WAS I FIND MY DAD AND GET THE HELL--"
I DON'T KNOW EXACTLY WHAT YOU THINK YOU'RE DOING...

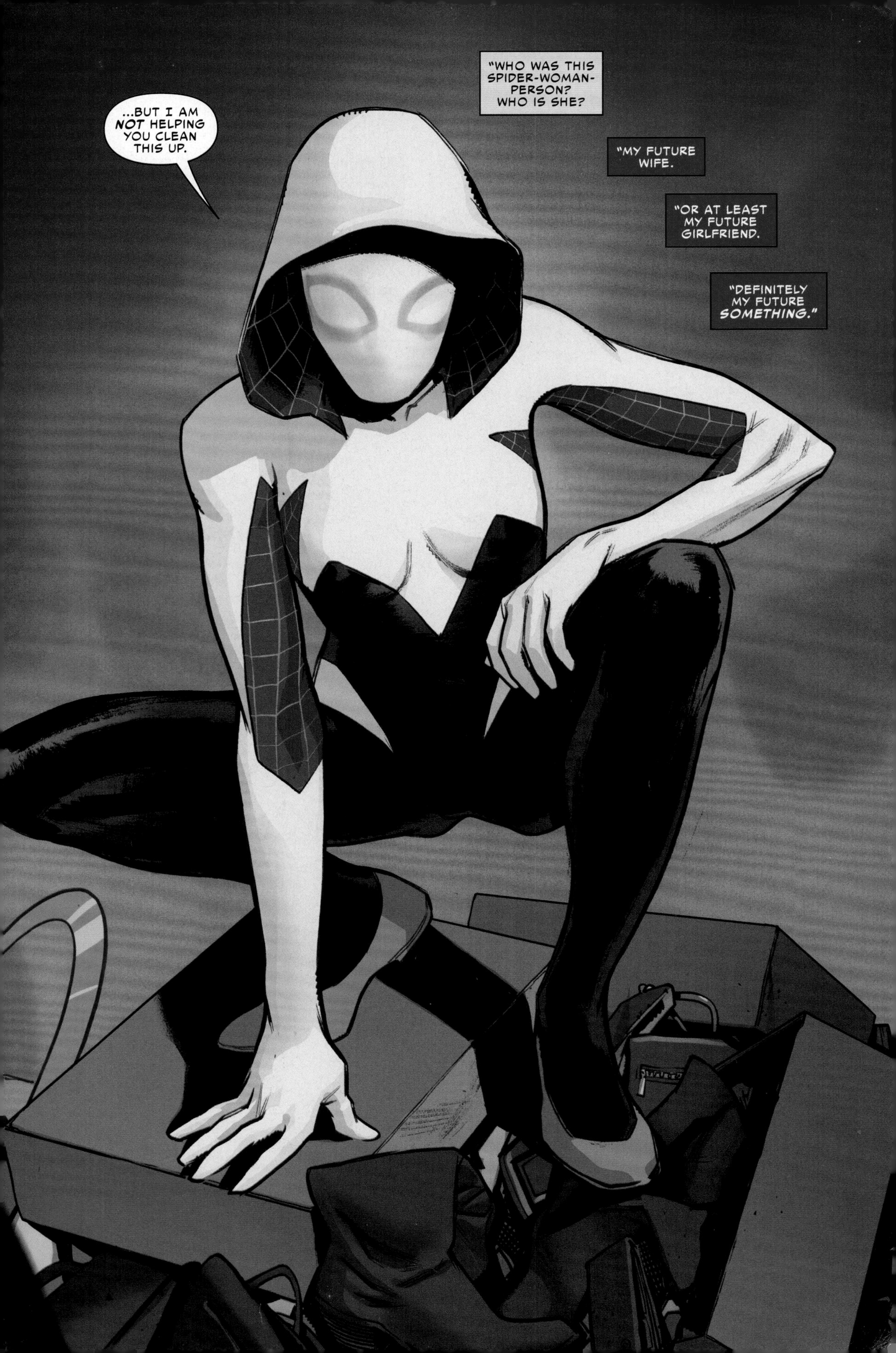
...BUT I AM *NOT* HELPING YOU CLEAN THIS UP.
"WHO WAS THIS SPIDER-WOMAN-PERSON? WHO IS SHE?
"MY FUTURE WIFE.
"OR AT LEAST MY FUTURE GIRLFRIEND.
"DEFINITELY MY FUTURE *SOMETHING.*"

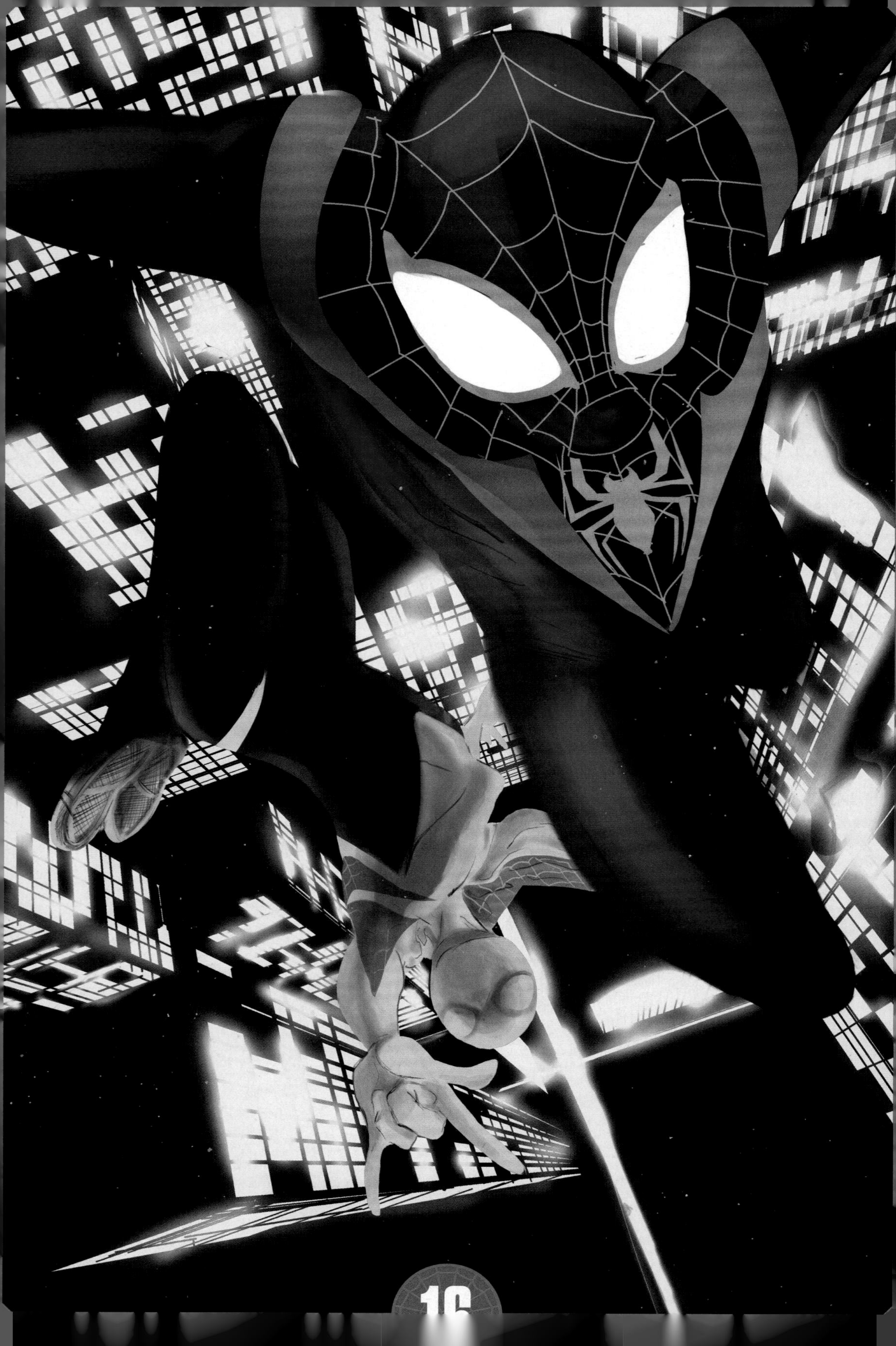

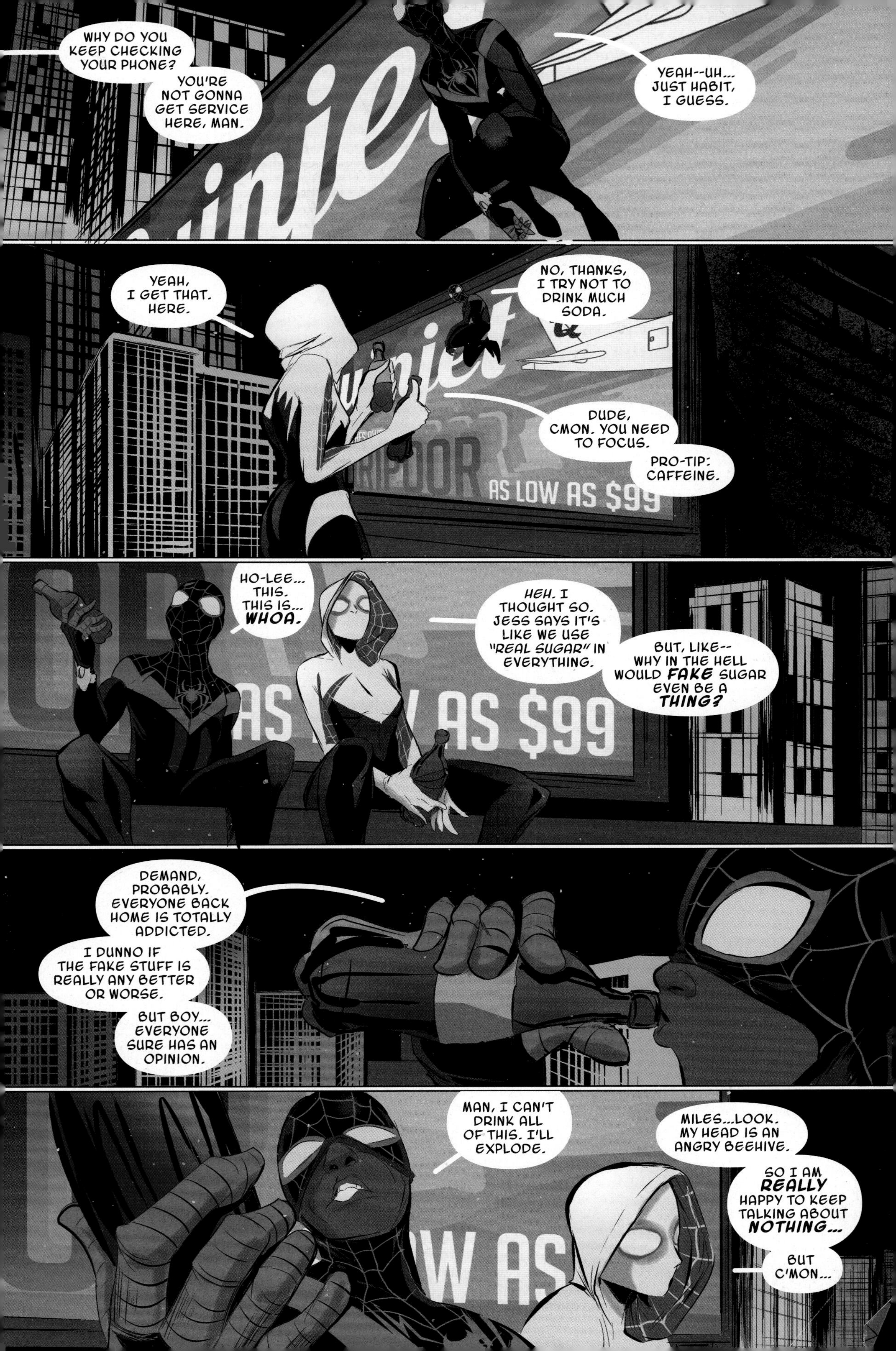
WHY DO YOU KEEP CHECKING YOUR PHONE?
YOU'RE NOT GONNA GET SERVICE HERE, MAN.
YEAH--UH... JUST HABIT, I GUESS.
YEAH, I GET THAT. HERE.
NO, THANKS, I TRY NOT TO DRINK MUCH SODA.
DUDE, CMON. YOU NEED TO FOCUS.
PRO-TIP: CAFFEINE.
AS LOW AS $99
HO-LEE... THIS. THIS IS... WHOA.
HEH. I THOUGHT SO. JESS SAYS IT'S LIKE WE USE "REAL SUGAR" IN EVERYTHING.
BUT, LIKE-- WHY IN THE HELL WOULD FAKE SUGAR EVEN BE A THING?
DEMAND, PROBABLY. EVERYONE BACK HOME IS TOTALLY ADDICTED.
I DUNNO IF THE FAKE STUFF IS REALLY ANY BETTER OR WORSE.
BUT BOY... EVERYONE SURE HAS AN OPINION.
MAN, I CAN'T DRINK ALL OF THIS. I'LL EXPLODE.
MILES...LOOK. MY HEAD IS AN ANGRY BEEHIVE.
SO I AM REALLY HAPPY TO KEEP TALKING ABOUT NOTHING...
BUT C'MON...

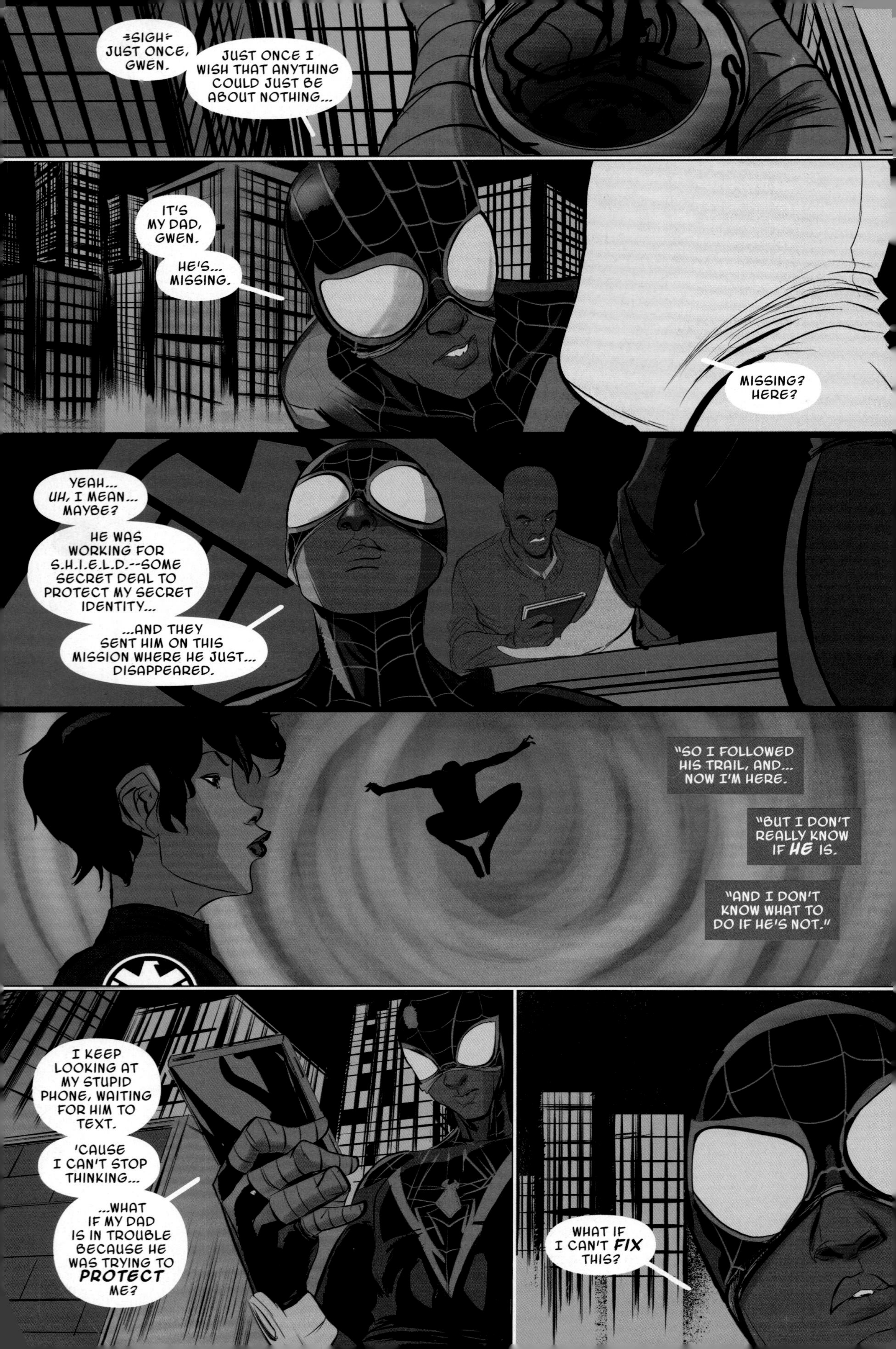
=SIGH= JUST ONCE, GWEN.
JUST ONCE I WISH THAT ANYTHING COULD JUST BE ABOUT NOTHING...
IT'S MY DAD, GWEN.
HE'S... MISSING.
MISSING? HERE?
YEAH... UH, I MEAN... MAYBE?
HE WAS WORKING FOR S.H.I.E.L.D.--SOME SECRET DEAL TO PROTECT MY SECRET IDENTITY...
...AND THEY SENT HIM ON THIS MISSION WHERE HE JUST... DISAPPEARED.
"SO I FOLLOWED HIS TRAIL, AND... NOW I'M HERE.
"BUT I DON'T REALLY KNOW IF HE IS.
"AND I DON'T KNOW WHAT TO DO IF HE'S NOT."
I KEEP LOOKING AT MY STUPID PHONE, WAITING FOR HIM TO TEXT.
'CAUSE I CAN'T STOP THINKING...
...WHAT IF MY DAD IS IN TROUBLE BECAUSE HE WAS TRYING TO PROTECT ME?
WHAT IF I CAN'T FIX THIS?

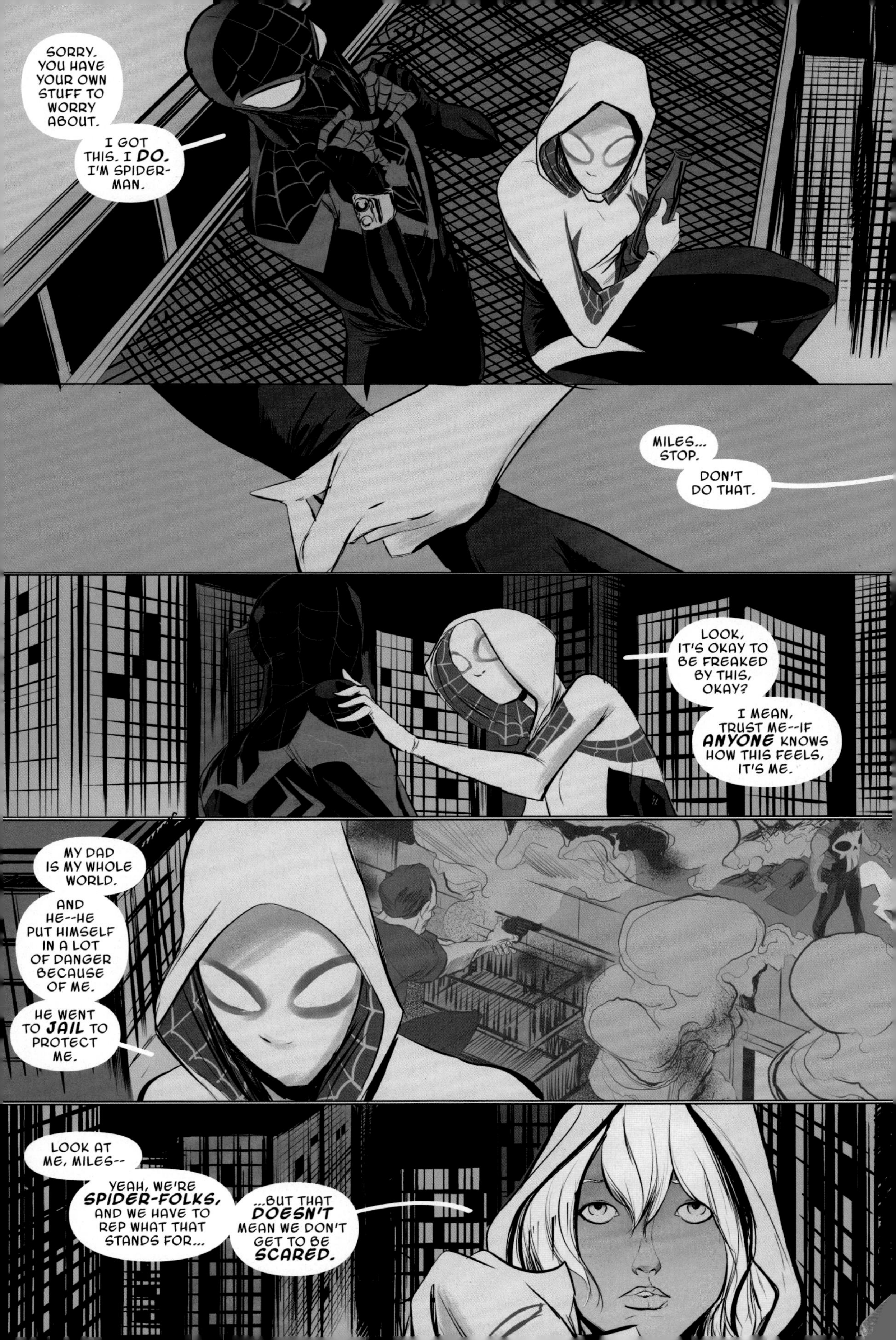
SORRY. YOU HAVE YOUR OWN STUFF TO WORRY ABOUT.
I GOT THIS. I DO. I'M SPIDER-MAN.
MILES... STOP.
DON'T DO THAT.
LOOK, IT'S OKAY TO BE FREAKED BY THIS, OKAY?
I MEAN, TRUST ME--IF ANYONE KNOWS HOW THIS FEELS, IT'S ME.
MY DAD IS MY WHOLE WORLD.
AND HE--HE PUT HIMSELF IN A LOT OF DANGER BECAUSE OF ME.
HE WENT TO JAIL TO PROTECT ME.
LOOK AT ME, MILES--
YEAH, WE'RE SPIDER-FOLKS, AND WE HAVE TO REP WHAT THAT STANDS FOR...
...BUT THAT DOESN'T MEAN WE DON'T GET TO BE SCARED.

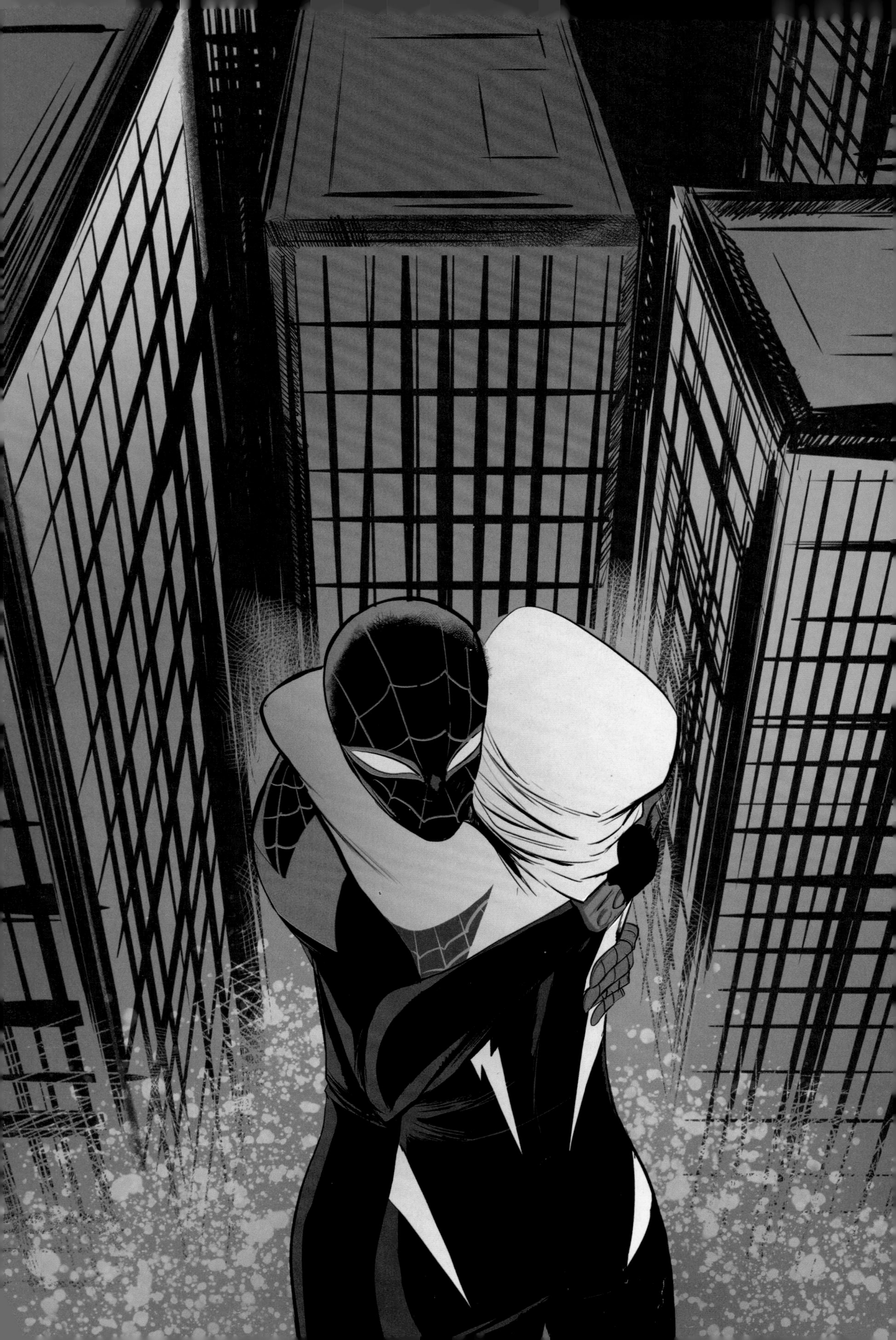

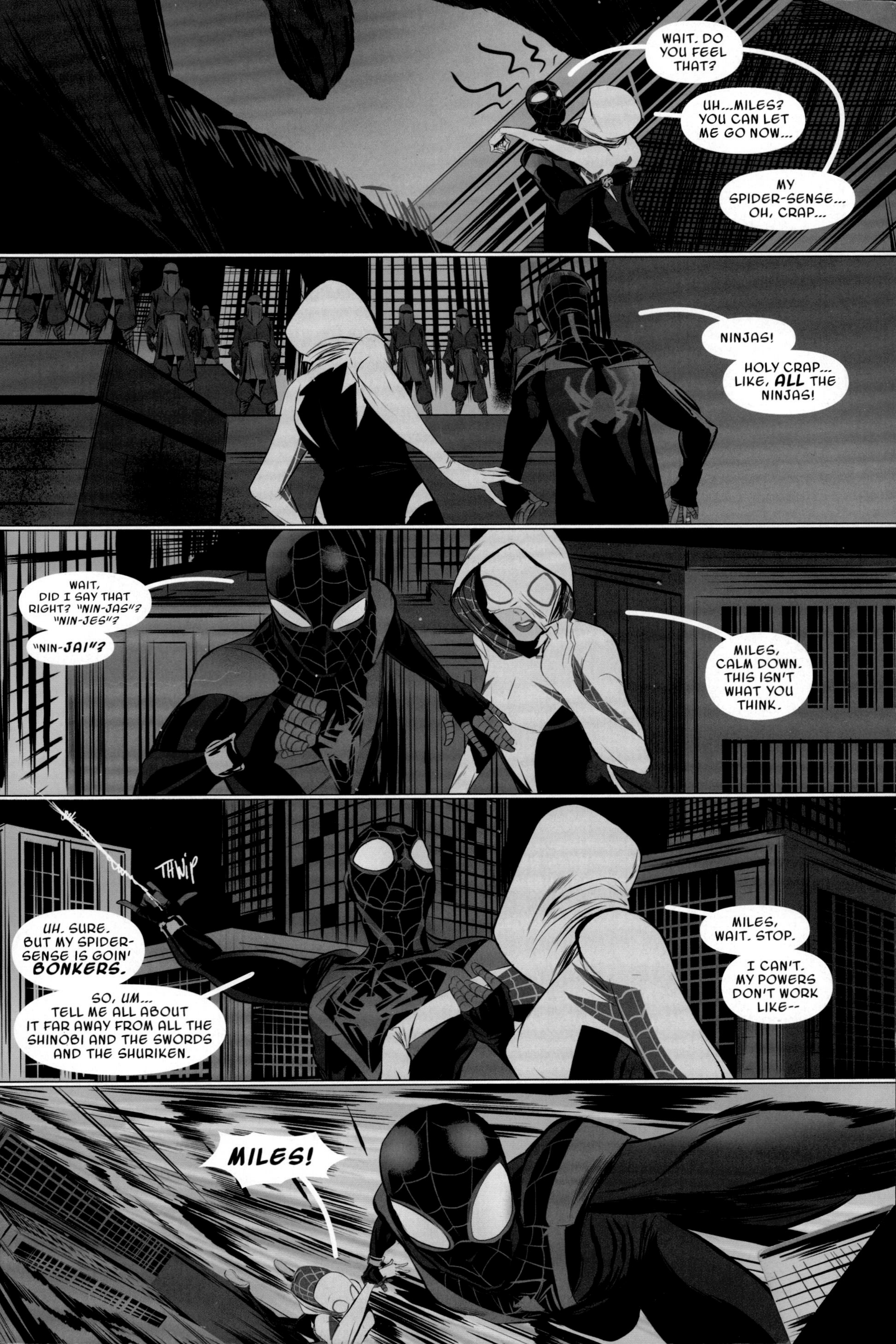

WAIT. DO YOU FEEL THAT?
UH...MILES? YOU CAN LET ME GO NOW...
MY SPIDER-SENSE... OH, CRAP...
NINJAS!
HOLY CRAP... LIKE, ALL THE NINJAS!
WAIT, DID I SAY THAT RIGHT? "NIN-JAS"? "NIN-JES"?
"NIN-JAI"?
MILES, CALM DOWN. THIS ISN'T WHAT YOU THINK.
THWIP
UH. SURE. BUT MY SPIDER-SENSE IS GOIN' BONKERS.
SO, UM... TELL ME ALL ABOUT IT FAR AWAY FROM ALL THE SHINOBI AND THE SWORDS AND THE SHURIKEN.
MILES, WAIT. STOP.
I CAN'T. MY POWERS DON'T WORK LIKE--
MILES!

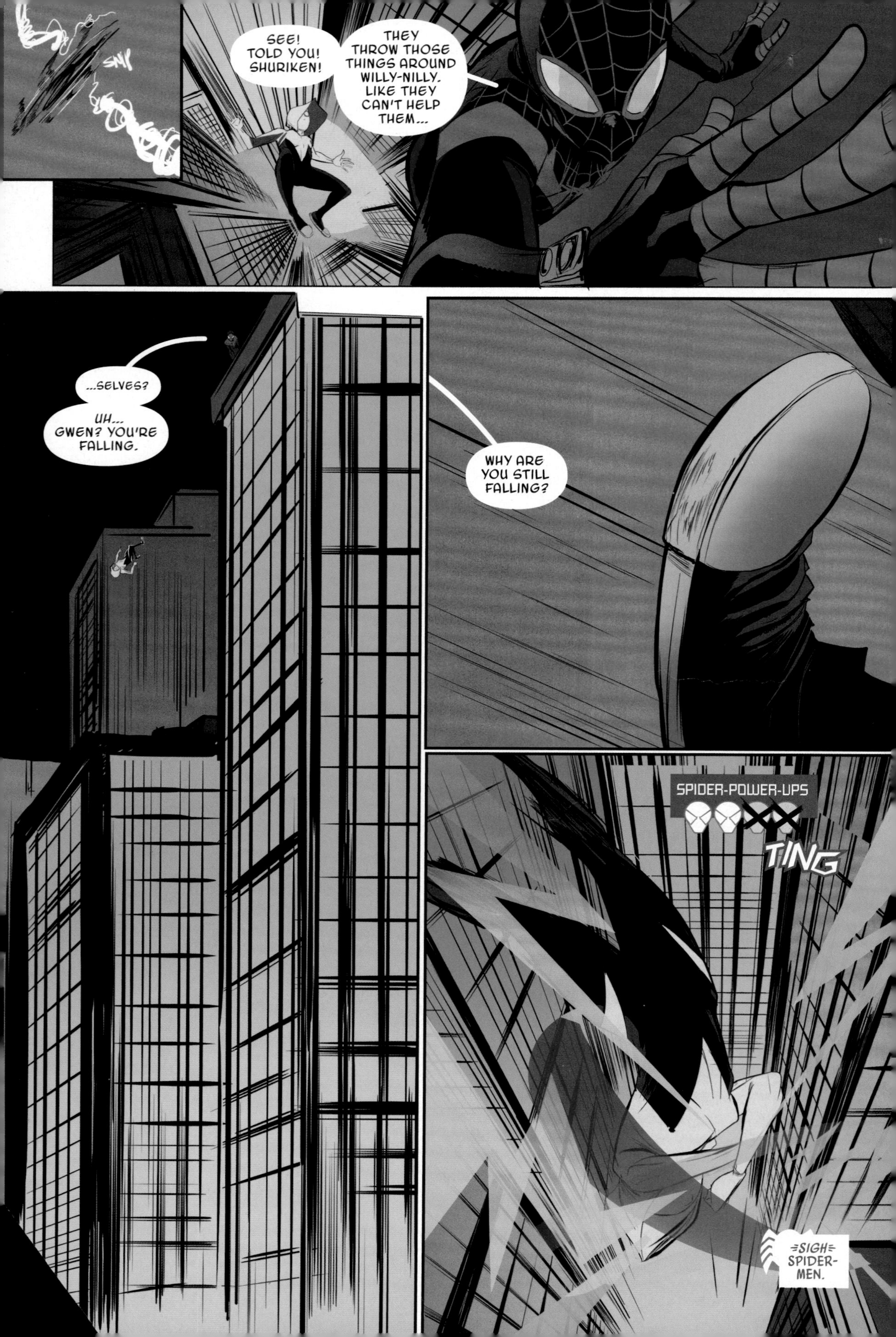
SNK
SEE! TOLD YOU! SHURIKEN!
THEY THROW THOSE THINGS AROUND WILLY-NILLY. LIKE THEY CAN'T HELP THEM...
...SELVES?
UH... GWEN? YOU'RE FALLING.
WHY ARE YOU STILL FALLING?
SPIDER-POWER-UPS
TING
SIGH SPIDER-MEN.

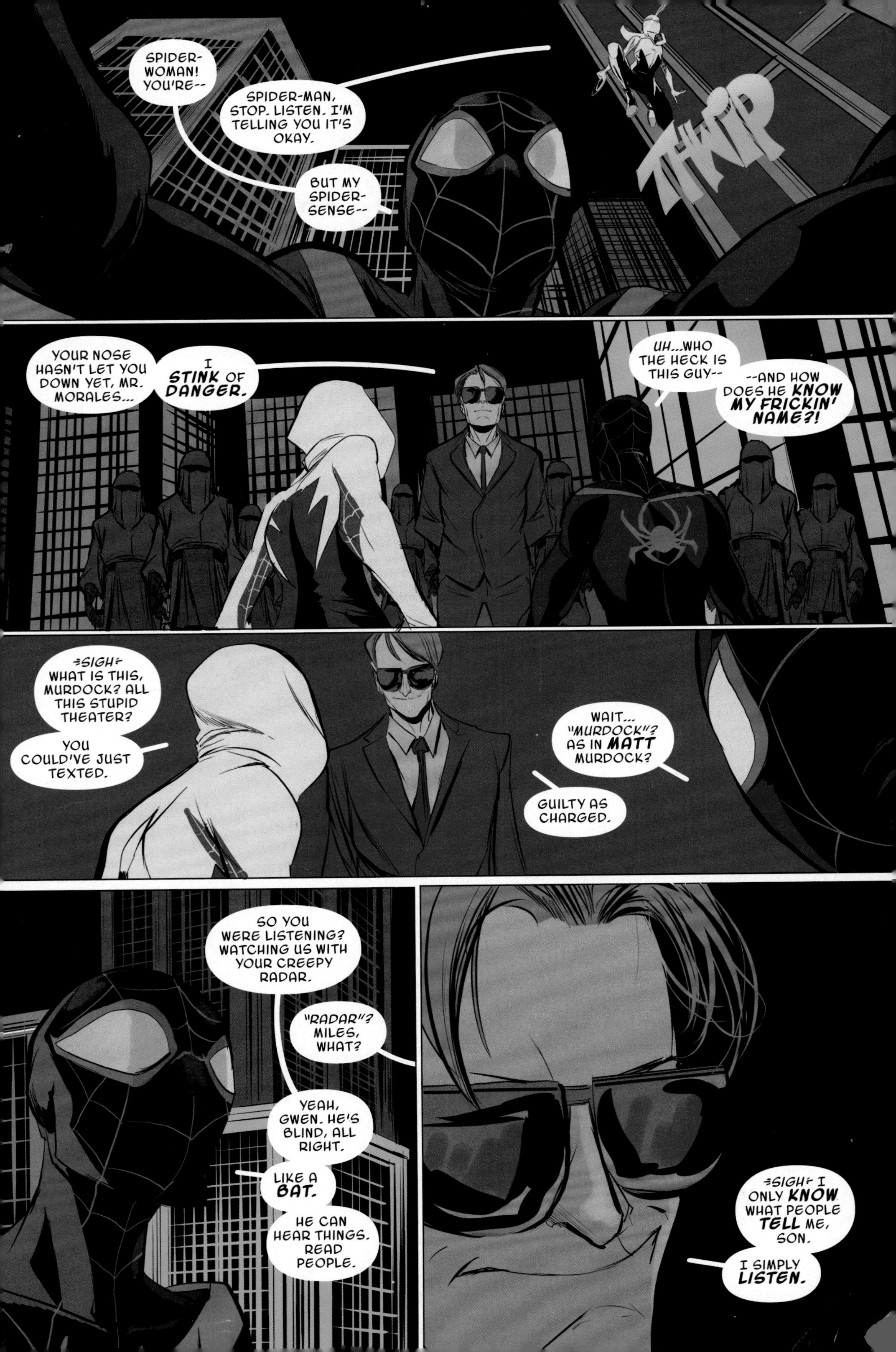
SPIDER-WOMAN! YOU'RE--
SPIDER-MAN, STOP. LISTEN. I'M TELLING YOU IT'S OKAY.
BUT MY SPIDER-SENSE--
THWIP
YOUR NOSE HASN'T LET YOU DOWN YET, MR. MORALES...
I STINK OF DANGER.
UH...WHO THE HECK IS THIS GUY--
--AND HOW DOES HE KNOW MY FRICKIN' NAME?!
=SIGH= WHAT IS THIS, MURDOCK? ALL THIS STUPID THEATER?
YOU COULD'VE JUST TEXTED.
WAIT... "MURDOCK"? AS IN MATT MURDOCK?
GUILTY AS CHARGED.
SO YOU WERE LISTENING? WATCHING US WITH YOUR CREEPY RADAR.
"RADAR"? MILES, WHAT?
YEAH, GWEN. HE'S BLIND, ALL RIGHT.
LIKE A BAT.
HE CAN HEAR THINGS. READ PEOPLE.
=SIGH= I ONLY KNOW WHAT PEOPLE TELL ME, SON.
I SIMPLY LISTEN.

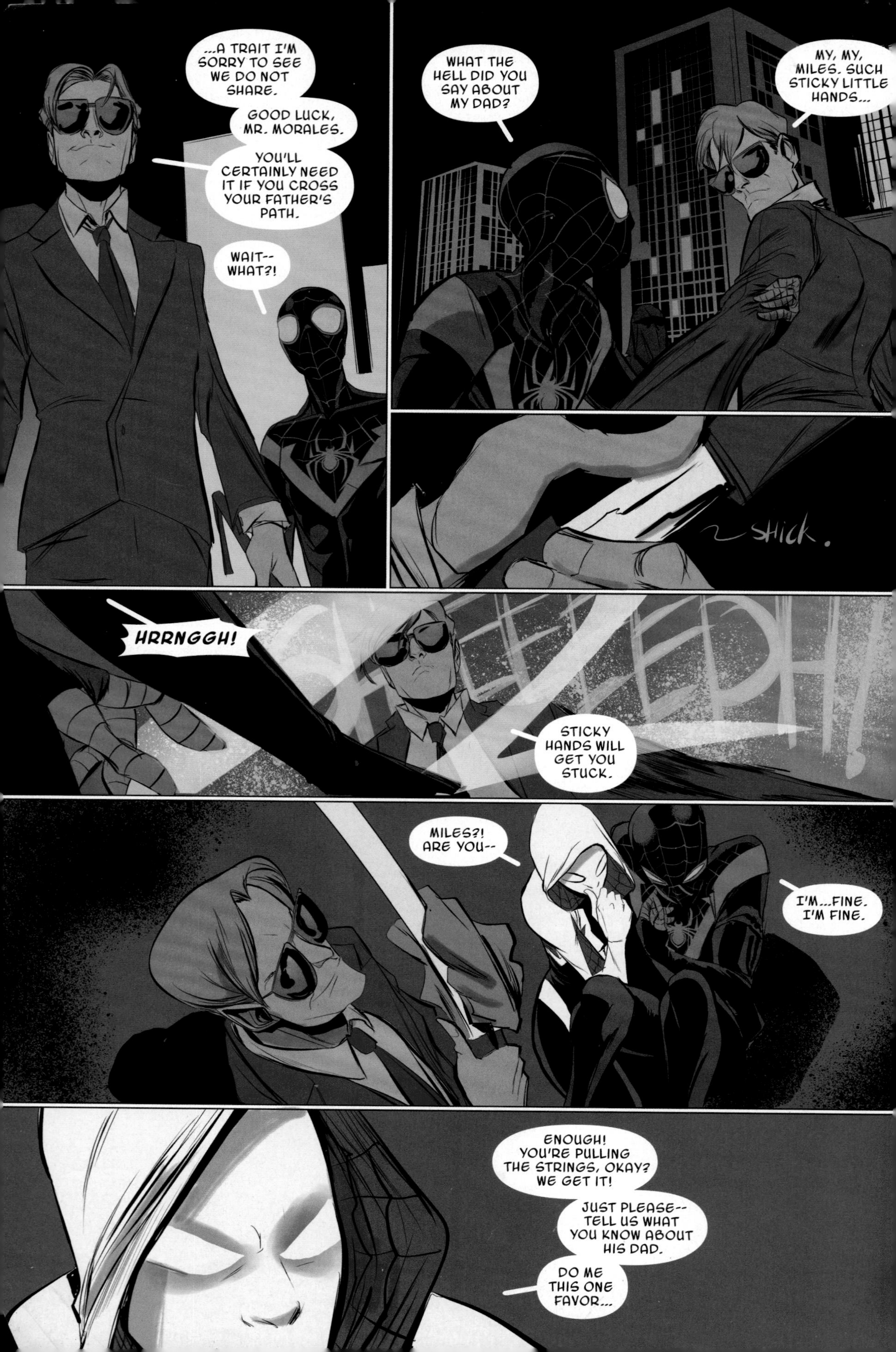

...A TRAIT I'M SORRY TO SEE WE DO NOT SHARE.
GOOD LUCK, MR. MORALES.
YOU'LL CERTAINLY NEED IT IF YOU CROSS YOUR FATHER'S PATH.
WAIT-- WHAT?!
WHAT THE HELL DID YOU SAY ABOUT MY DAD?
MY, MY, MILES. SUCH STICKY LITTLE HANDS...
SHICK.
HRRNGGH!
STICKY HANDS WILL GET YOU STUCK.
MILES?! ARE YOU--
I'M...FINE. I'M FINE.
ENOUGH! YOU'RE PULLING THE STRINGS, OKAY? WE GET IT!
JUST PLEASE-- TELL US WHAT YOU KNOW ABOUT HIS DAD.
DO ME THIS ONE FAVOR...

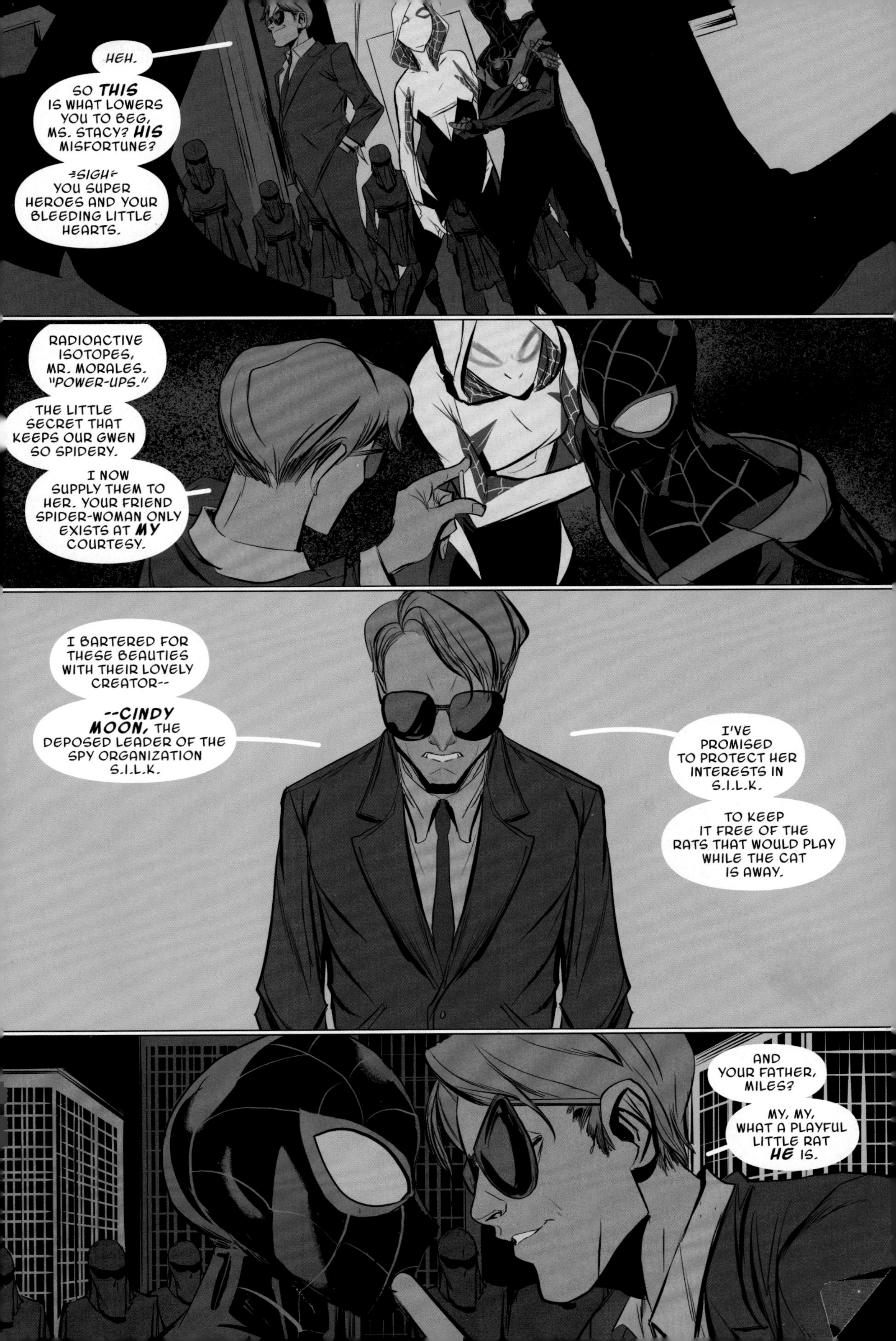
HEH.
SO THIS IS WHAT LOWERS YOU TO BEG, MS. STACY? HIS MISFORTUNE?
=SIGH= YOU SUPER HEROES AND YOUR BLEEDING LITTLE HEARTS.
RADIOACTIVE ISOTOPES, MR. MORALES. "POWER-UPS."
THE LITTLE SECRET THAT KEEPS OUR GWEN SO SPIDERY.
I NOW SUPPLY THEM TO HER. YOUR FRIEND SPIDER-WOMAN ONLY EXISTS AT MY COURTESY.
I BARTERED FOR THESE BEAUTIES WITH THEIR LOVELY CREATOR--
--CINDY MOON, THE DEPOSED LEADER OF THE SPY ORGANIZATION S.I.L.K.
I'VE PROMISED TO PROTECT HER INTERESTS IN S.I.L.K.
TO KEEP IT FREE OF THE RATS THAT WOULD PLAY WHILE THE CAT IS AWAY.
AND YOUR FATHER, MILES?
MY, MY, WHAT A PLAYFUL LITTLE RAT HE IS.

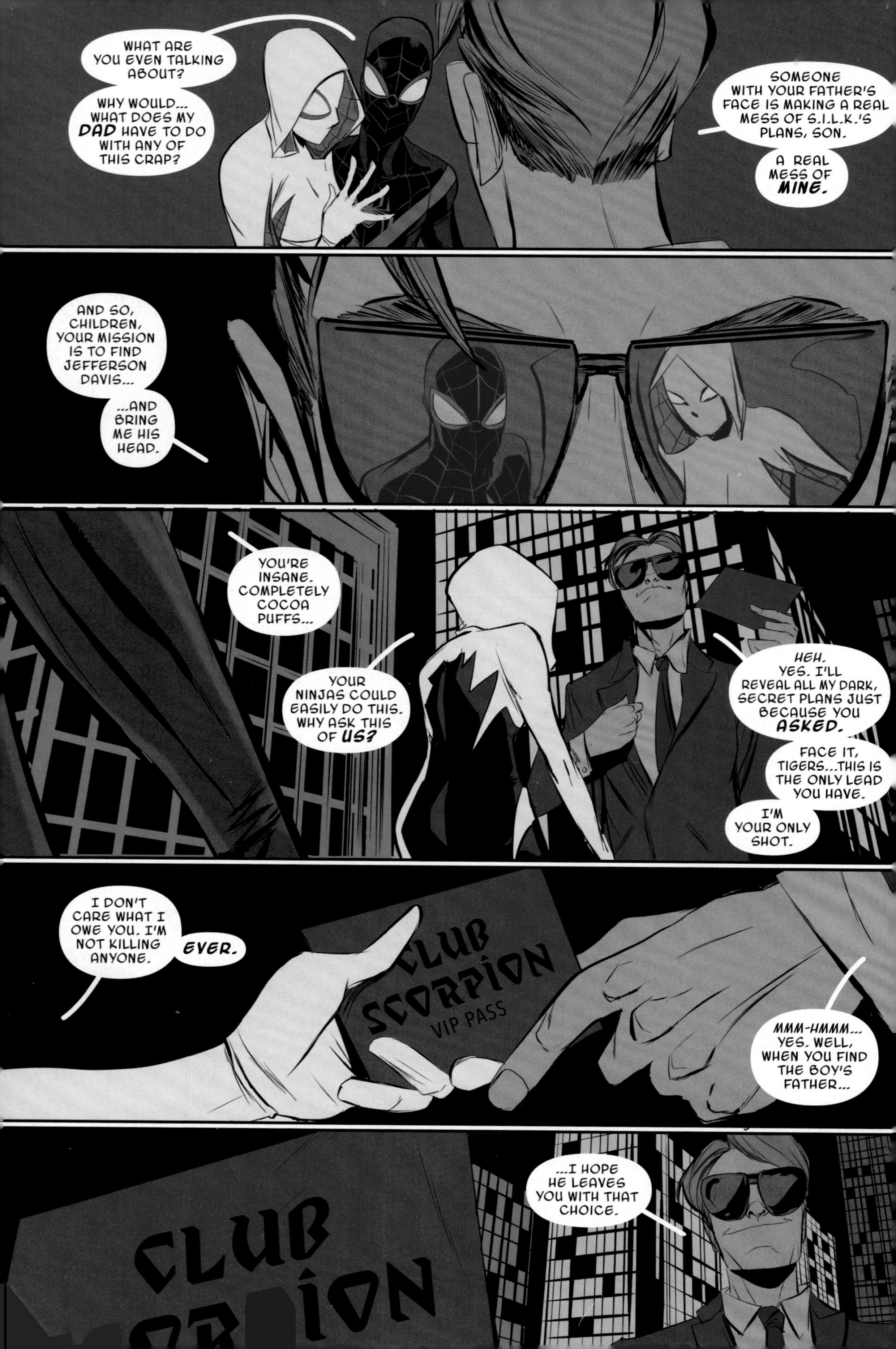
WHAT ARE YOU EVEN TALKING ABOUT?
WHY WOULD... WHAT DOES MY DAD HAVE TO DO WITH ANY OF THIS CRAP?
SOMEONE WITH YOUR FATHER'S FACE IS MAKING A REAL MESS OF S.I.L.K.'S PLANS, SON.
A REAL MESS OF MINE.
AND SO, CHILDREN, YOUR MISSION IS TO FIND JEFFERSON DAVIS...
...AND BRING ME HIS HEAD.
YOU'RE INSANE. COMPLETELY COCOA PUFFS...
YOUR NINJAS COULD EASILY DO THIS. WHY ASK THIS OF US?
HEH. YES. I'LL REVEAL ALL MY DARK, SECRET PLANS JUST BECAUSE YOU ASKED.
FACE IT, TIGERS...THIS IS THE ONLY LEAD YOU HAVE.
I'M YOUR ONLY SHOT.
I DON'T CARE WHAT I OWE YOU. I'M NOT KILLING ANYONE.
EVER.
CLUB SCORPION
VIP PASS
MMM-HMMM... YES. WELL, WHEN YOU FIND THE BOY'S FATHER...
...I HOPE HE LEAVES YOU WITH THAT CHOICE.

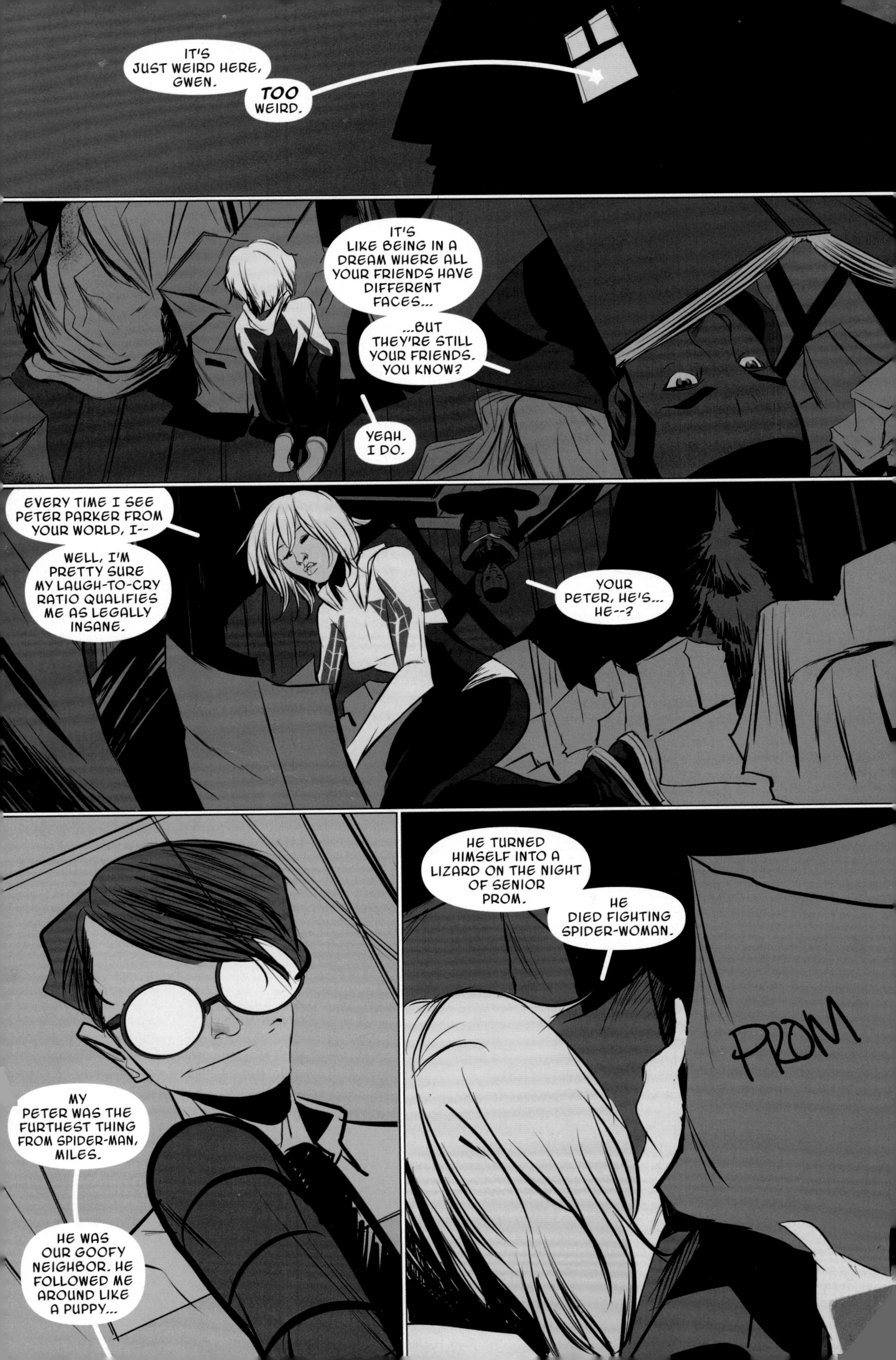
IT'S JUST WEIRD HERE, GWEN.
TOO WEIRD.
IT'S LIKE BEING IN A DREAM WHERE ALL YOUR FRIENDS HAVE DIFFERENT FACES...
...BUT THEY'RE STILL YOUR FRIENDS. YOU KNOW?
YEAH. I DO.
EVERY TIME I SEE PETER PARKER FROM YOUR WORLD, I--
WELL, I'M PRETTY SURE MY LAUGH-TO-CRY RATIO QUALIFIES ME AS LEGALLY INSANE.
YOUR PETER, HE'S... HE--?
MY PETER WAS THE FURTHEST THING FROM SPIDER-MAN, MILES.
HE WAS OUR GOOFY NEIGHBOR. HE FOLLOWED ME AROUND LIKE A PUPPY...
HE TURNED HIMSELF INTO A LIZARD ON THE NIGHT OF SENIOR PROM.
HE DIED FIGHTING SPIDER-WOMAN.
PROM

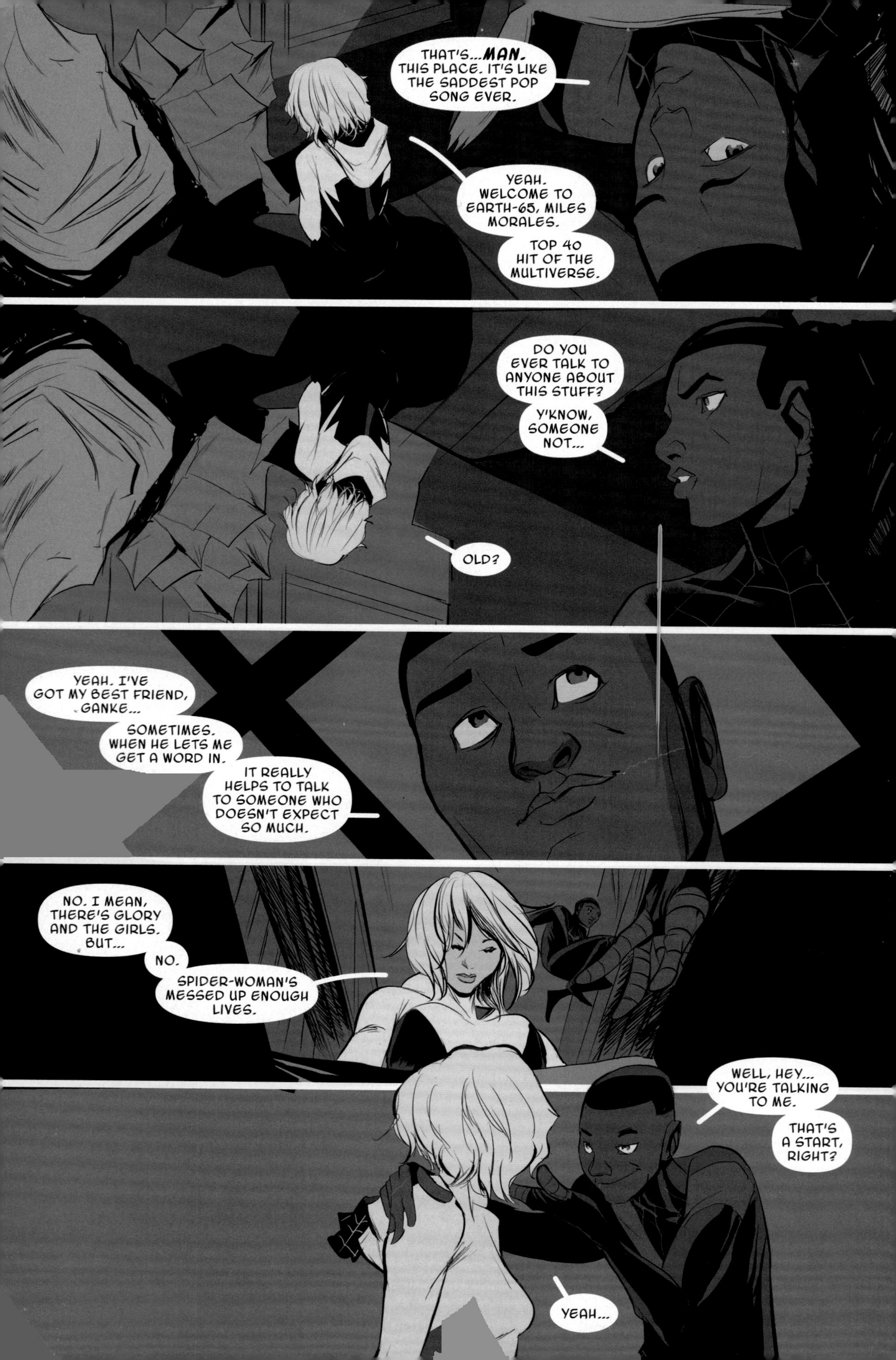
THAT'S...MAN. THIS PLACE. IT'S LIKE THE SADDEST POP SONG EVER.
YEAH. WELCOME TO EARTH-65, MILES MORALES.
TOP 40 HIT OF THE MULTIVERSE.
DO YOU EVER TALK TO ANYONE ABOUT THIS STUFF?
Y'KNOW, SOMEONE NOT...
OLD?
YEAH. I'VE GOT MY BEST FRIEND, GANKE...
SOMETIMES. WHEN HE LETS ME GET A WORD IN.
IT REALLY HELPS TO TALK TO SOMEONE WHO DOESN'T EXPECT SO MUCH.
NO. I MEAN, THERE'S GLORY AND THE GIRLS. BUT...
NO.
SPIDER-WOMAN'S MESSED UP ENOUGH LIVES.
WELL, HEY... YOU'RE TALKING TO ME.
THAT'S A START, RIGHT?
YEAH...

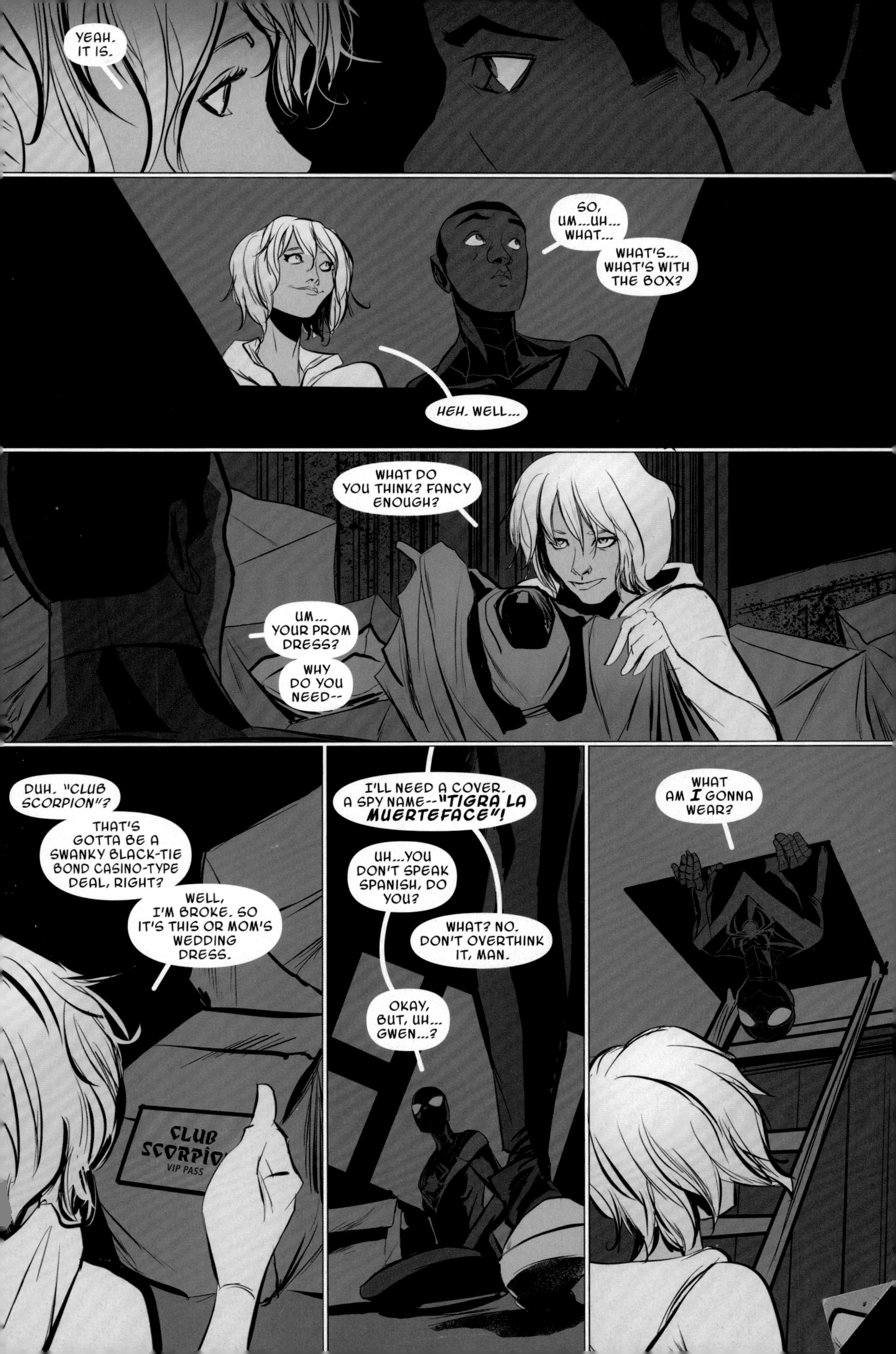
YEAH. IT IS.
SO, UM...UH... WHAT...
WHAT'S... WHAT'S WITH THE BOX?
HEH. WELL...
WHAT DO YOU THINK? FANCY ENOUGH?
UM... YOUR PROM DRESS?
WHY DO YOU NEED--
DUH. "CLUB SCORPION"?
THAT'S GOTTA BE A SWANKY BLACK-TIE BOND CASINO-TYPE DEAL, RIGHT?
WELL, I'M BROKE. SO IT'S THIS OR MOM'S WEDDING DRESS.
CLUB SCORPIO
VIP PASS
I'LL NEED A COVER. A SPY NAME--"TIGRA LA MUERTEFACE"!
UH...YOU DON'T SPEAK SPANISH, DO YOU?
WHAT? NO. DON'T OVERTHINK IT, MAN.
OKAY, BUT, UH... GWEN...?
WHAT AM I GONNA WEAR?

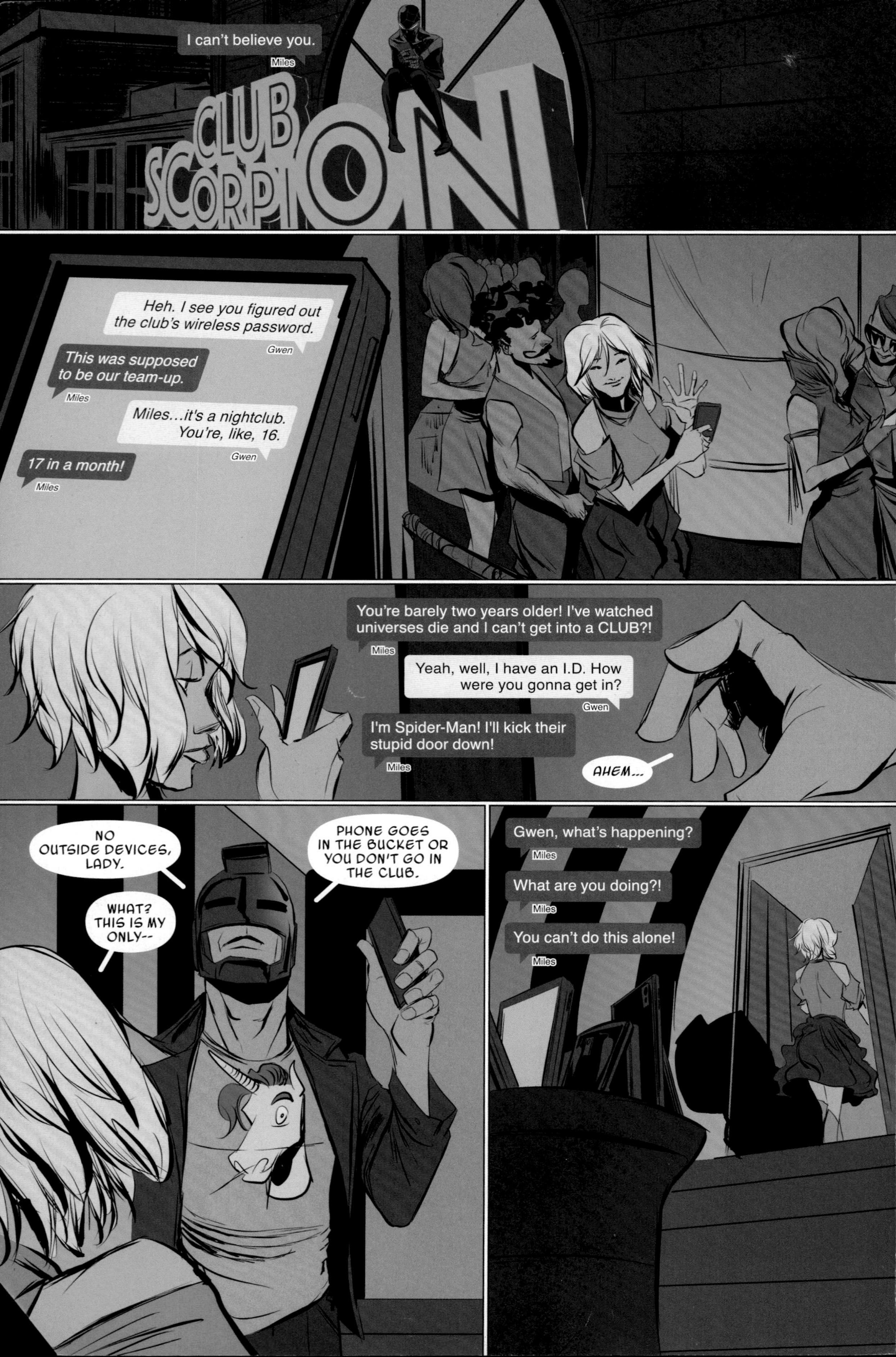
I can't believe you.
Miles
CLUB SCORPION
Heh. I see you figured out the club's wireless password.
Gwen
This was supposed to be our team-up.
Miles
Miles...it's a nightclub. You're, like, 16.
Gwen
17 in a month!
Miles
You're barely two years older! I've watched universes die and I can't get into a CLUB?!
Miles
Yeah, well, I have an I.D. How were you gonna get in?
Gwen
I'm Spider-Man! I'll kick their stupid door down!
Miles
AHEM...
NO OUTSIDE DEVICES, LADY.
WHAT? THIS IS MY ONLY--
PHONE GOES IN THE BUCKET OR YOU DON'T GO IN THE CLUB.
Gwen, what's happening?
Miles
What are you doing?!
Miles
You can't do this alone!
Miles

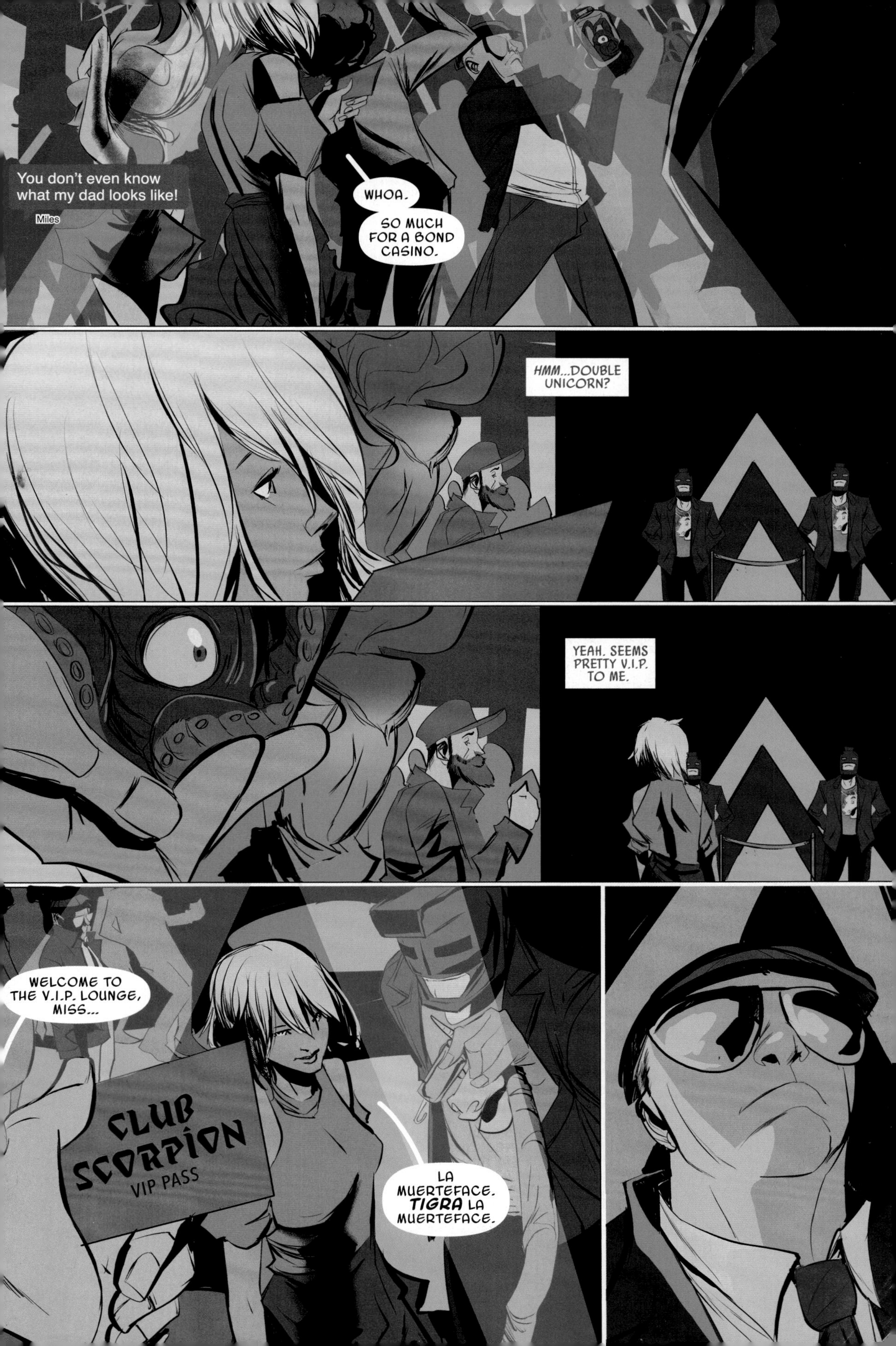
You don't even know what my dad looks like!
Miles
WHOA.
SO MUCH FOR A BOND CASINO.
HMM...DOUBLE UNICORN?
YEAH. SEEMS PRETTY V.I.P. TO ME.
WELCOME TO THE V.I.P. LOUNGE, MISS...
CLUB SCORPION
VIP PASS
LA MUERTEFACE. **TIGRA** LA MUERTEFACE.

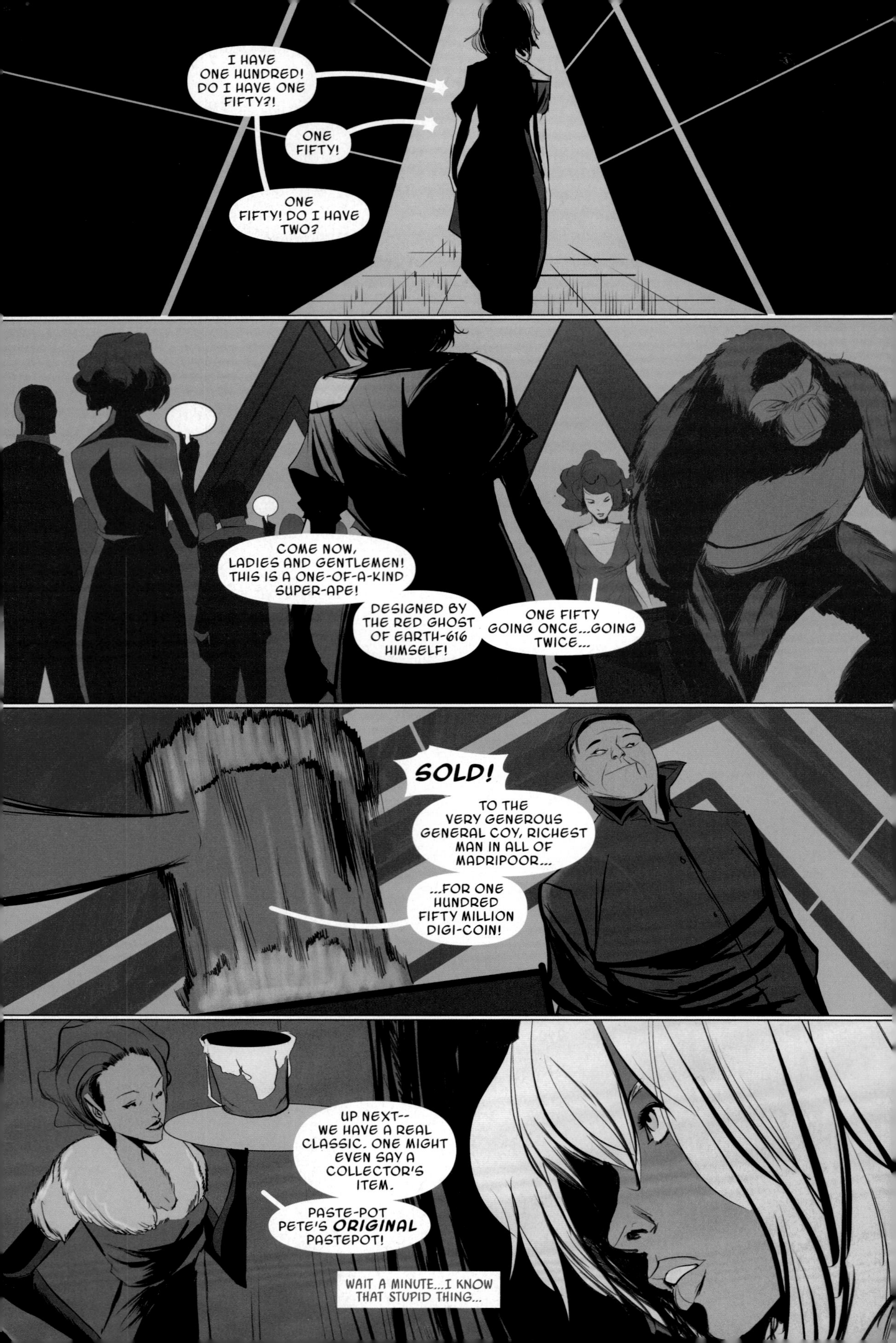
I HAVE ONE HUNDRED! DO I HAVE ONE FIFTY?!
ONE FIFTY!
ONE FIFTY! DO I HAVE TWO?
COME NOW, LADIES AND GENTLEMEN! THIS IS A ONE-OF-A-KIND SUPER-APE!
DESIGNED BY THE RED GHOST OF EARTH-616 HIMSELF!
ONE FIFTY GOING ONCE...GOING TWICE...
SOLD!
TO THE VERY GENEROUS GENERAL COY, RICHEST MAN IN ALL OF MADRIPOOR...
...FOR ONE HUNDRED FIFTY MILLION DIGI-COIN!
UP NEXT-- WE HAVE A REAL CLASSIC. ONE MIGHT EVEN SAY A COLLECTOR'S ITEM.
PASTE-POT PETE'S ORIGINAL PASTEPOT!
WAIT A MINUTE...I KNOW THAT STUPID THING...

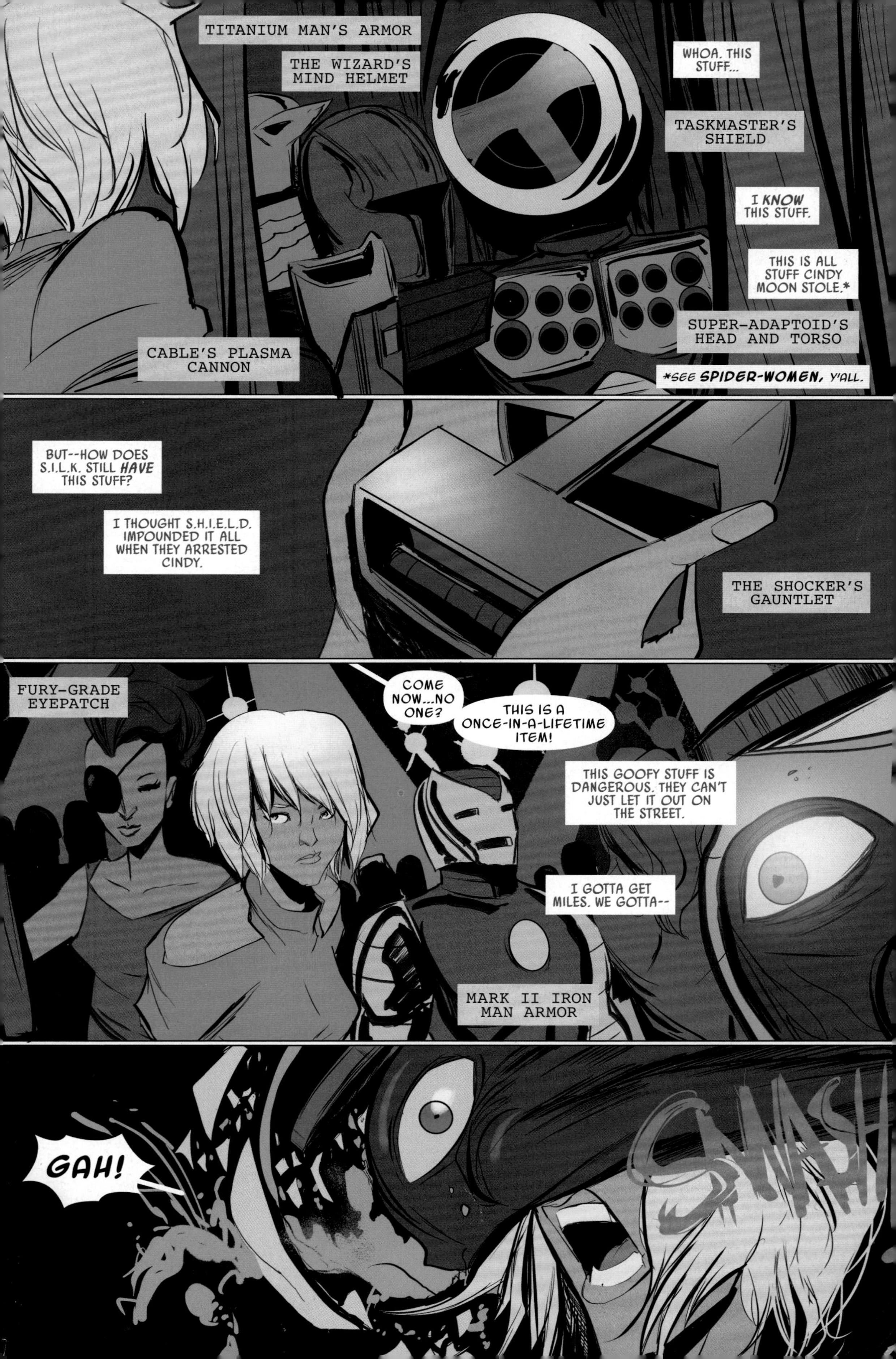
TITANIUM MAN'S ARMOR
THE WIZARD'S MIND HELMET
WHOA. THIS STUFF...
TASKMASTER'S SHIELD
I KNOW THIS STUFF.
THIS IS ALL STUFF CINDY MOON STOLE.*
SUPER-ADAPTOID'S HEAD AND TORSO
CABLE'S PLASMA CANNON
*SEE SPIDER-WOMEN, Y'ALL.
BUT--HOW DOES S.I.L.K. STILL HAVE THIS STUFF?
I THOUGHT S.H.I.E.L.D. IMPOUNDED IT ALL WHEN THEY ARRESTED CINDY.
THE SHOCKER'S GAUNTLET
FURY-GRADE EYEPATCH
COME NOW...NO ONE?
THIS IS A ONCE-IN-A-LIFETIME ITEM!
THIS GOOFY STUFF IS DANGEROUS. THEY CAN'T JUST LET IT OUT ON THE STREET.
I GOTTA GET MILES. WE GOTTA--
MARK II IRON MAN ARMOR
GAH!
SMASH!

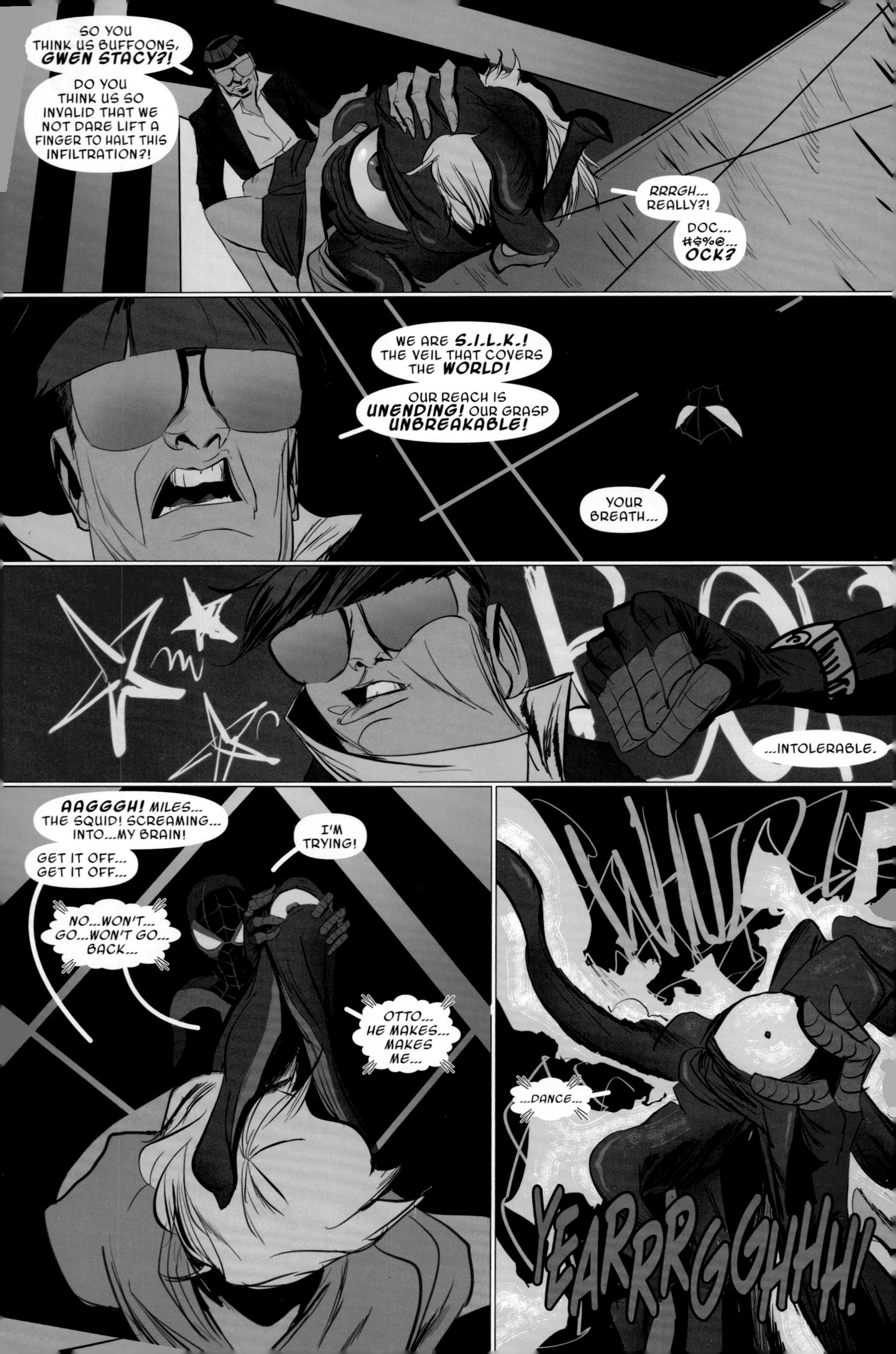
SO YOU THINK US BUFFOONS, GWEN STACY?!
DO YOU THINK US SO INVALID THAT WE NOT DARE LIFT A FINGER TO HALT THIS INFILTRATION?!
RRRGH... REALLY?!
DOC... #$%@... OCK?
WE ARE S.I.L.K.! THE VEIL THAT COVERS THE WORLD!
OUR REACH IS UNENDING! OUR GRASP UNBREAKABLE!
YOUR BREATH...
...INTOLERABLE.
AAGGGH! MILES... THE SQUID! SCREAMING... INTO...MY BRAIN!
I'M TRYING!
GET IT OFF... GET IT OFF...
NO...WON'T... GO...WON'T GO... BACK...
OTTO... HE MAKES... MAKES ME...
...DANCE...
YEARRRGGHHH!

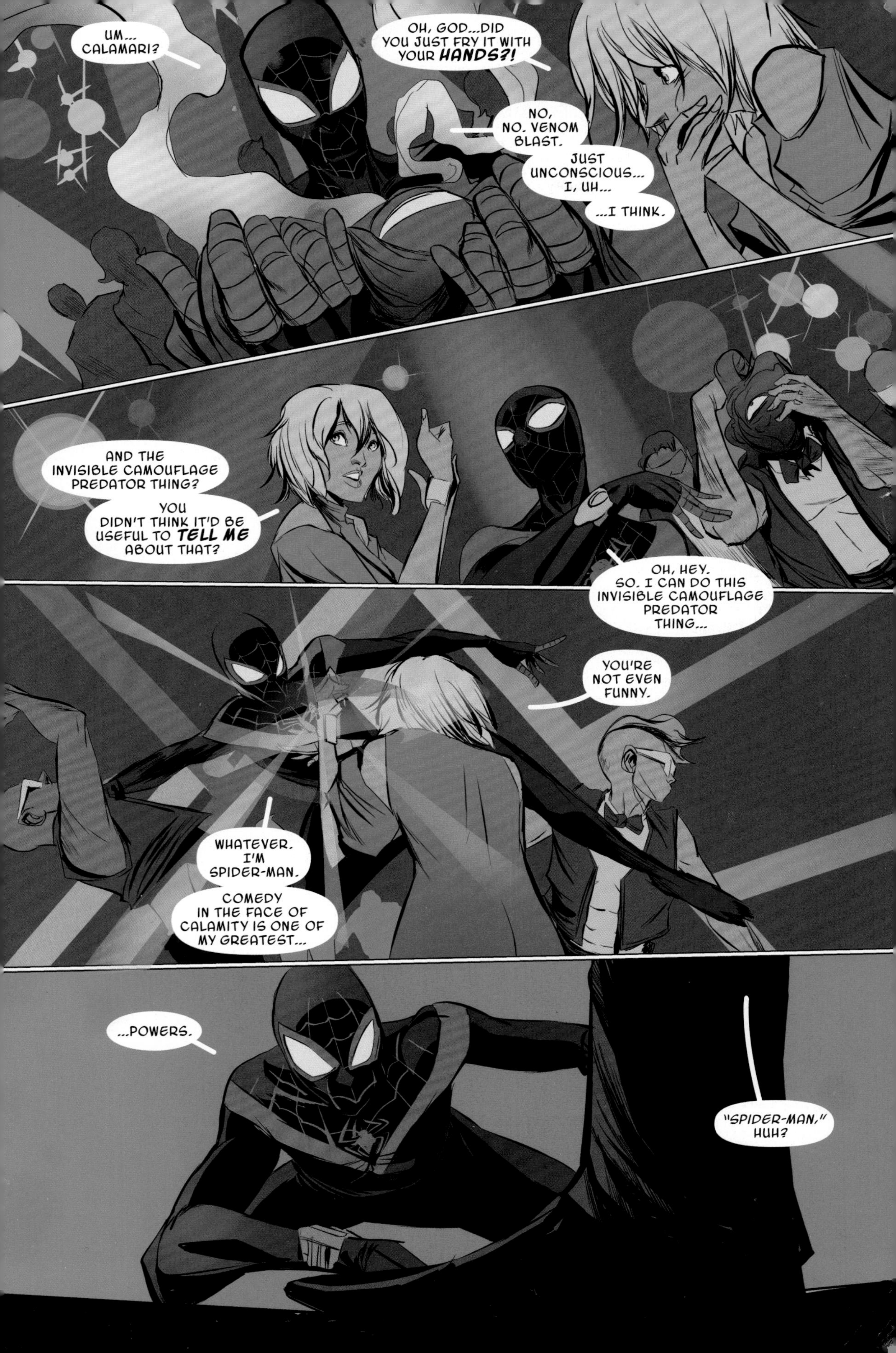
UM... CALAMARI?
OH, GOD...DID YOU JUST FRY IT WITH YOUR HANDS?!
NO, NO. VENOM BLAST.
JUST UNCONSCIOUS... I, UH...
...I THINK.
AND THE INVISIBLE CAMOUFLAGE PREDATOR THING?
YOU DIDN'T THINK IT'D BE USEFUL TO TELL ME ABOUT THAT?
OH, HEY. SO. I CAN DO THIS INVISIBLE CAMOUFLAGE PREDATOR THING...
YOU'RE NOT EVEN FUNNY.
WHATEVER. I'M SPIDER-MAN.
COMEDY IN THE FACE OF CALAMITY IS ONE OF MY GREATEST...
...POWERS.
"SPIDER-MAN," HUH?

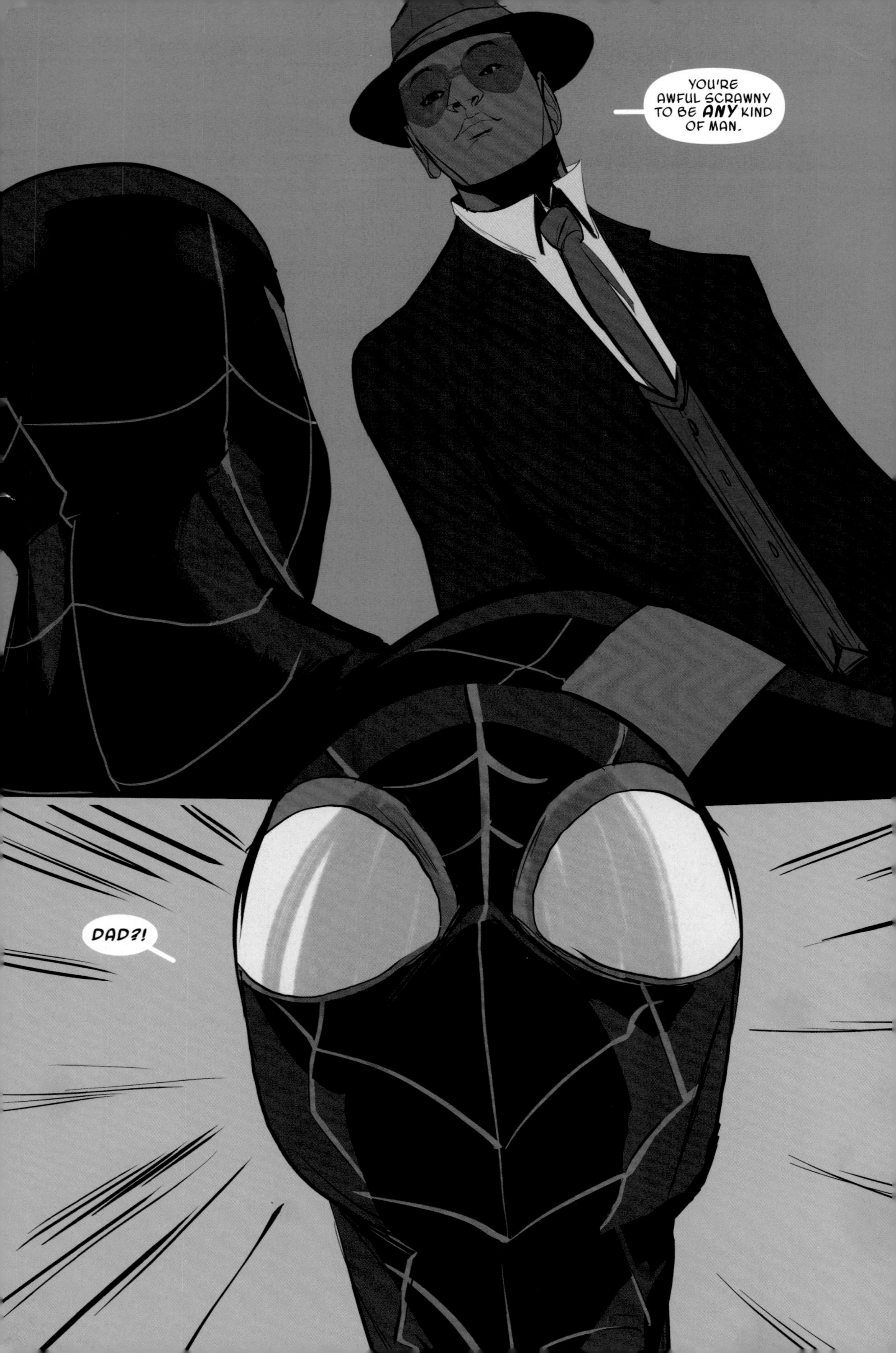
YOU'RE AWFUL SCRAWNY TO BE ANY KIND OF MAN.
DAD?!

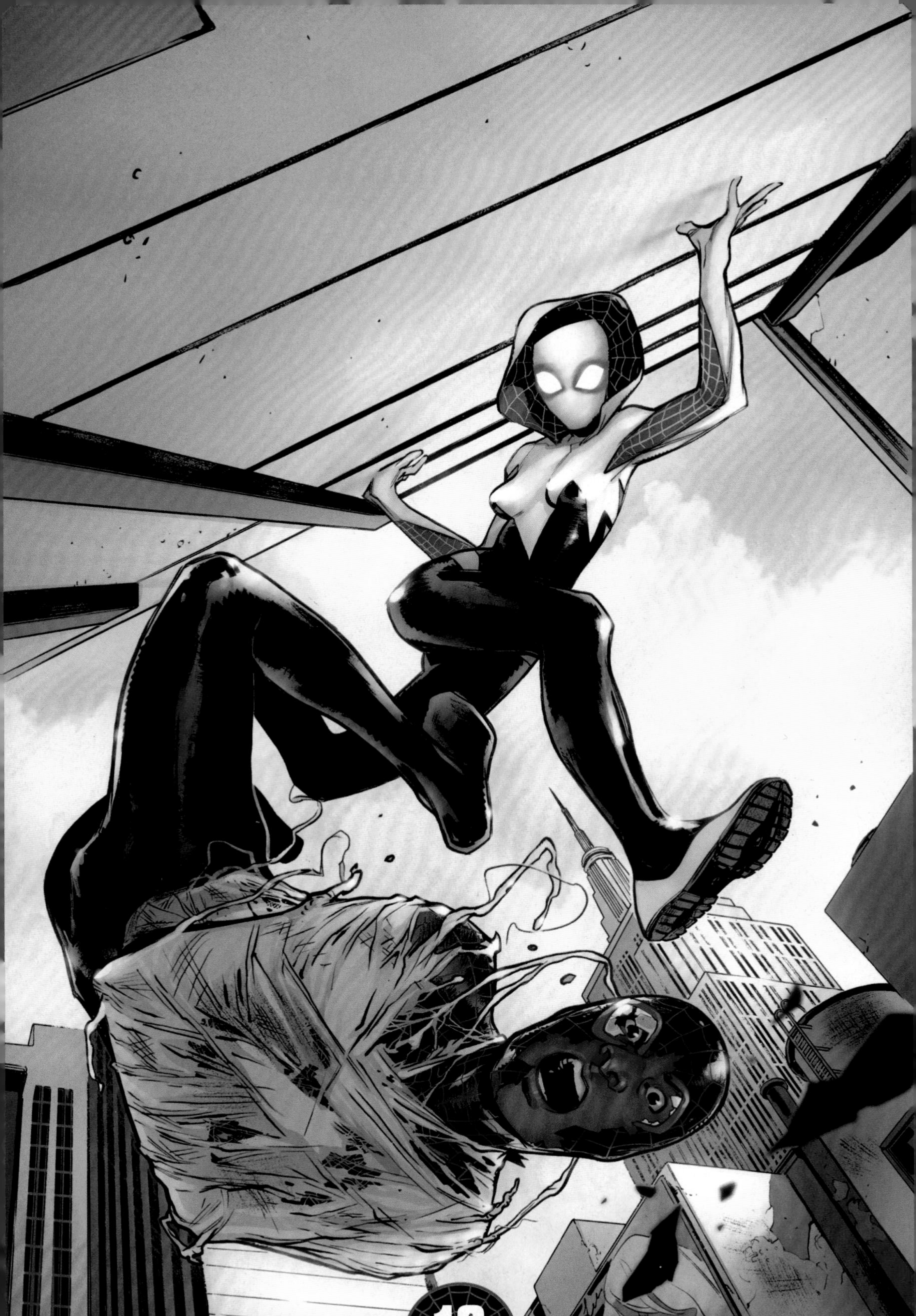

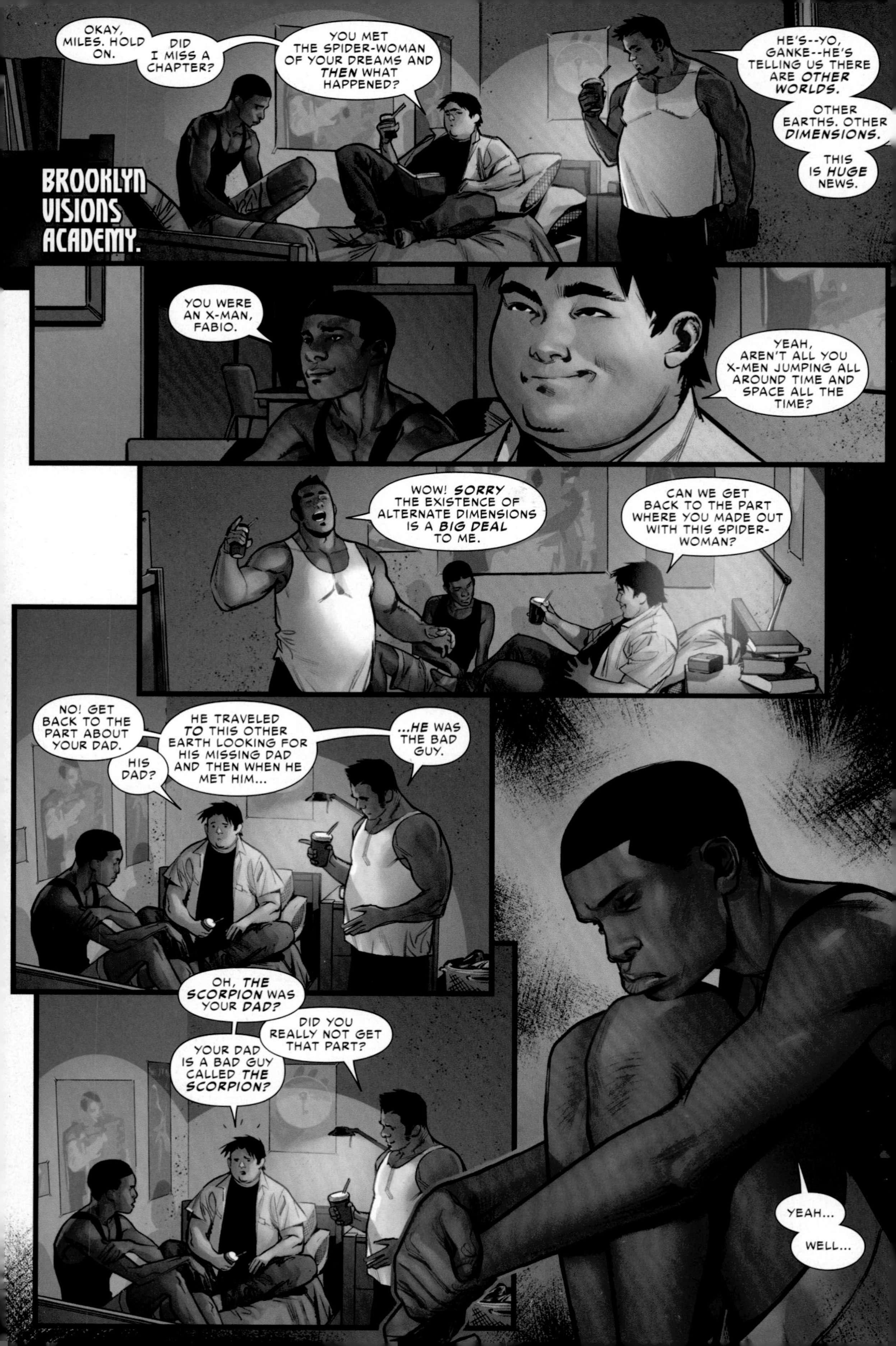
BROOKLYN VISIONS ACADEMY.
OKAY, MILES. HOLD ON.
DID I MISS A CHAPTER?
YOU MET THE SPIDER-WOMAN OF YOUR DREAMS AND THEN WHAT HAPPENED?
HE'S--YO, GANKE--HE'S TELLING US THERE ARE OTHER WORLDS.
OTHER EARTHS. OTHER DIMENSIONS.
THIS IS HUGE NEWS.
YOU WERE AN X-MAN, FABIO.
YEAH, AREN'T ALL YOU X-MEN JUMPING ALL AROUND TIME AND SPACE ALL THE TIME?
WOW! SORRY THE EXISTENCE OF ALTERNATE DIMENSIONS IS A BIG DEAL TO ME.
CAN WE GET BACK TO THE PART WHERE YOU MADE OUT WITH THIS SPIDER-WOMAN?
NO! GET BACK TO THE PART ABOUT YOUR DAD.
HIS DAD?
HE TRAVELED TO THIS OTHER EARTH LOOKING FOR HIS MISSING DAD AND THEN WHEN HE MET HIM...
...HE WAS THE BAD GUY.
OH, THE SCORPION WAS YOUR DAD?
YOUR DAD IS A BAD GUY CALLED THE SCORPION?
DID YOU REALLY NOT GET THAT PART?
YEAH...
WELL...

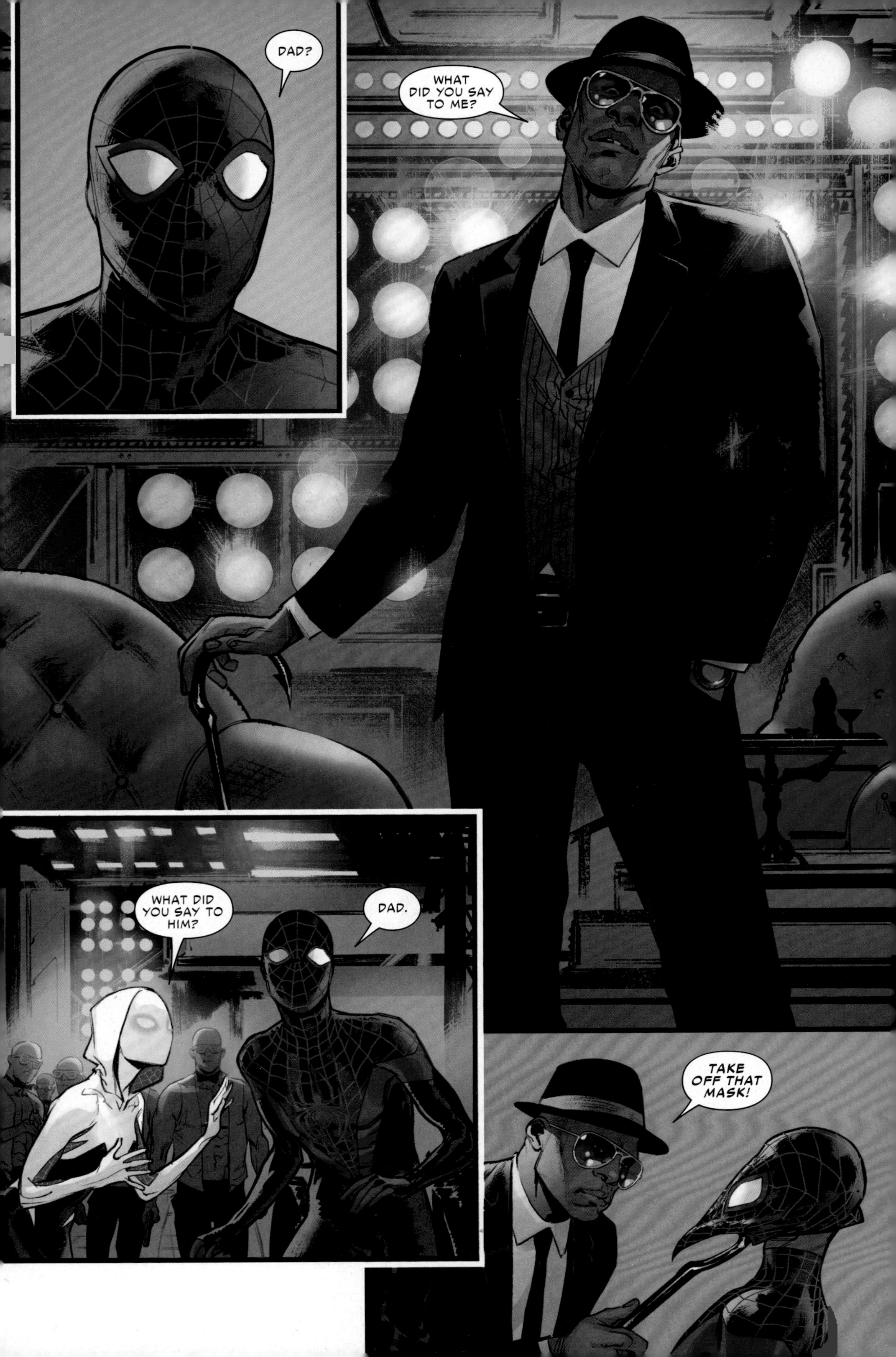
DAD?
WHAT DID YOU SAY TO ME?
WHAT DID YOU SAY TO HIM?
DAD.
TAKE OFF THAT MASK!

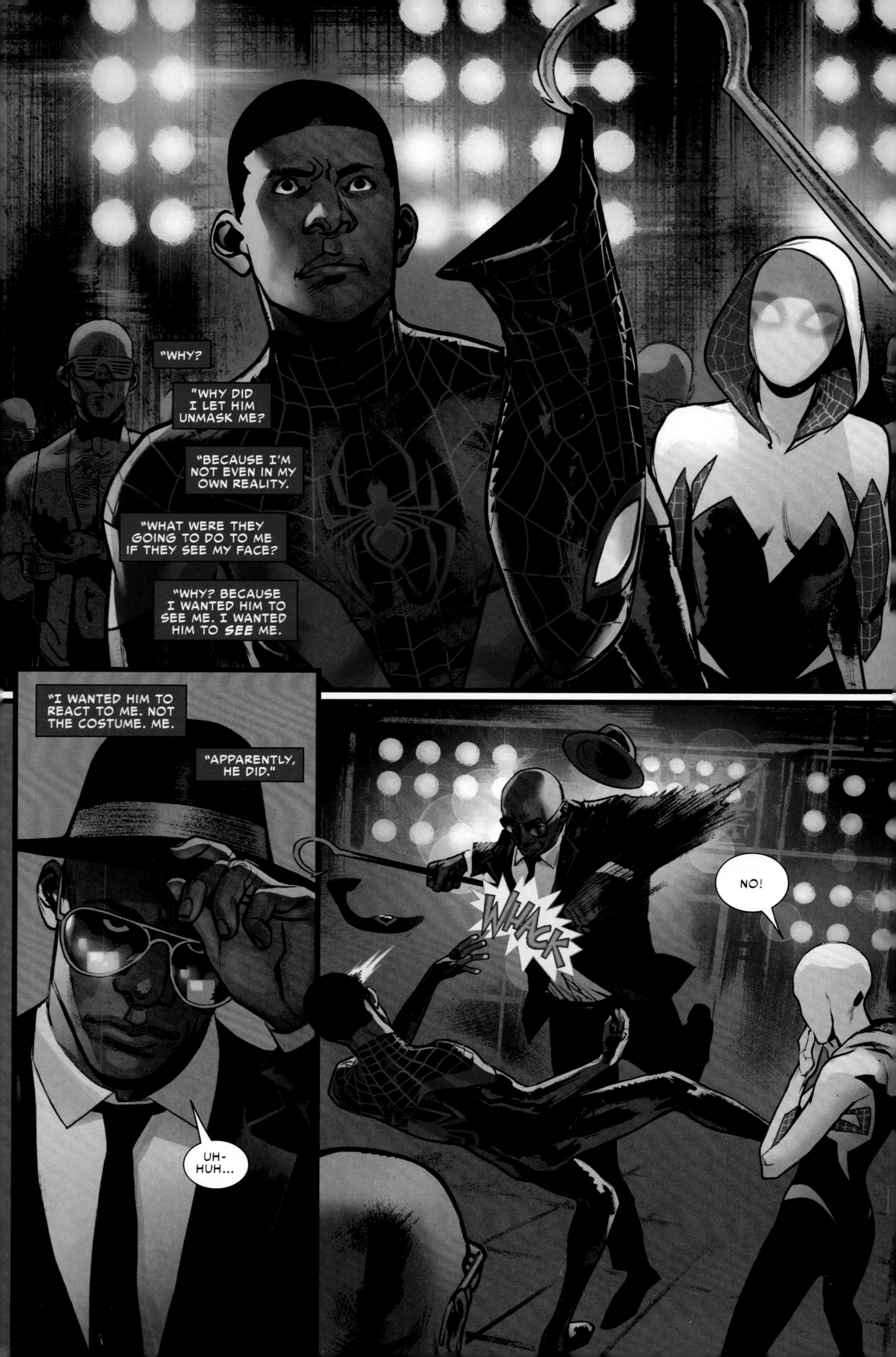
"WHY?
"WHY DID I LET HIM UNMASK ME?
"BECAUSE I'M NOT EVEN IN MY OWN REALITY.
"WHAT WERE THEY GOING TO DO TO ME IF THEY SEE MY FACE?
"WHY? BECAUSE I WANTED HIM TO SEE ME. I WANTED HIM TO *SEE* ME.
"I WANTED HIM TO REACT TO ME. NOT THE COSTUME. ME.
"APPARENTLY, HE DID."
UH-HUH...
WHACK
NO!

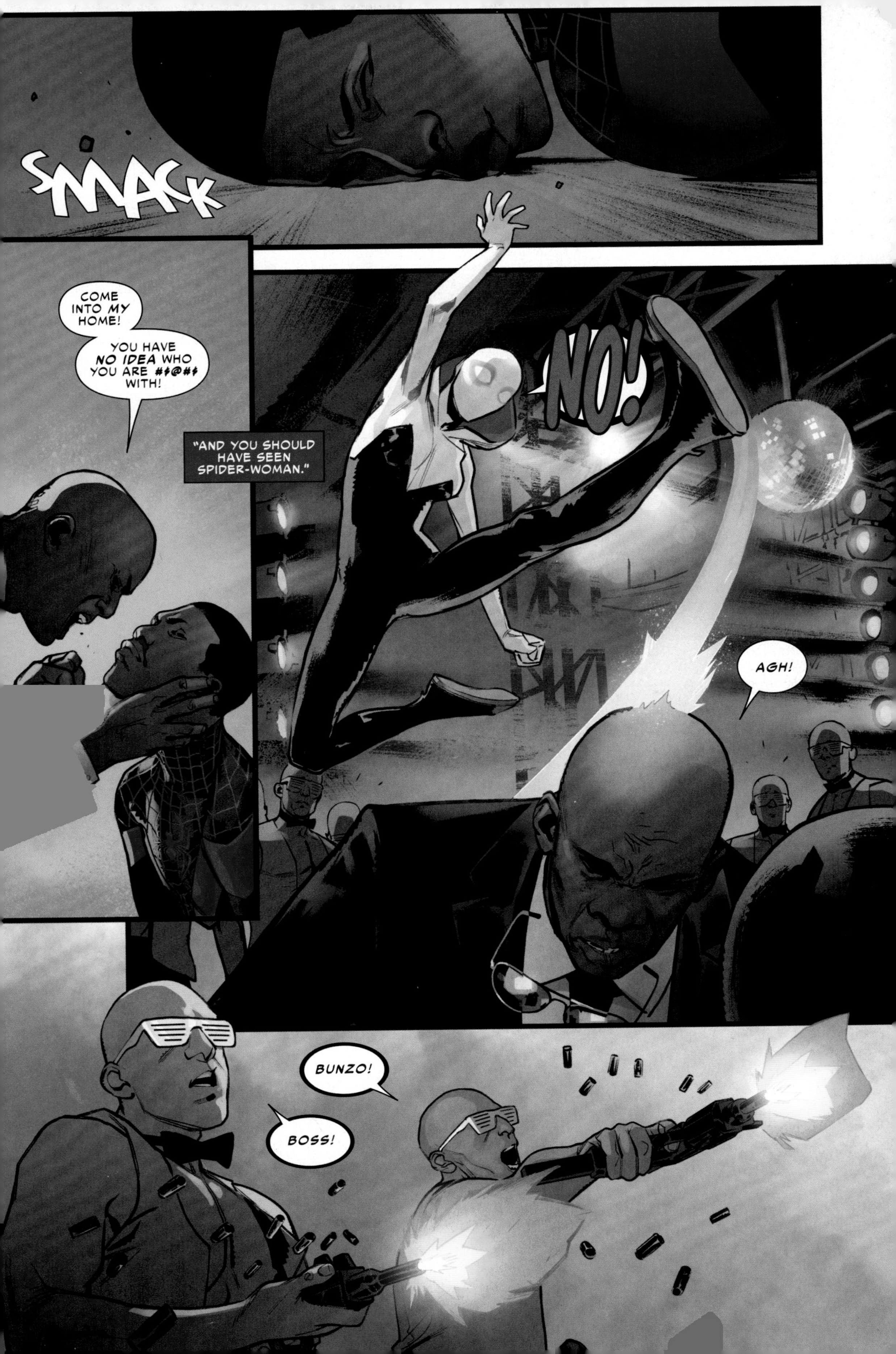
SMACK
COME INTO MY HOME!
YOU HAVE NO IDEA WHO YOU ARE #$@#$ WITH!
"AND YOU SHOULD HAVE SEEN SPIDER-WOMAN."
NO!
AGH!
BUNZO!
BOSS!

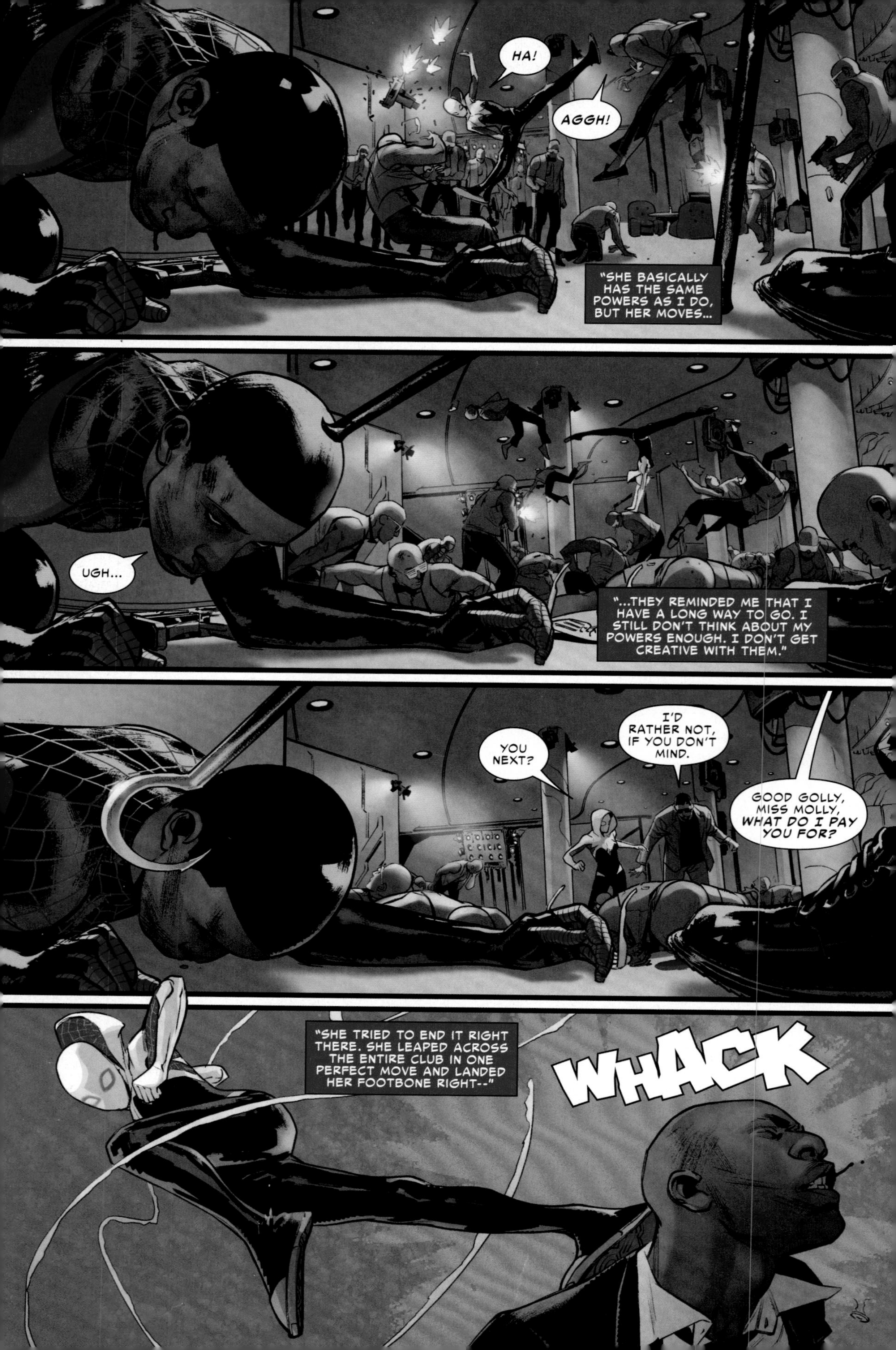
HA!
AGGH!
"SHE BASICALLY HAS THE SAME POWERS AS I DO, BUT HER MOVES...
UGH...
"...THEY REMINDED ME THAT I HAVE A LONG WAY TO GO. I STILL DON'T THINK ABOUT MY POWERS ENOUGH. I DON'T GET CREATIVE WITH THEM."
YOU NEXT?
I'D RATHER NOT, IF YOU DON'T MIND.
GOOD GOLLY, MISS MOLLY, WHAT DO I PAY YOU FOR?
"SHE TRIED TO END IT RIGHT THERE. SHE LEAPED ACROSS THE ENTIRE CLUB IN ONE PERFECT MOVE AND LANDED HER FOOTBONE RIGHT--"
WHACK

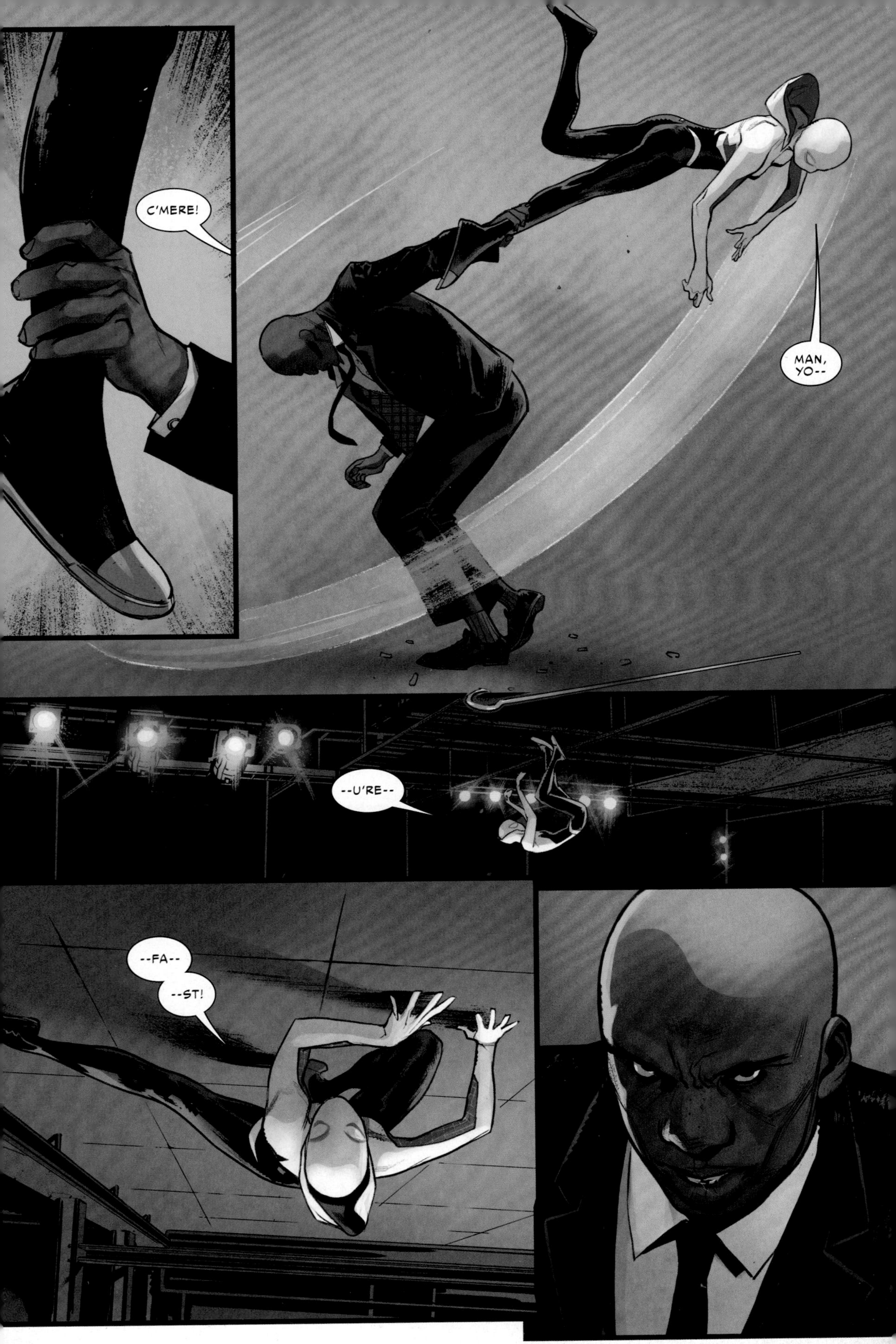
C'MERE!
MAN, YO--
--U'RE--
--FA--
--ST!

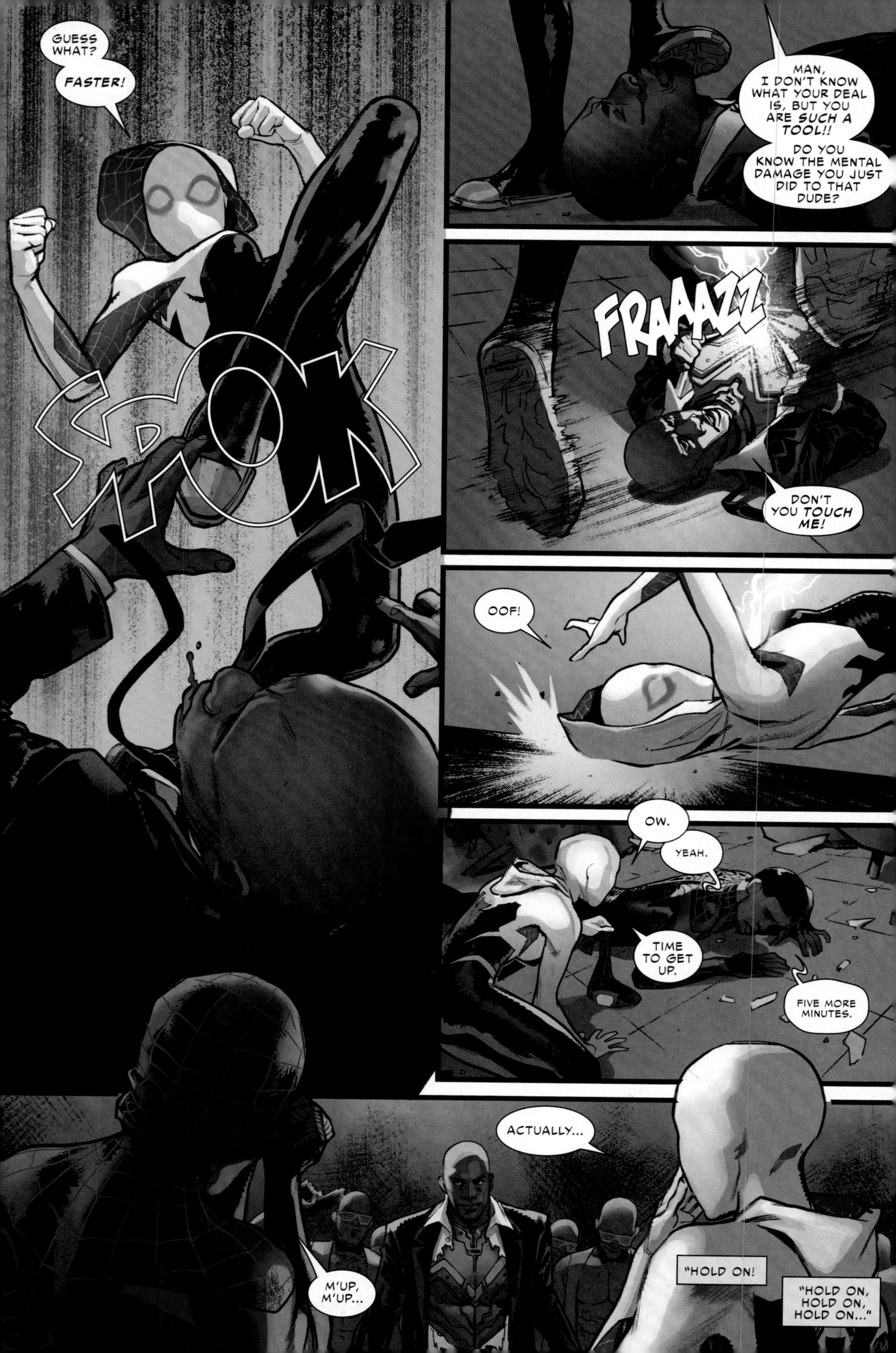
GUESS WHAT?
FASTER!
SPOK
MAN, I DON'T KNOW WHAT YOUR DEAL IS, BUT YOU ARE SUCH A TOOL!!
DO YOU KNOW THE MENTAL DAMAGE YOU JUST DID TO THAT DUDE?
FRAAAZZ
DON'T YOU TOUCH ME!
OOF!
OW.
YEAH.
TIME TO GET UP.
FIVE MORE MINUTES.
ACTUALLY...
M'UP, M'UP...
"HOLD ON!
"HOLD ON, HOLD ON, HOLD ON..."

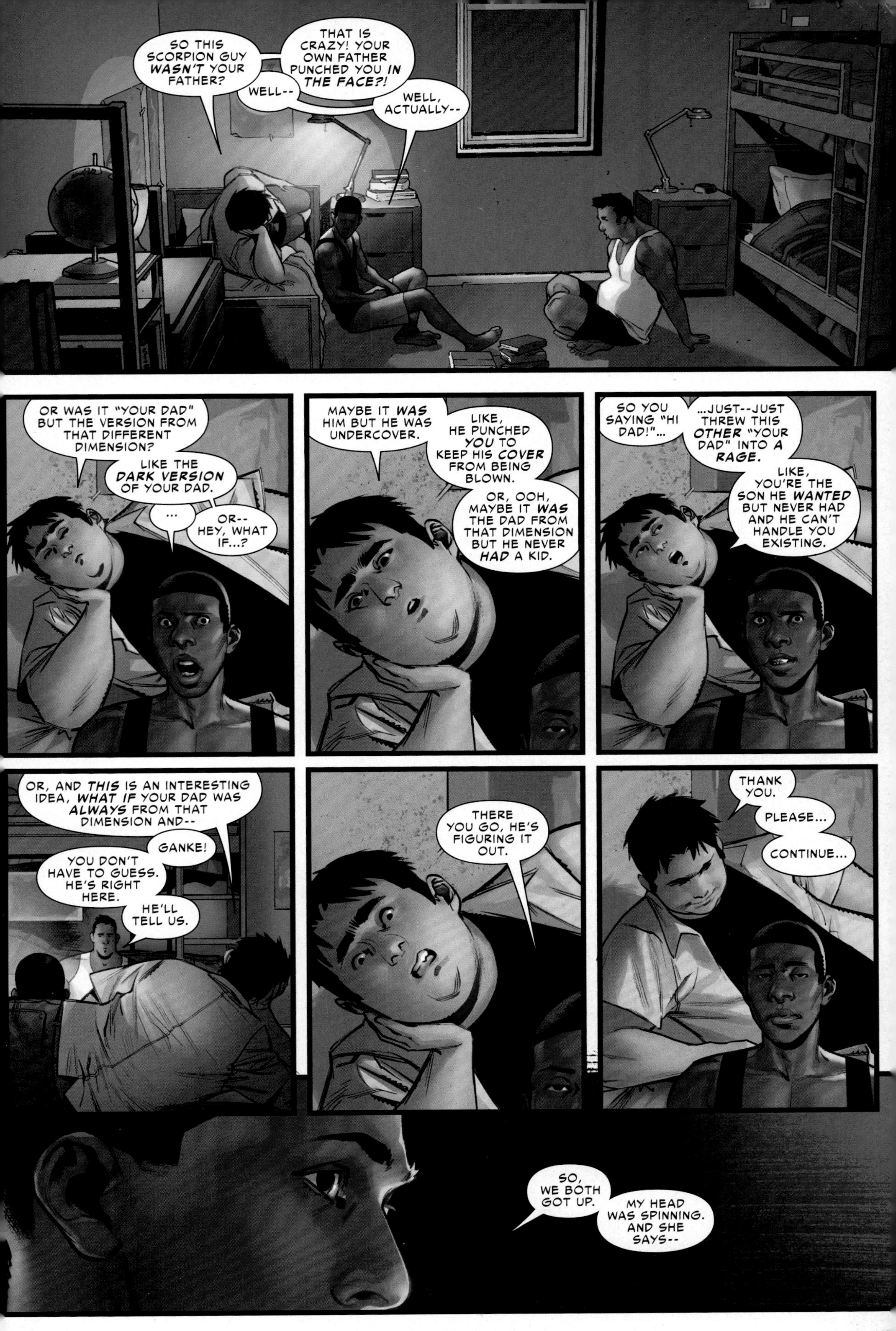
SO THIS SCORPION GUY WASN'T YOUR FATHER?
THAT IS CRAZY! YOUR OWN FATHER PUNCHED YOU IN THE FACE?!
WELL--
WELL, ACTUALLY--
OR WAS IT "YOUR DAD" BUT THE VERSION FROM THAT DIFFERENT DIMENSION?
LIKE THE DARK VERSION OF YOUR DAD.
...
OR-- HEY, WHAT IF...?
MAYBE IT WAS HIM BUT HE WAS UNDERCOVER.
LIKE, HE PUNCHED YOU TO KEEP HIS COVER FROM BEING BLOWN.
OR, OOH, MAYBE IT WAS THE DAD FROM THAT DIMENSION BUT HE NEVER HAD A KID.
SO YOU SAYING "HI DAD!"...
...JUST--JUST THREW THIS OTHER "YOUR DAD" INTO A RAGE.
LIKE, YOU'RE THE SON HE WANTED BUT NEVER HAD AND HE CAN'T HANDLE YOU EXISTING.
OR, AND THIS IS AN INTERESTING IDEA, WHAT IF YOUR DAD WAS ALWAYS FROM THAT DIMENSION AND--
GANKE!
YOU DON'T HAVE TO GUESS. HE'S RIGHT HERE.
HE'LL TELL US.
THERE YOU GO, HE'S FIGURING IT OUT.
THANK YOU.
PLEASE...
CONTINUE...
SO, WE BOTH GOT UP.
MY HEAD WAS SPINNING. AND SHE SAYS--

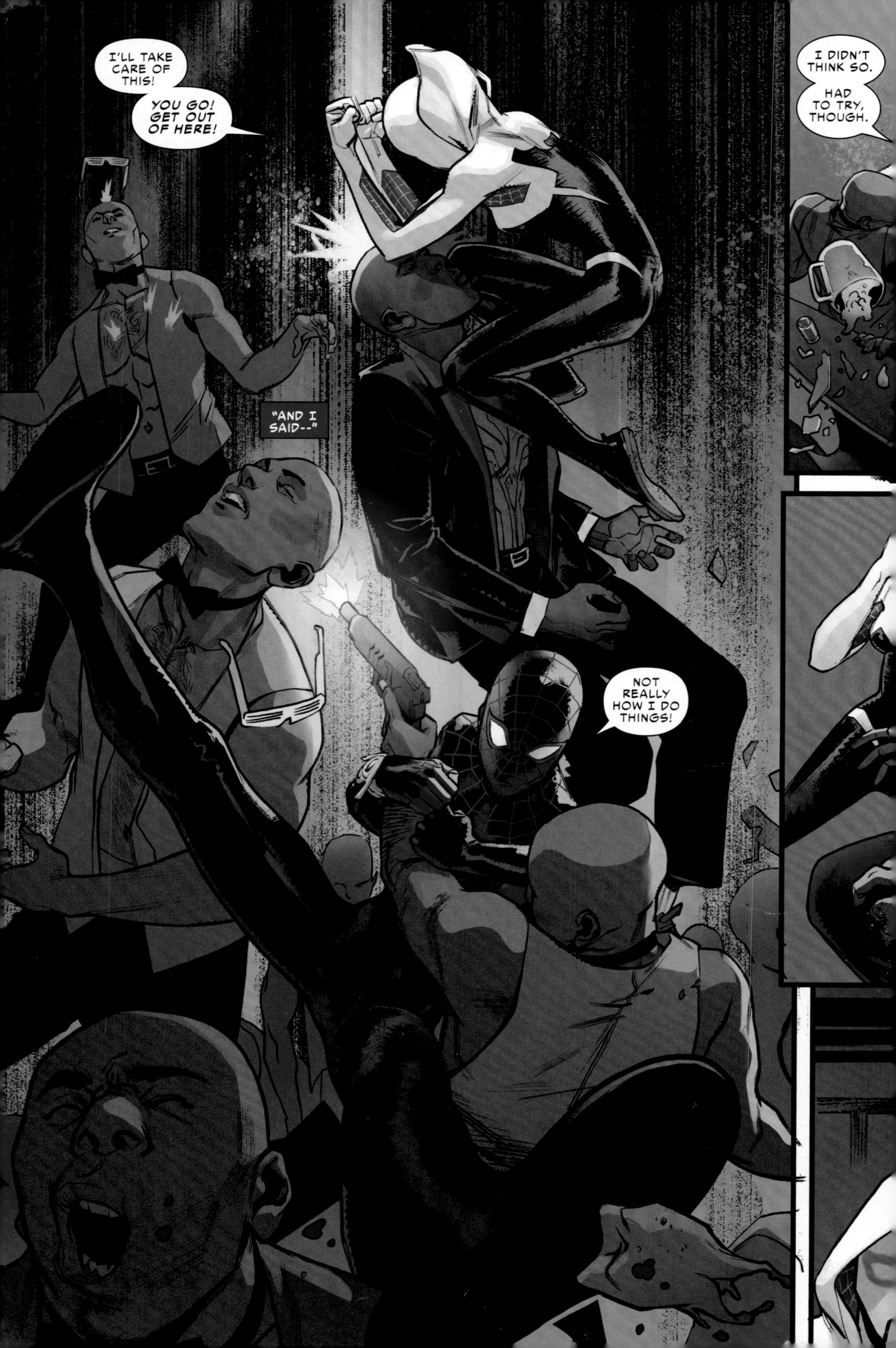
I'LL TAKE CARE OF THIS!
YOU GO! GET OUT OF HERE!
"AND I SAID--"
NOT REALLY HOW I DO THINGS!
I DIDN'T THINK SO.
HAD TO TRY, THOUGH.

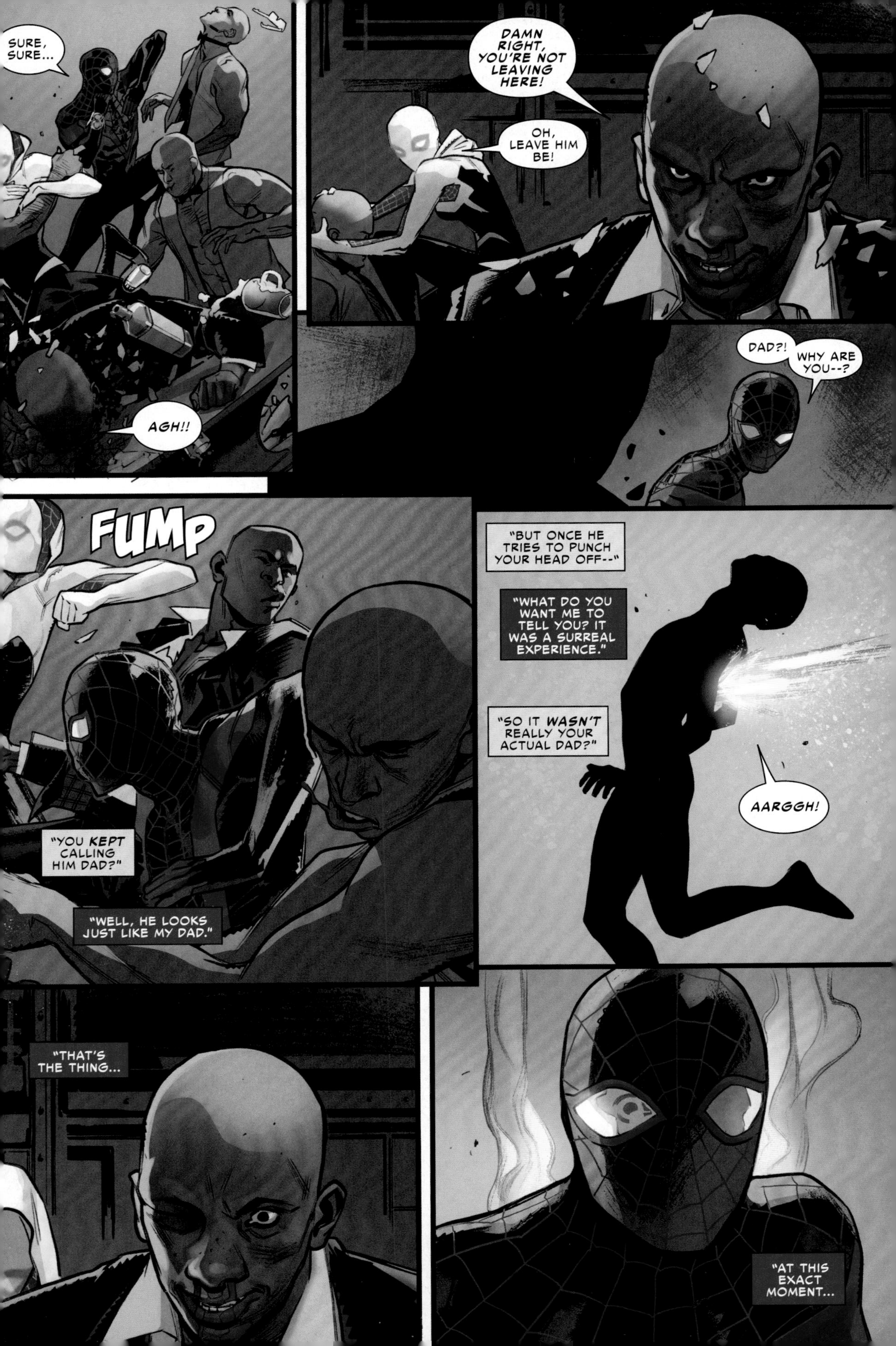
SURE, SURE...
AGH!!
DAMN RIGHT, YOU'RE NOT LEAVING HERE!
OH, LEAVE HIM BE!
DAD?!
WHY ARE YOU--?
FUMP
"YOU KEPT CALLING HIM DAD?"
"WELL, HE LOOKS JUST LIKE MY DAD."
"BUT ONCE HE TRIES TO PUNCH YOUR HEAD OFF--"
"WHAT DO YOU WANT ME TO TELL YOU? IT WAS A SURREAL EXPERIENCE."
"SO IT WASN'T REALLY YOUR ACTUAL DAD?"
AARGGH!
"THAT'S THE THING...
"AT THIS EXACT MOMENT...

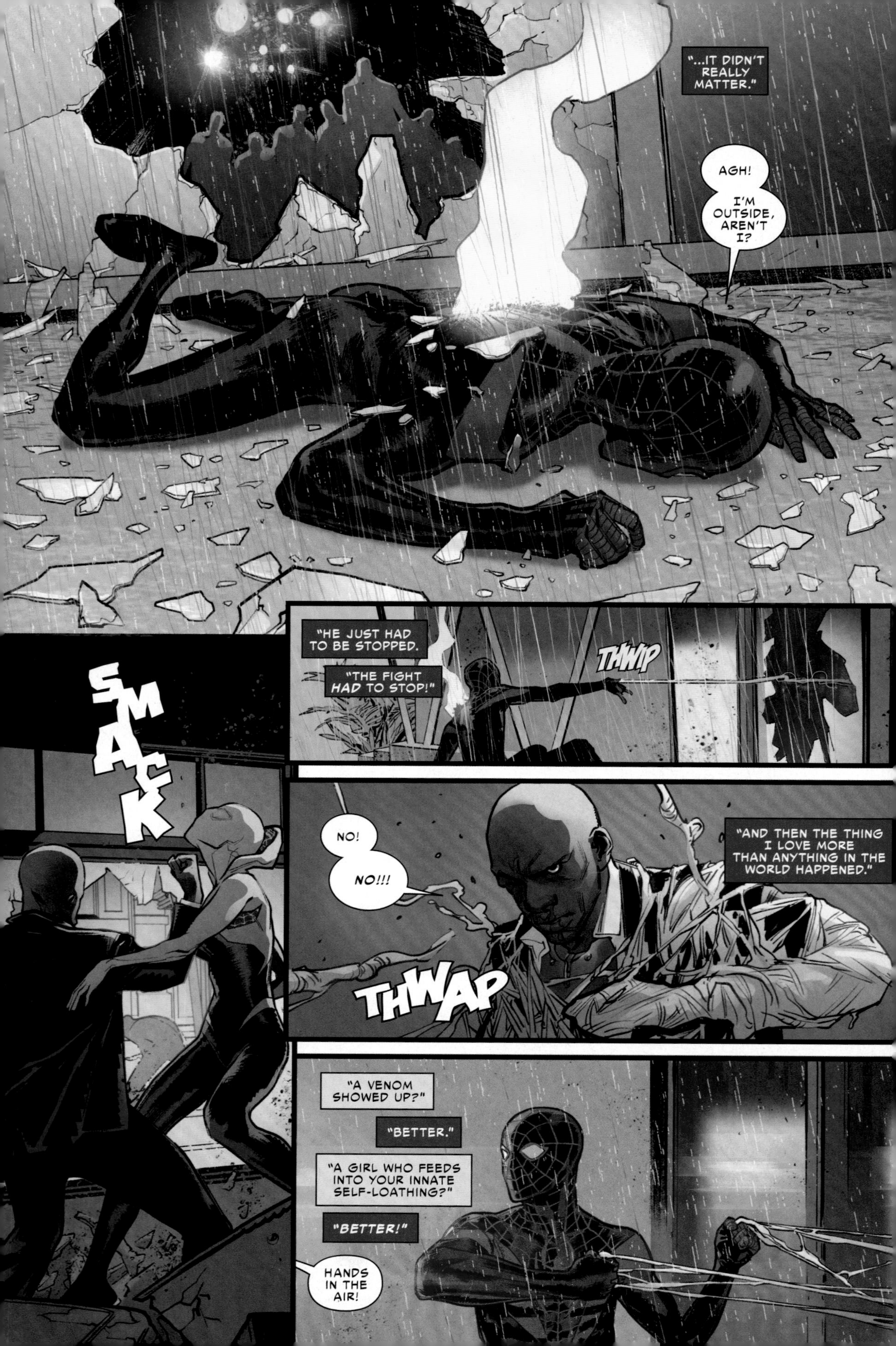
"...IT DIDN'T REALLY MATTER."
AGH!
I'M OUTSIDE, AREN'T I?
"HE JUST HAD TO BE STOPPED.
"THE FIGHT HAD TO STOP!"
THWIP
SMACK
NO!
NO!!!
"AND THEN THE THING I LOVE MORE THAN ANYTHING IN THE WORLD HAPPENED."
THWAP
"A VENOM SHOWED UP?"
"BETTER."
"A GIRL WHO FEEDS INTO YOUR INNATE SELF-LOATHING?"
"BETTER!"
HANDS IN THE AIR!

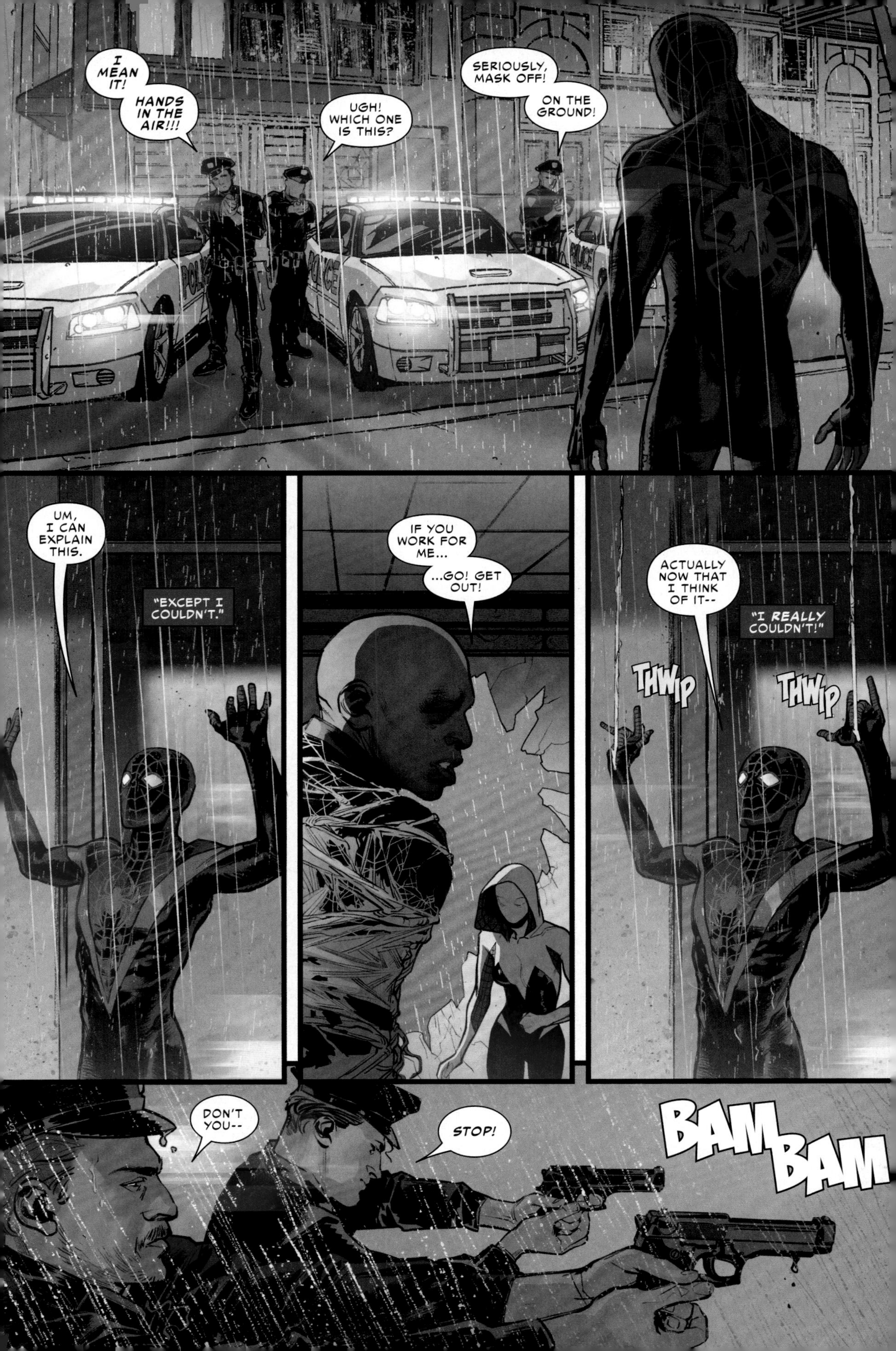
I MEAN IT! HANDS IN THE AIR!!!
UGH! WHICH ONE IS THIS?
SERIOUSLY, MASK OFF! ON THE GROUND!
POLICE
UM, I CAN EXPLAIN THIS.
"EXCEPT I COULDN'T."
IF YOU WORK FOR ME... ...GO! GET OUT!
ACTUALLY NOW THAT I THINK OF IT--
"I REALLY COULDN'T!"
THWIP
THWIP
DON'T YOU--
STOP!
BAM BAM

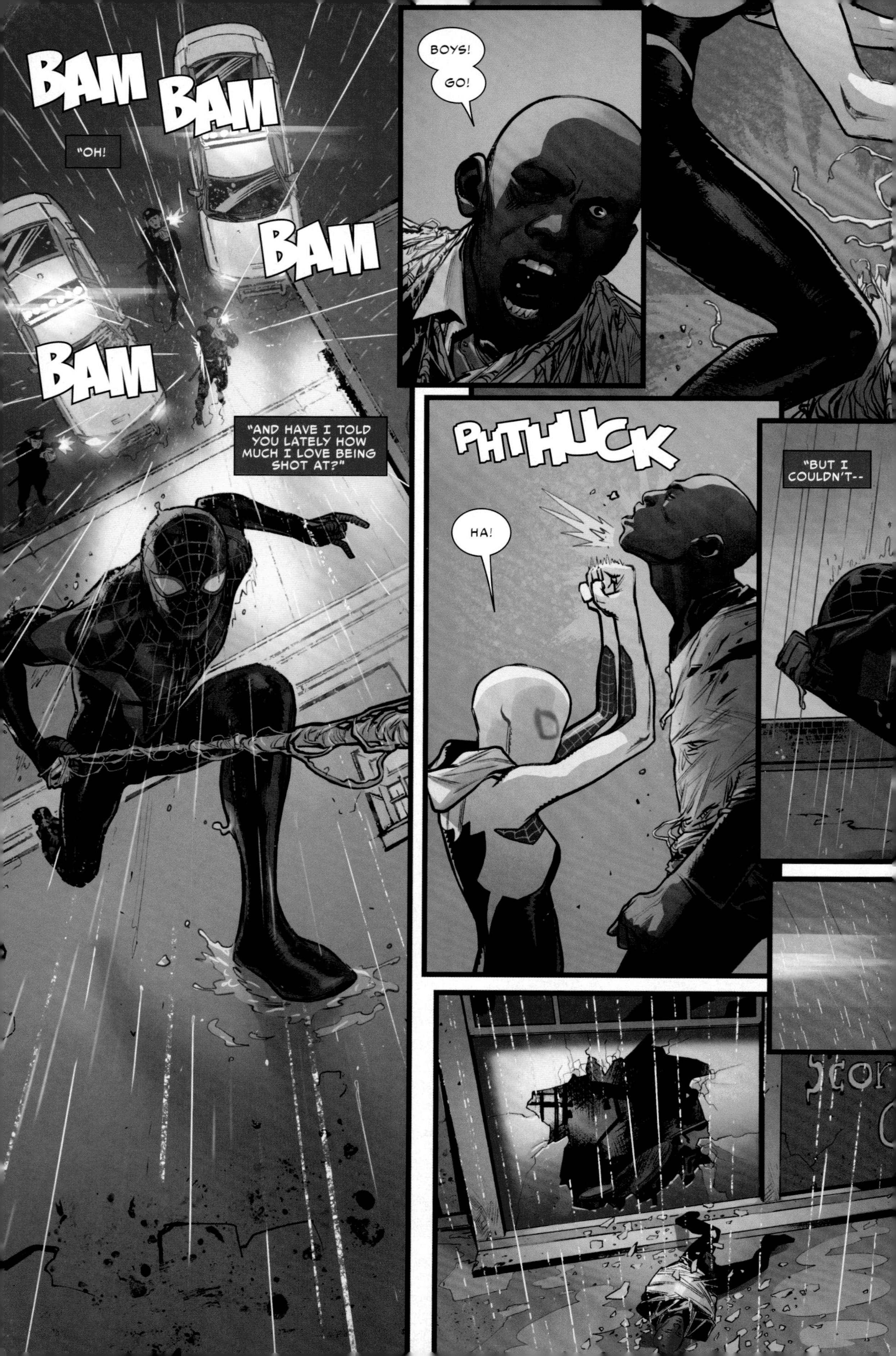
BAM BAM
"OH!
BAM
BAM
"AND HAVE I TOLD YOU LATELY HOW MUCH I LOVE BEING SHOT AT?"
BOYS!
GO!
PHTHUCK
HA!
"BUT I COULDN'T--

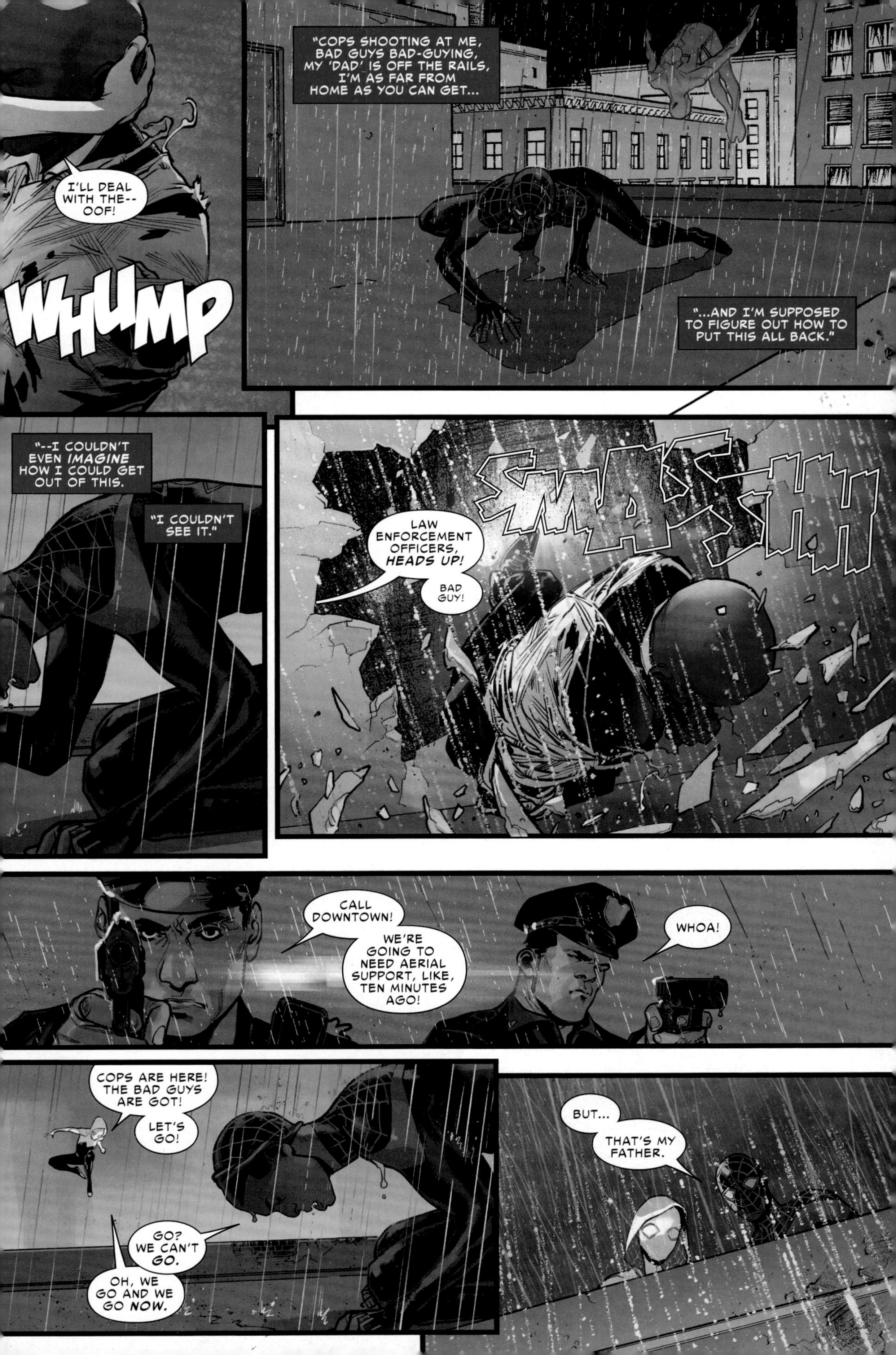
I'LL DEAL WITH THE-- OOF!
WHUMP
"COPS SHOOTING AT ME, BAD GUYS BAD-GUYING, MY 'DAD' IS OFF THE RAILS, I'M AS FAR FROM HOME AS YOU CAN GET...
"...AND I'M SUPPOSED TO FIGURE OUT HOW TO PUT THIS ALL BACK."
"--I COULDN'T EVEN IMAGINE HOW I COULD GET OUT OF THIS.
"I COULDN'T SEE IT."
SMASH
LAW ENFORCEMENT OFFICERS, HEADS UP!
BAD GUY!
CALL DOWNTOWN!
WE'RE GOING TO NEED AERIAL SUPPORT, LIKE, TEN MINUTES AGO!
WHOA!
COPS ARE HERE! THE BAD GUYS ARE GOT!
LET'S GO!
GO? WE CAN'T GO.
OH, WE GO AND WE GO NOW.
BUT...
THAT'S MY FATHER.

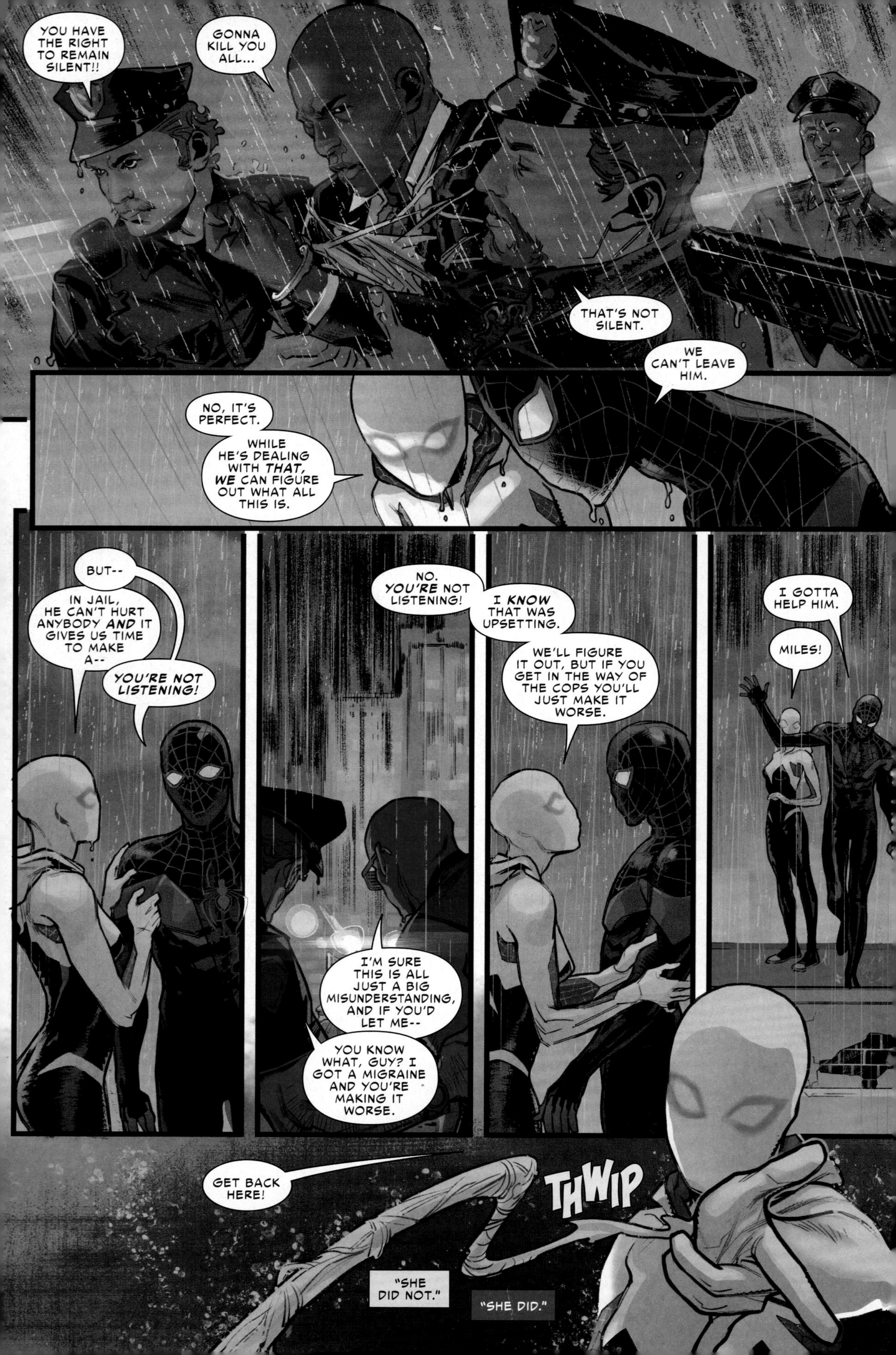
YOU HAVE THE RIGHT TO REMAIN SILENT!!
GONNA KILL YOU ALL...
THAT'S NOT SILENT.
WE CAN'T LEAVE HIM.
NO, IT'S PERFECT.
WHILE HE'S DEALING WITH THAT, WE CAN FIGURE OUT WHAT ALL THIS IS.
BUT--
IN JAIL, HE CAN'T HURT ANYBODY AND IT GIVES US TIME TO MAKE A--
YOU'RE NOT LISTENING!
NO. YOU'RE NOT LISTENING!
I'M SURE THIS IS ALL JUST A BIG MISUNDERSTANDING, AND IF YOU'D LET ME--
YOU KNOW WHAT, GUY? I GOT A MIGRAINE AND YOU'RE MAKING IT WORSE.
I KNOW THAT WAS UPSETTING.
WE'LL FIGURE IT OUT, BUT IF YOU GET IN THE WAY OF THE COPS YOU'LL JUST MAKE IT WORSE.
I GOTTA HELP HIM.
MILES!
GET BACK HERE!
THWIP
"SHE DID NOT."
"SHE DID."

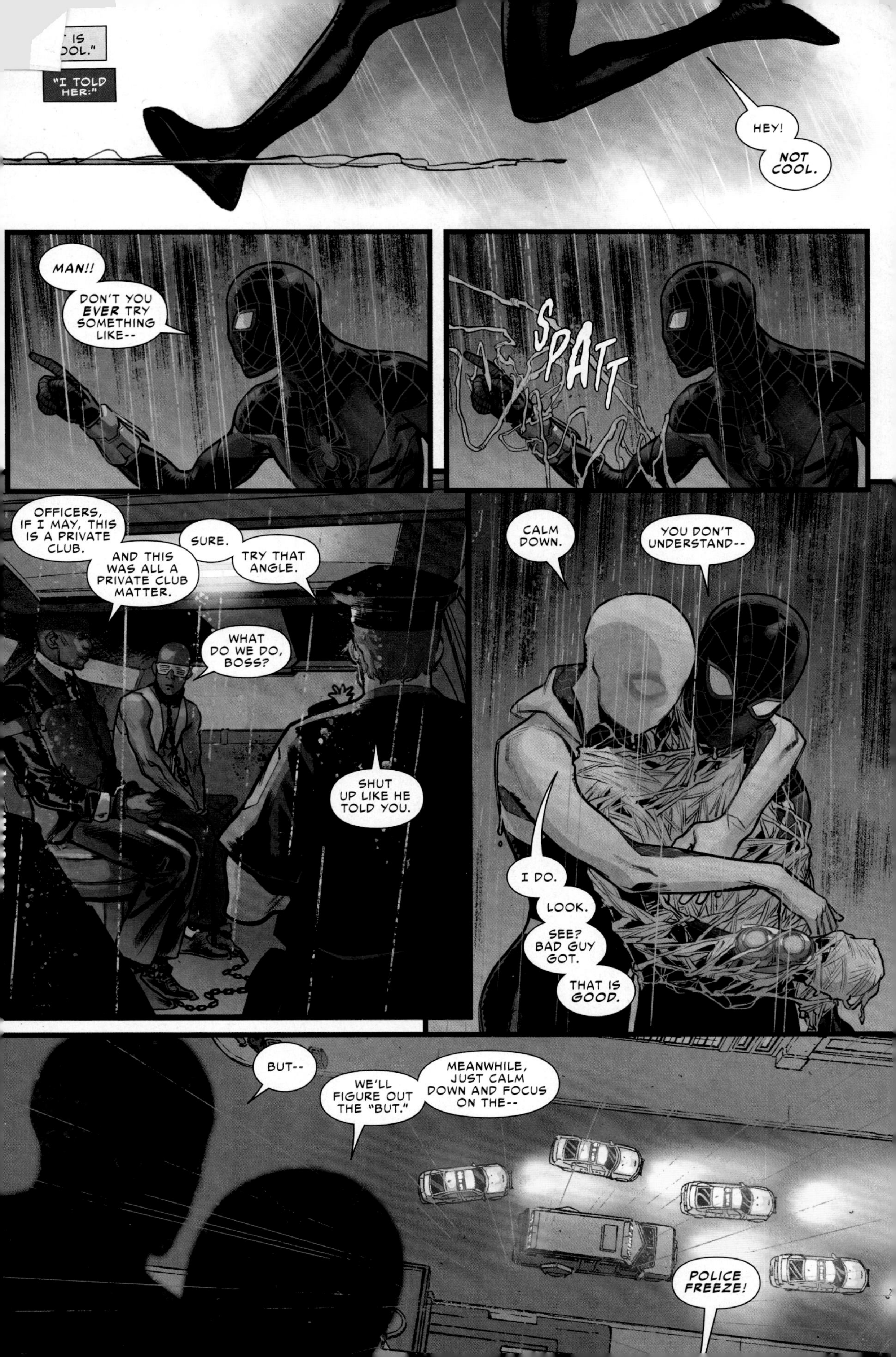
"I TOLD HER:"
HEY!
NOT COOL.
MAN!!
DON'T YOU EVER TRY SOMETHING LIKE--
SPATT
OFFICERS, IF I MAY, THIS IS A PRIVATE CLUB.
AND THIS WAS ALL A PRIVATE CLUB MATTER.
SURE.
TRY THAT ANGLE.
WHAT DO WE DO, BOSS?
SHUT UP LIKE HE TOLD YOU.
CALM DOWN.
YOU DON'T UNDERSTAND--
I DO.
LOOK.
SEE? BAD GUY GOT.
THAT IS GOOD.
BUT--
WE'LL FIGURE OUT THE "BUT."
MEANWHILE, JUST CALM DOWN AND FOCUS ON THE--
POLICE FREEZE!

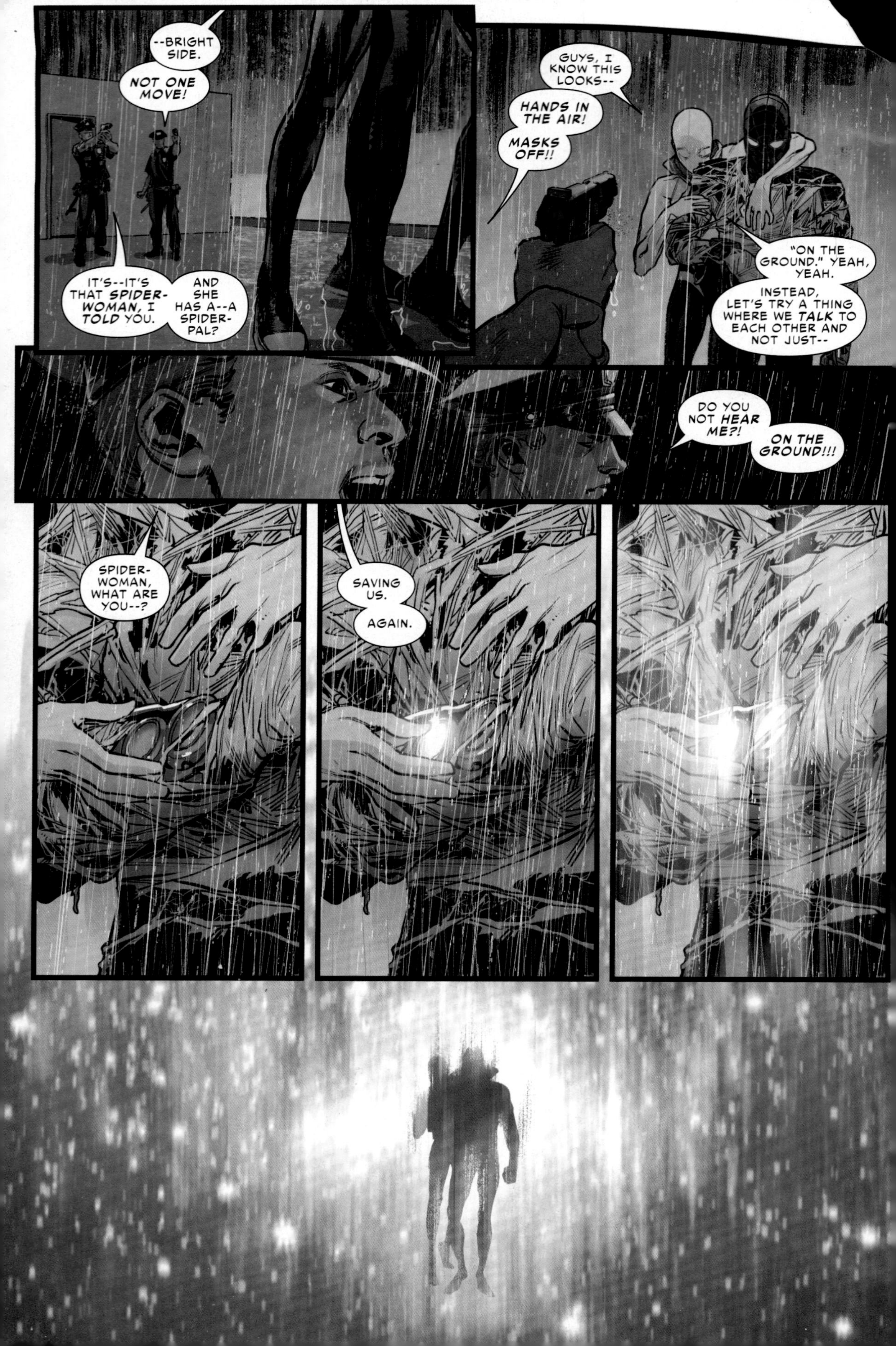
--BRIGHT SIDE.
NOT ONE MOVE!
IT'S--IT'S THAT SPIDER-WOMAN, I TOLD YOU.
AND SHE HAS A--A SPIDER-PAL?
GUYS, I KNOW THIS LOOKS--
HANDS IN THE AIR!
MASKS OFF!!
"ON THE GROUND." YEAH, YEAH.
INSTEAD, LET'S TRY A THING WHERE WE TALK TO EACH OTHER AND NOT JUST--
DO YOU NOT HEAR ME?!
ON THE GROUND!!!
SPIDER-WOMAN, WHAT ARE YOU--?
SAVING US.
AGAIN.

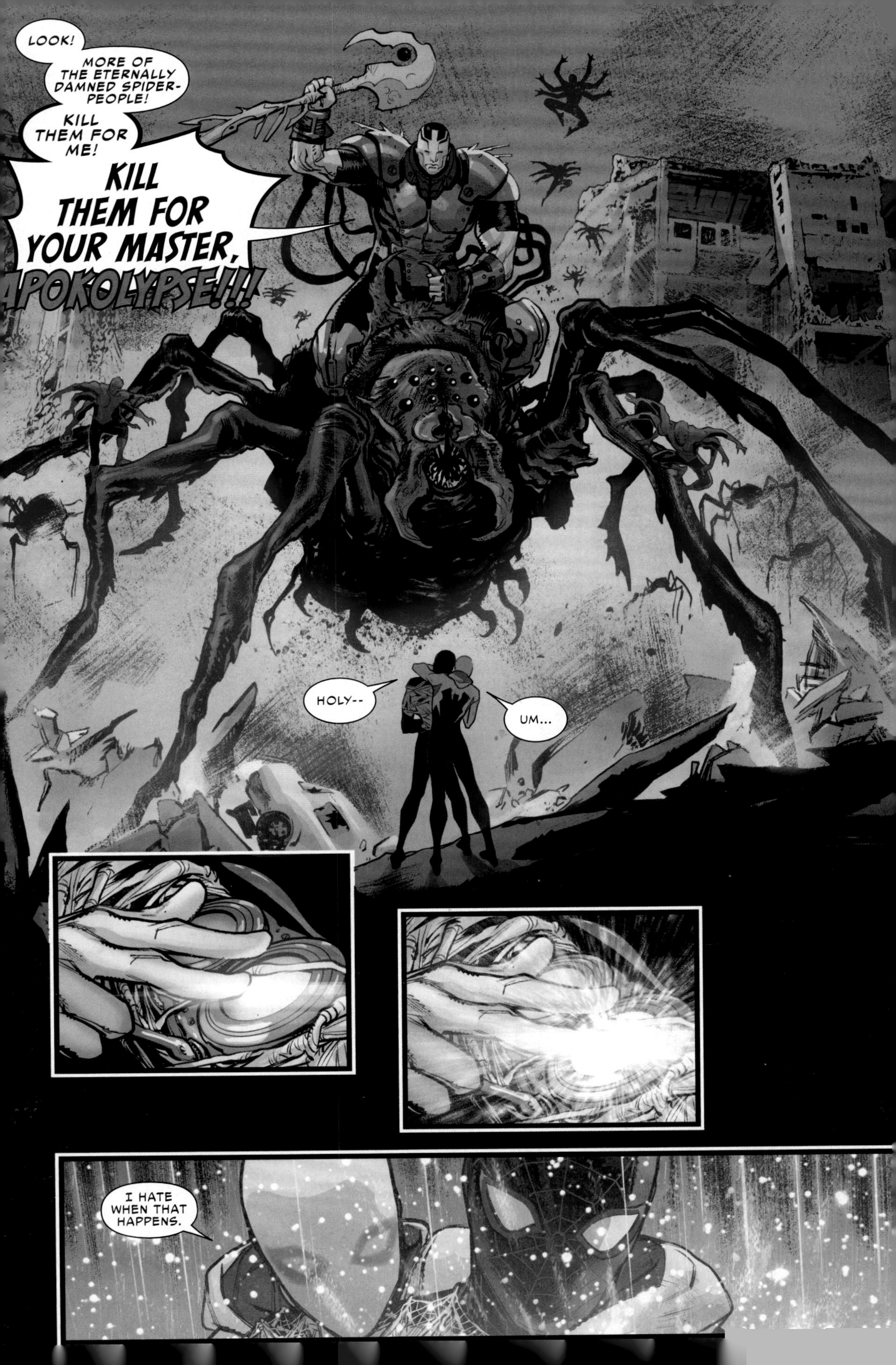
LOOK!
MORE OF THE ETERNALLY DAMNED SPIDER-PEOPLE!
KILL THEM FOR ME!
KILL THEM FOR YOUR MASTER, APOKOLYPSE!!!
HOLY--
UM...
I HATE WHEN THAT HAPPENS.

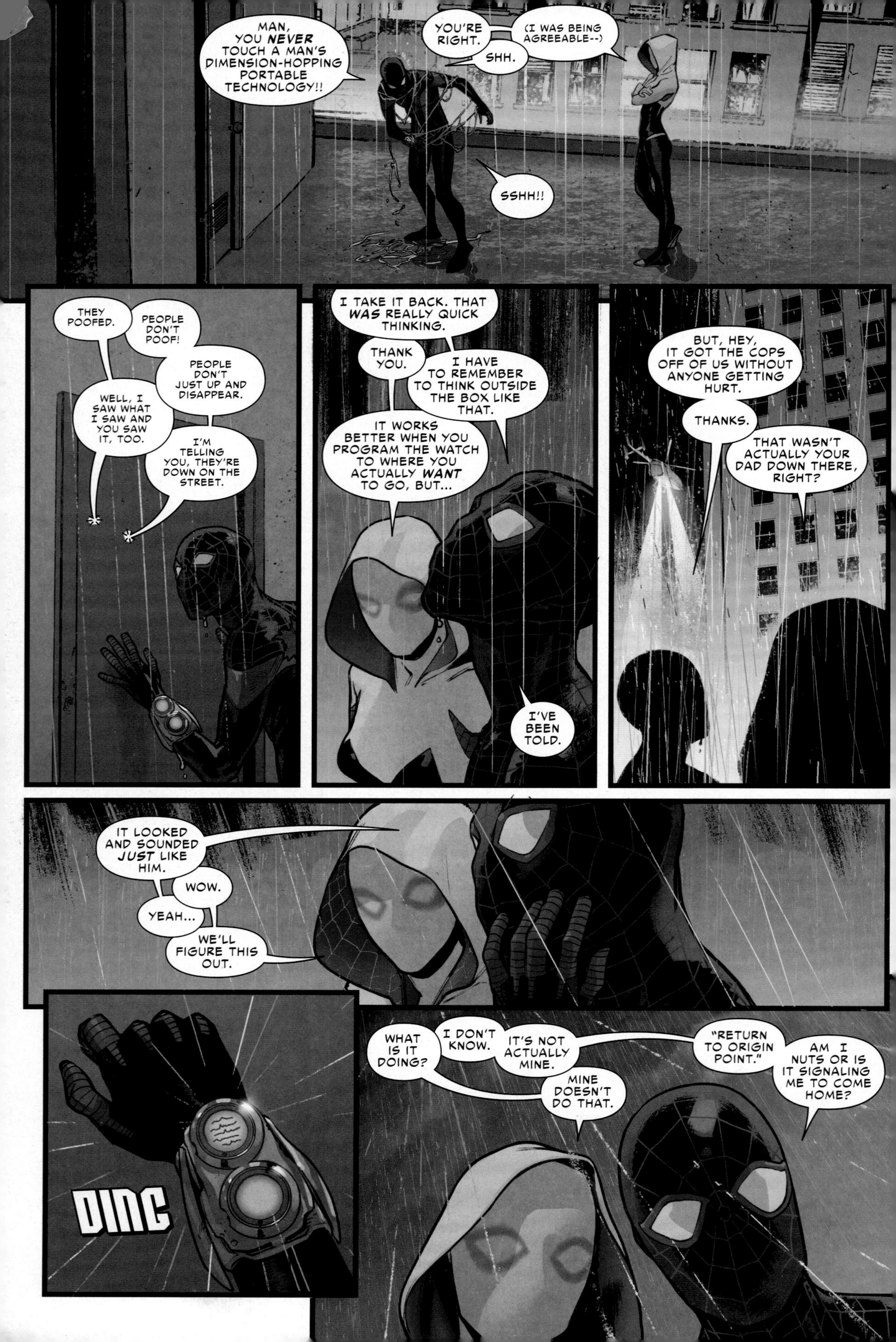
MAN, YOU NEVER TOUCH A MAN'S DIMENSION-HOPPING PORTABLE TECHNOLOGY!!
YOU'RE RIGHT.
(I WAS BEING AGREEABLE--)
SHH.
SSHH!!
THEY POOFED.
PEOPLE DON'T POOF!
PEOPLE DON'T JUST UP AND DISAPPEAR.
WELL, I SAW WHAT I SAW AND YOU SAW IT, TOO.
I'M TELLING YOU, THEY'RE DOWN ON THE STREET.
I TAKE IT BACK. THAT WAS REALLY QUICK THINKING.
THANK YOU.
I HAVE TO REMEMBER TO THINK OUTSIDE THE BOX LIKE THAT.
IT WORKS BETTER WHEN YOU PROGRAM THE WATCH TO WHERE YOU ACTUALLY WANT TO GO, BUT...
I'VE BEEN TOLD.
BUT, HEY, IT GOT THE COPS OFF OF US WITHOUT ANYONE GETTING HURT.
THANKS.
THAT WASN'T ACTUALLY YOUR DAD DOWN THERE, RIGHT?
IT LOOKED AND SOUNDED JUST LIKE HIM.
WOW.
YEAH...
WE'LL FIGURE THIS OUT.
DING
WHAT IS IT DOING?
I DON'T KNOW.
IT'S NOT ACTUALLY MINE.
MINE DOESN'T DO THAT.
"RETURN TO ORIGIN POINT."
AM I NUTS OR IS IT SIGNALING ME TO COME HOME?

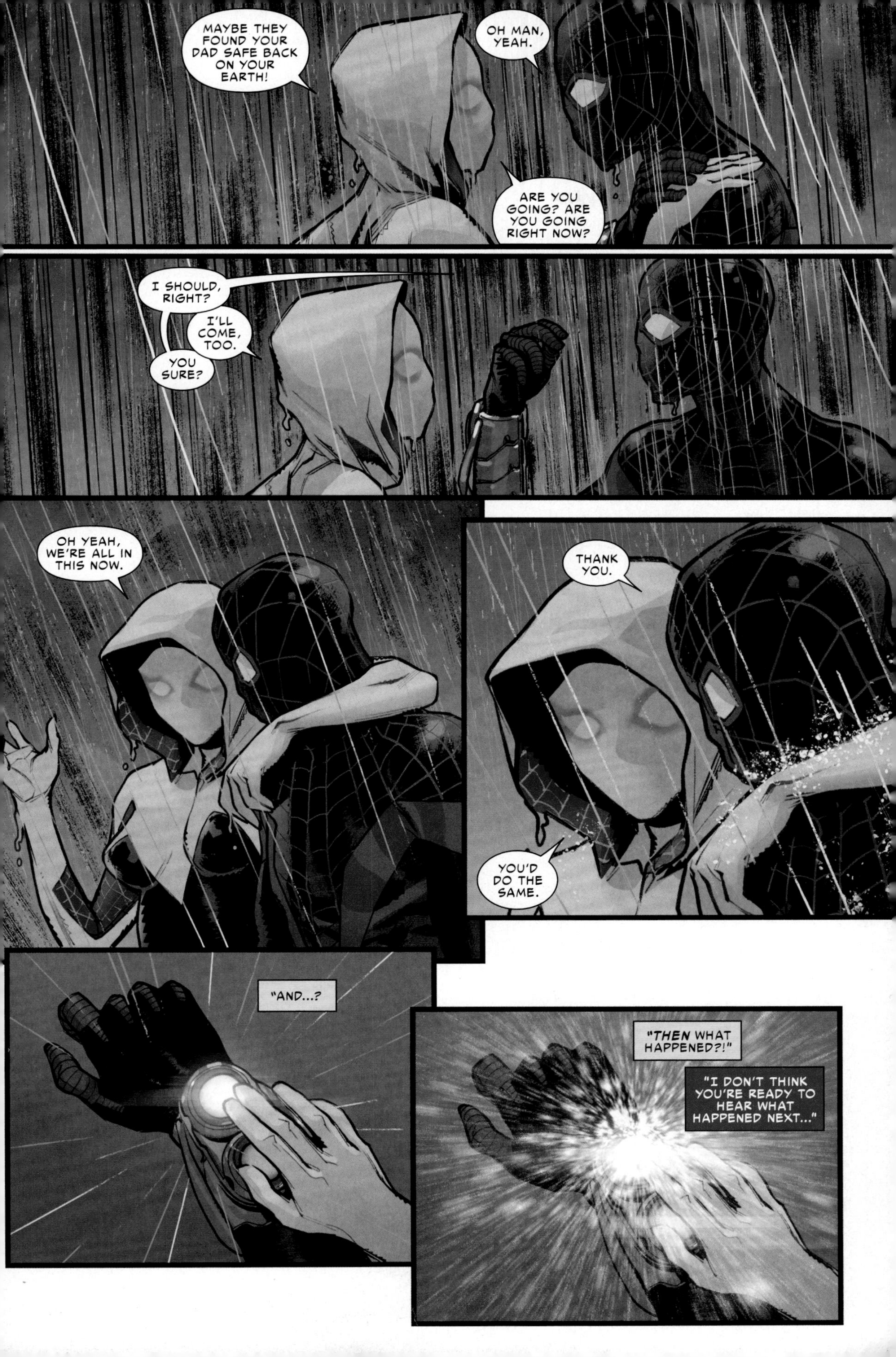
MAYBE THEY FOUND YOUR DAD SAFE BACK ON YOUR EARTH!
OH MAN, YEAH.
ARE YOU GOING? ARE YOU GOING RIGHT NOW?
I SHOULD, RIGHT?
I'LL COME, TOO.
YOU SURE?
OH YEAH, WE'RE ALL IN THIS NOW.
THANK YOU.
YOU'D DO THE SAME.
"AND...?
"THEN WHAT HAPPENED?!"
"I DON'T THINK YOU'RE READY TO HEAR WHAT HAPPENED NEXT..."

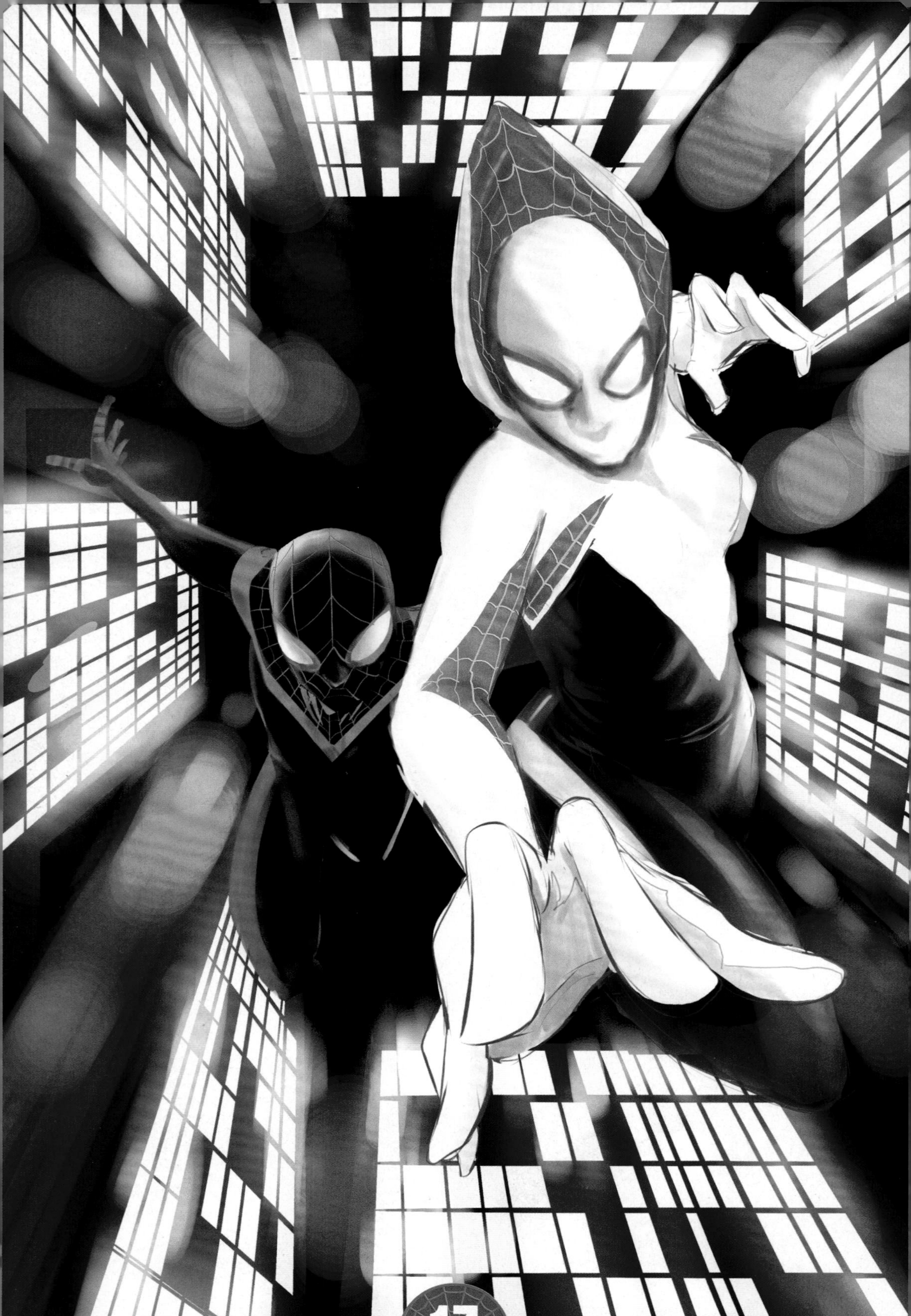

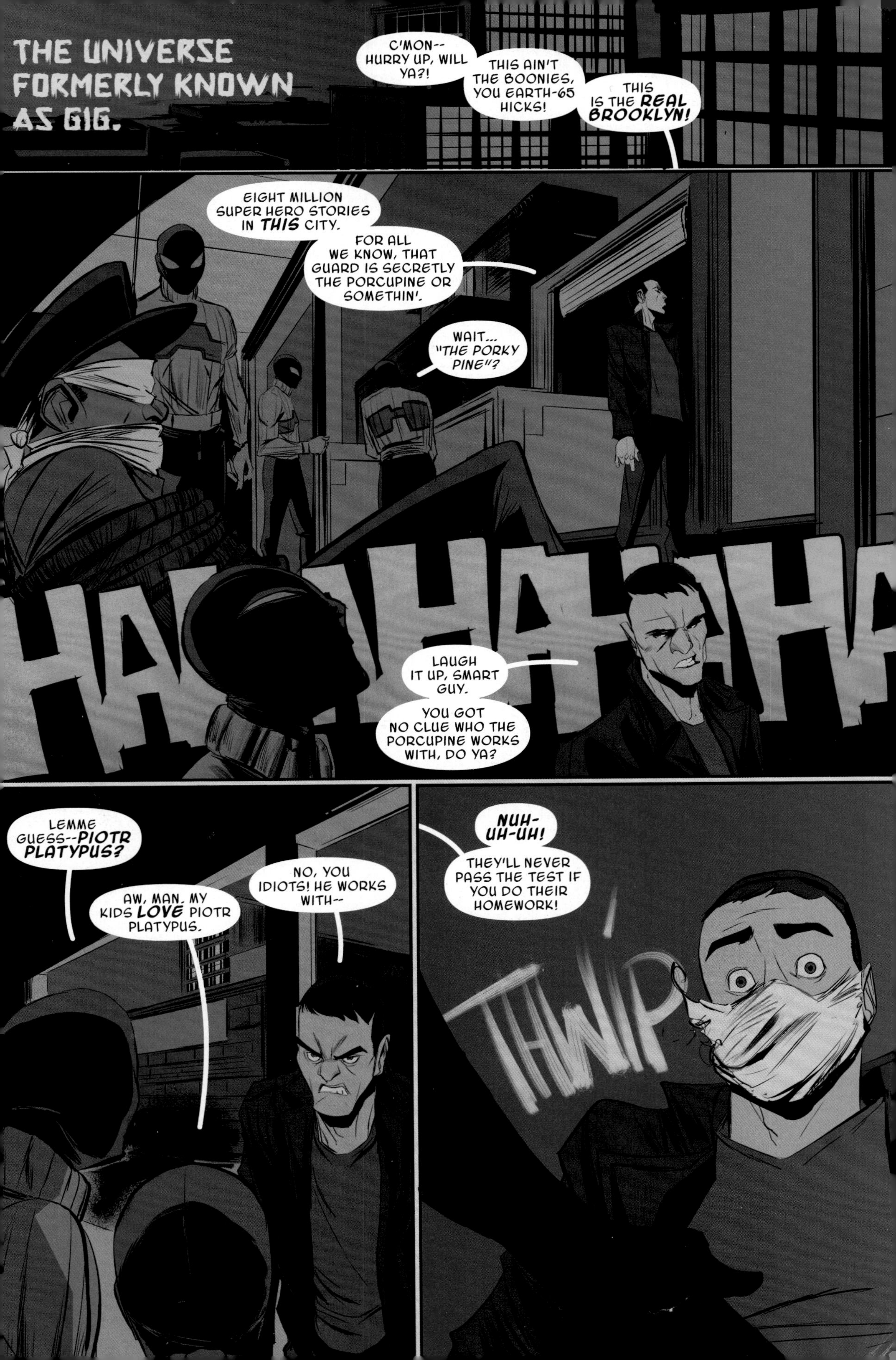
THE UNIVERSE FORMERLY KNOWN AS 616.
C'MON-- HURRY UP, WILL YA?!
THIS AIN'T THE BOONIES, YOU EARTH-65 HICKS!
THIS IS THE REAL BROOKLYN!
EIGHT MILLION SUPER HERO STORIES IN THIS CITY.
FOR ALL WE KNOW, THAT GUARD IS SECRETLY THE PORCUPINE OR SOMETHIN'.
WAIT... "THE PORKY PINE"?
HAHAHAHA
LAUGH IT UP, SMART GUY.
YOU GOT NO CLUE WHO THE PORCUPINE WORKS WITH, DO YA?
LEMME GUESS--PIOTR PLATYPUS?
AW, MAN. MY KIDS LOVE PIOTR PLATYPUS.
NO, YOU IDIOTS! HE WORKS WITH--
NUH-UH-UH!
THEY'LL NEVER PASS THE TEST IF YOU DO THEIR HOMEWORK!
THWIP

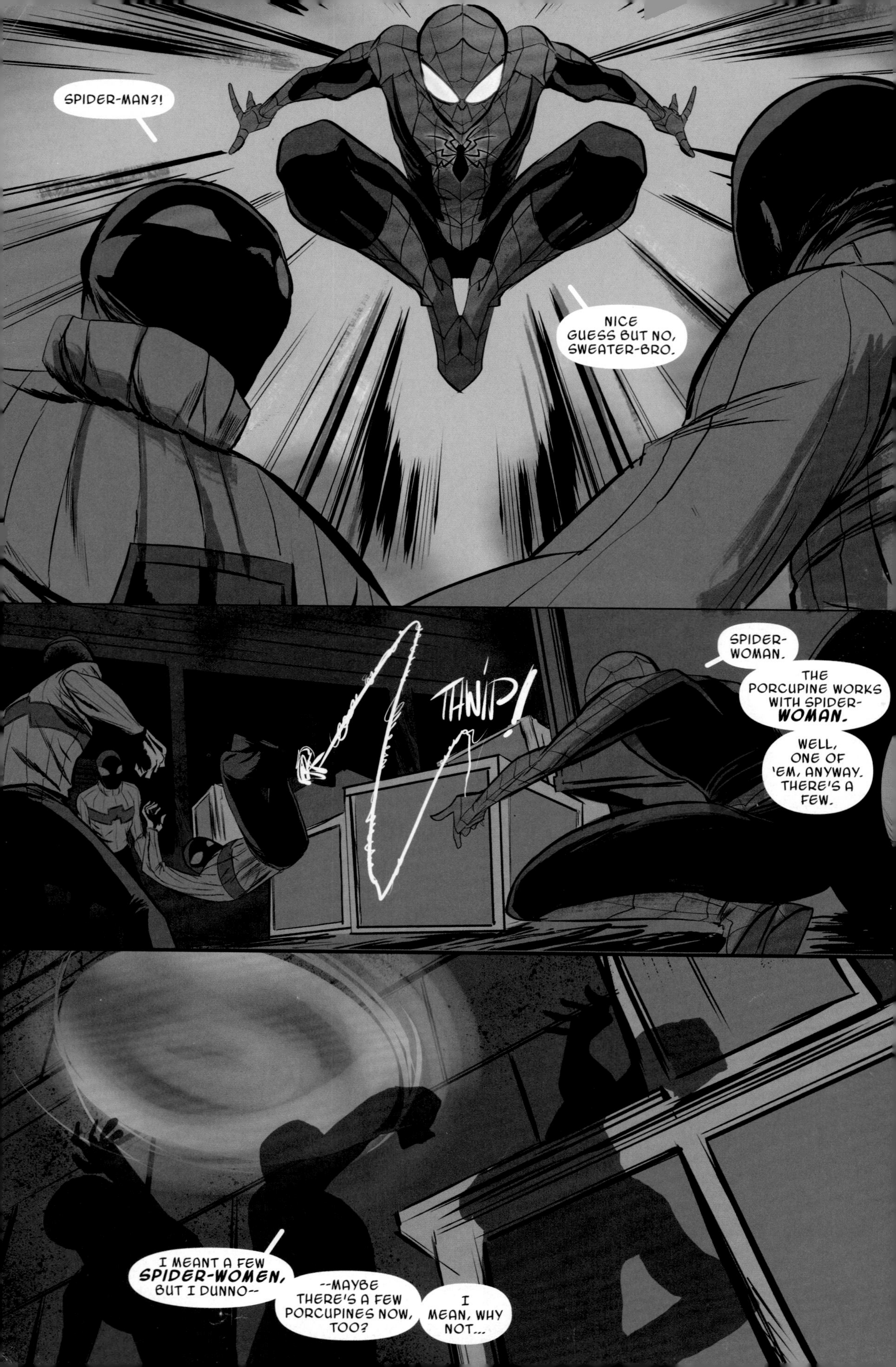
SPIDER-MAN?!
NICE GUESS BUT NO, SWEATER-BRO.
THWIP!
SPIDER-WOMAN.
THE PORCUPINE WORKS WITH SPIDER-WOMAN.
WELL, ONE OF 'EM, ANYWAY. THERE'S A FEW.
I MEANT A FEW SPIDER-WOMEN, BUT I DUNNO--
--MAYBE THERE'S A FEW PORCUPINES NOW, TOO?
I MEAN, WHY NOT...

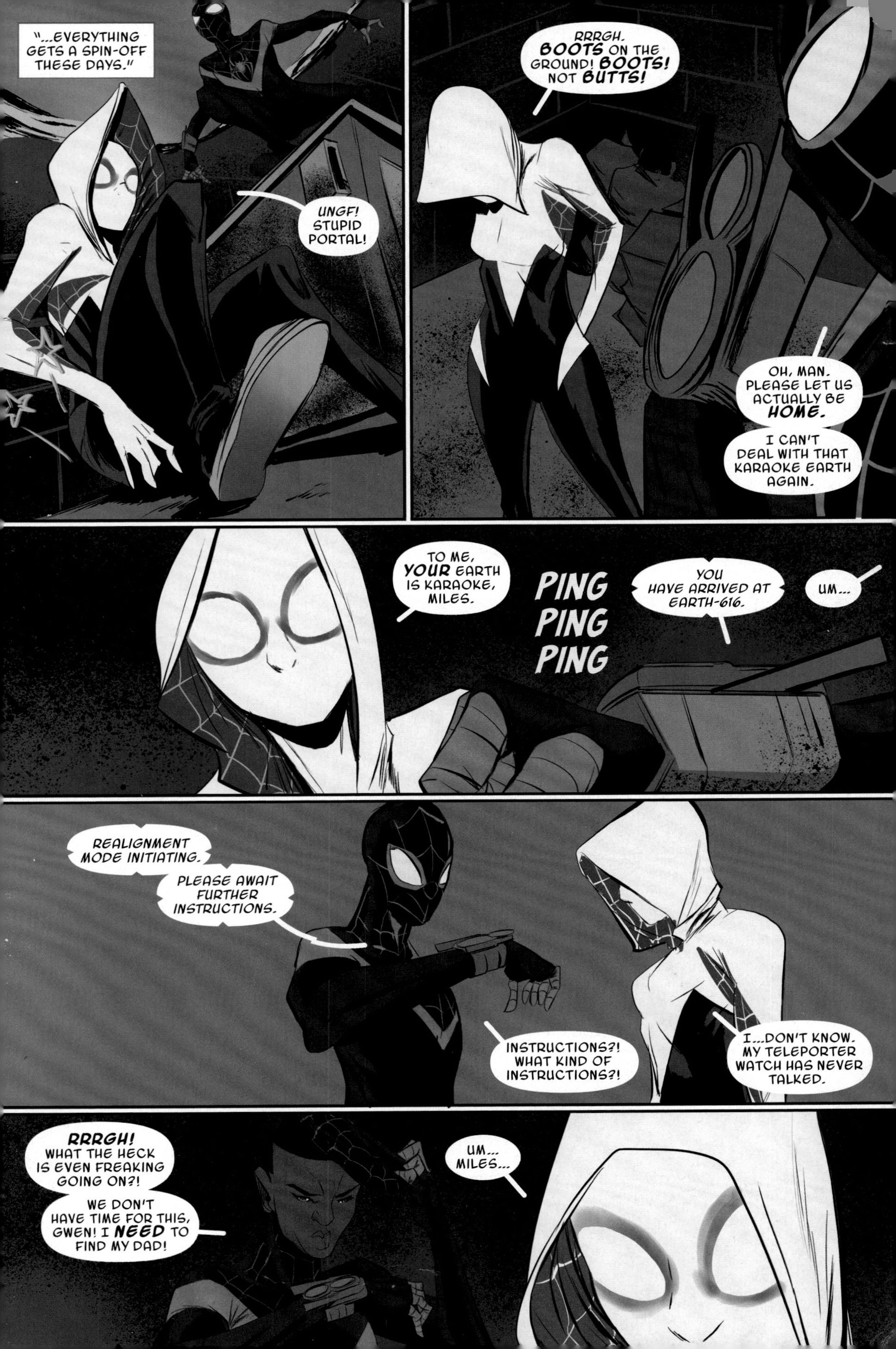
"...EVERYTHING GETS A SPIN-OFF THESE DAYS."
UNGF! STUPID PORTAL!
RRRGH. BOOTS ON THE GROUND! BOOTS! NOT BUTTS!
OH, MAN. PLEASE LET US ACTUALLY BE HOME.
I CAN'T DEAL WITH THAT KARAOKE EARTH AGAIN.
TO ME, YOUR EARTH IS KARAOKE, MILES.
PING PING PING
YOU HAVE ARRIVED AT EARTH-616.
UM...
REALIGNMENT MODE INITIATING.
PLEASE AWAIT FURTHER INSTRUCTIONS.
INSTRUCTIONS?! WHAT KIND OF INSTRUCTIONS?!
I...DON'T KNOW. MY TELEPORTER WATCH HAS NEVER TALKED.
RRRGH! WHAT THE HECK IS EVEN FREAKING GOING ON?!
WE DON'T HAVE TIME FOR THIS, GWEN! I NEED TO FIND MY DAD!
UM... MILES...

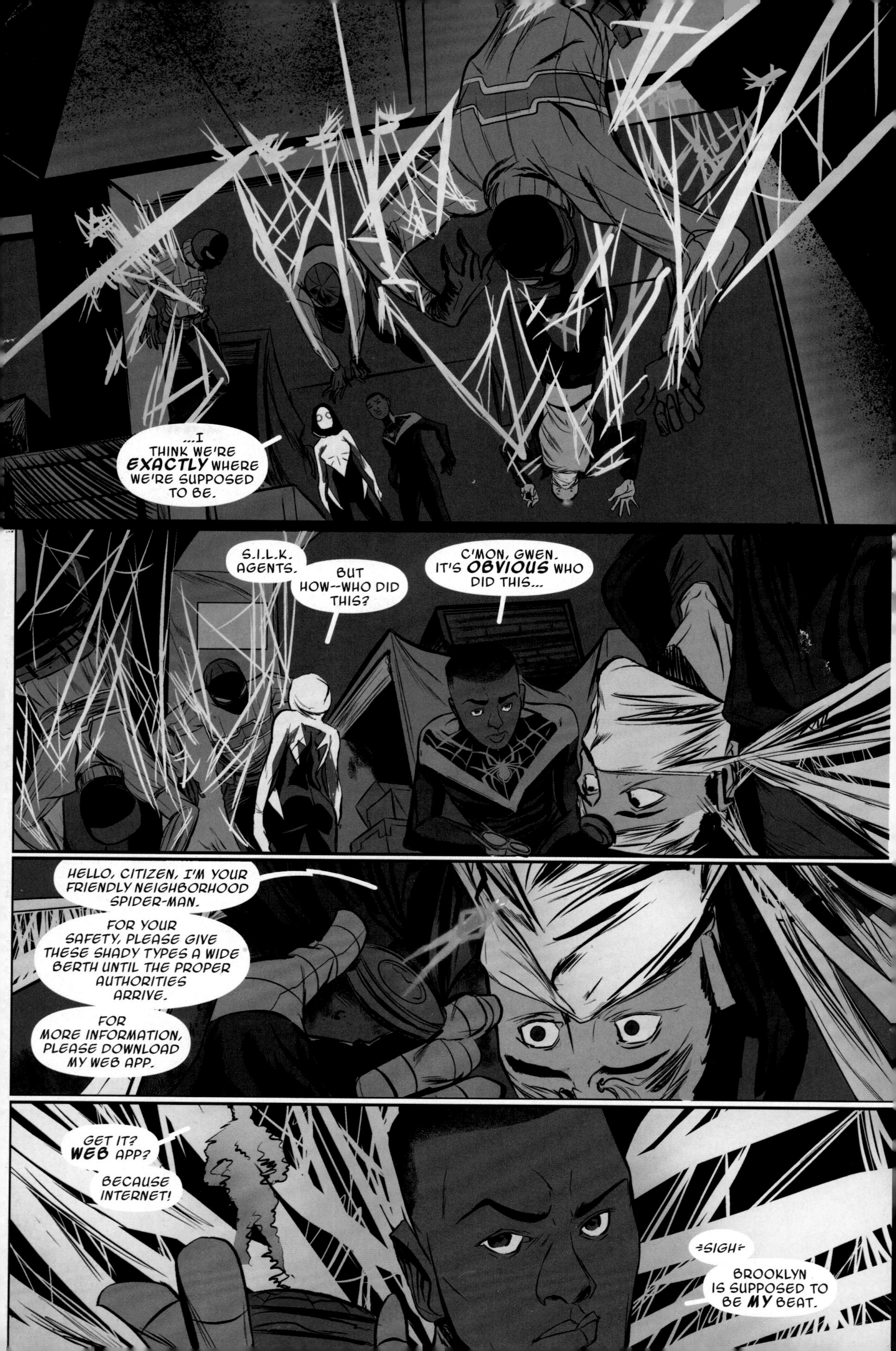
...I THINK WE'RE EXACTLY WHERE WE'RE SUPPOSED TO BE.
S.I.L.K. AGENTS.
BUT HOW--WHO DID THIS?
C'MON, GWEN. IT'S OBVIOUS WHO DID THIS...
HELLO, CITIZEN, I'M YOUR FRIENDLY NEIGHBORHOOD SPIDER-MAN.
FOR YOUR SAFETY, PLEASE GIVE THESE SHADY TYPES A WIDE BERTH UNTIL THE PROPER AUTHORITIES ARRIVE.
FOR MORE INFORMATION, PLEASE DOWNLOAD MY WEB APP.
GET IT? WEB APP?
BECAUSE INTERNET!
=SIGH=
BROOKLYN IS SUPPOSED TO BE MY BEAT.

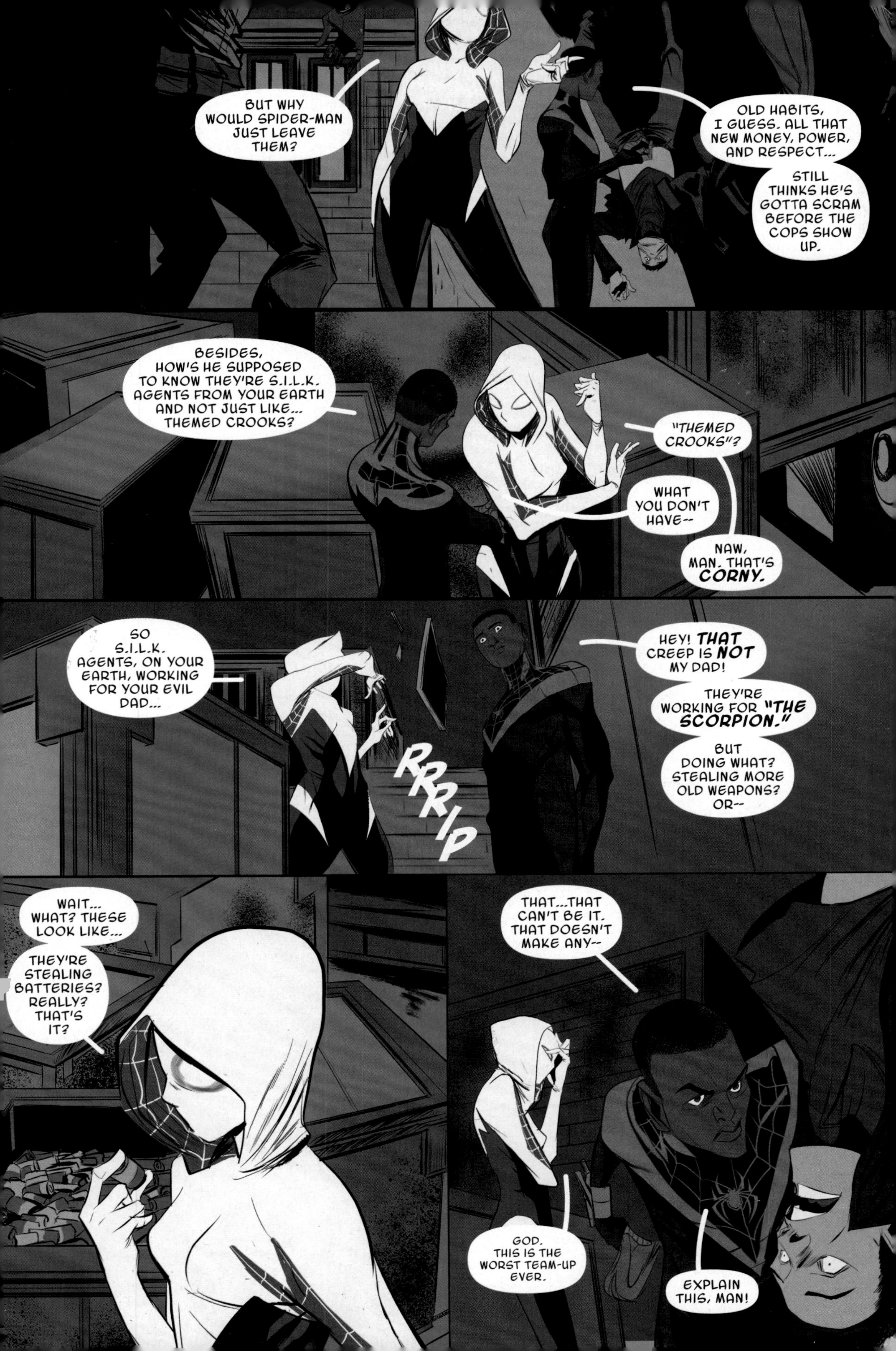
BUT WHY WOULD SPIDER-MAN JUST LEAVE THEM?
OLD HABITS, I GUESS. ALL THAT NEW MONEY, POWER, AND RESPECT...
STILL THINKS HE'S GOTTA SCRAM BEFORE THE COPS SHOW UP.
BESIDES, HOW'S HE SUPPOSED TO KNOW THEY'RE S.I.L.K. AGENTS FROM YOUR EARTH AND NOT JUST LIKE... THEMED CROOKS?
"THEMED CROOKS"?
WHAT YOU DON'T HAVE--
NAW, MAN. THAT'S CORNY.
SO S.I.L.K. AGENTS, ON YOUR EARTH, WORKING FOR YOUR EVIL DAD...
RRRIP
HEY! THAT CREEP IS NOT MY DAD!
THEY'RE WORKING FOR "THE SCORPION."
BUT DOING WHAT? STEALING MORE OLD WEAPONS? OR--
WAIT... WHAT? THESE LOOK LIKE...
THEY'RE STEALING BATTERIES? REALLY? THAT'S IT?
THAT...THAT CAN'T BE IT. THAT DOESN'T MAKE ANY--
GOD. THIS IS THE WORST TEAM-UP EVER.
EXPLAIN THIS, MAN!

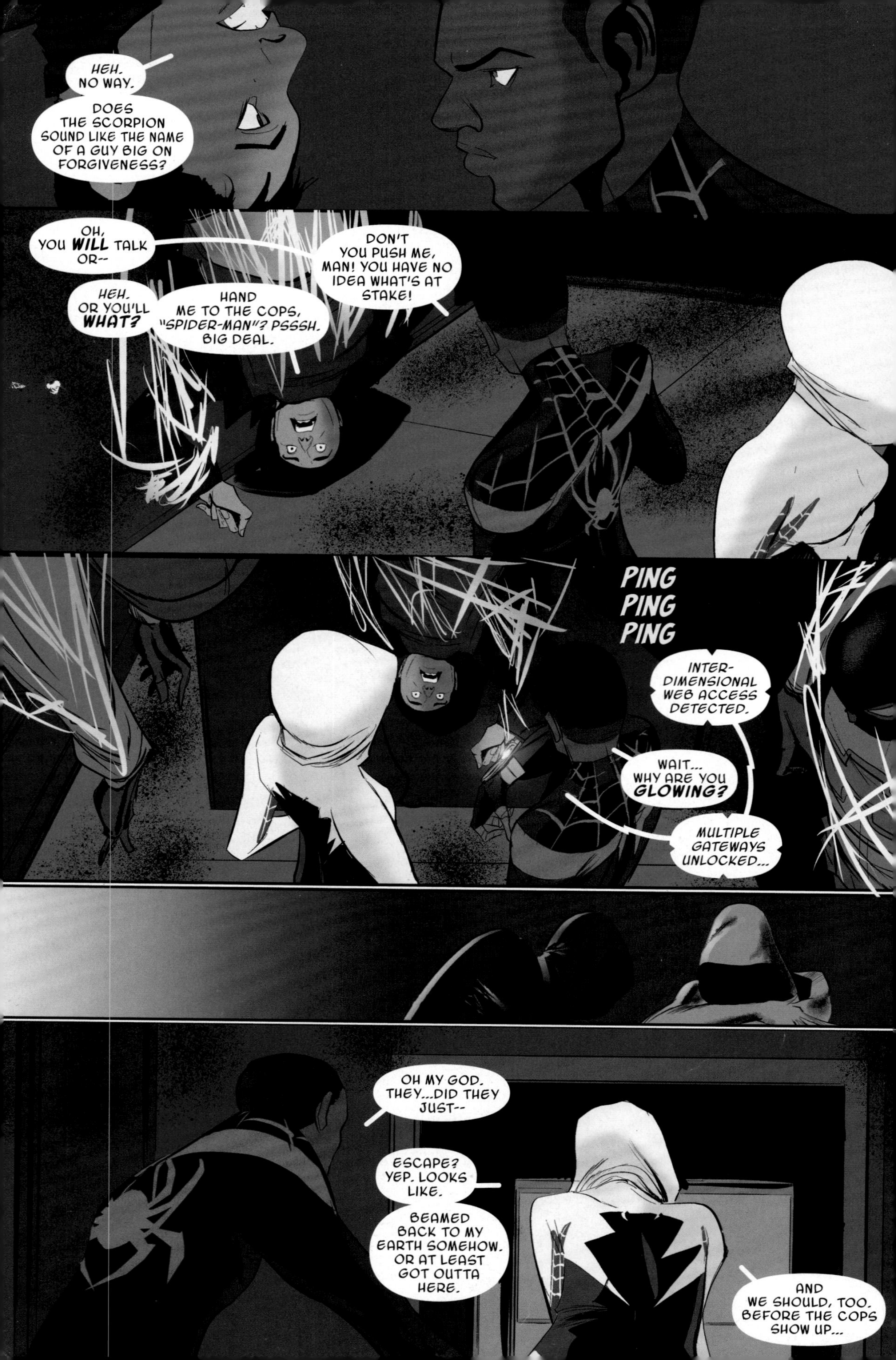
HEH. NO WAY.
DOES THE SCORPION SOUND LIKE THE NAME OF A GUY BIG ON FORGIVENESS?
OH, YOU WILL TALK OR--
DON'T YOU PUSH ME, MAN! YOU HAVE NO IDEA WHAT'S AT STAKE!
HEH. OR YOU'LL WHAT?
HAND ME TO THE COPS, "SPIDER-MAN"? PSSSH. BIG DEAL.
PING PING PING
INTER-DIMENSIONAL WEB ACCESS DETECTED.
WAIT... WHY ARE YOU GLOWING?
MULTIPLE GATEWAYS UNLOCKED...
OH MY GOD. THEY...DID THEY JUST--
ESCAPE? YEP. LOOKS LIKE.
BEAMED BACK TO MY EARTH SOMEHOW. OR AT LEAST GOT OUTTA HERE.
AND WE SHOULD, TOO. BEFORE THE COPS SHOW UP...

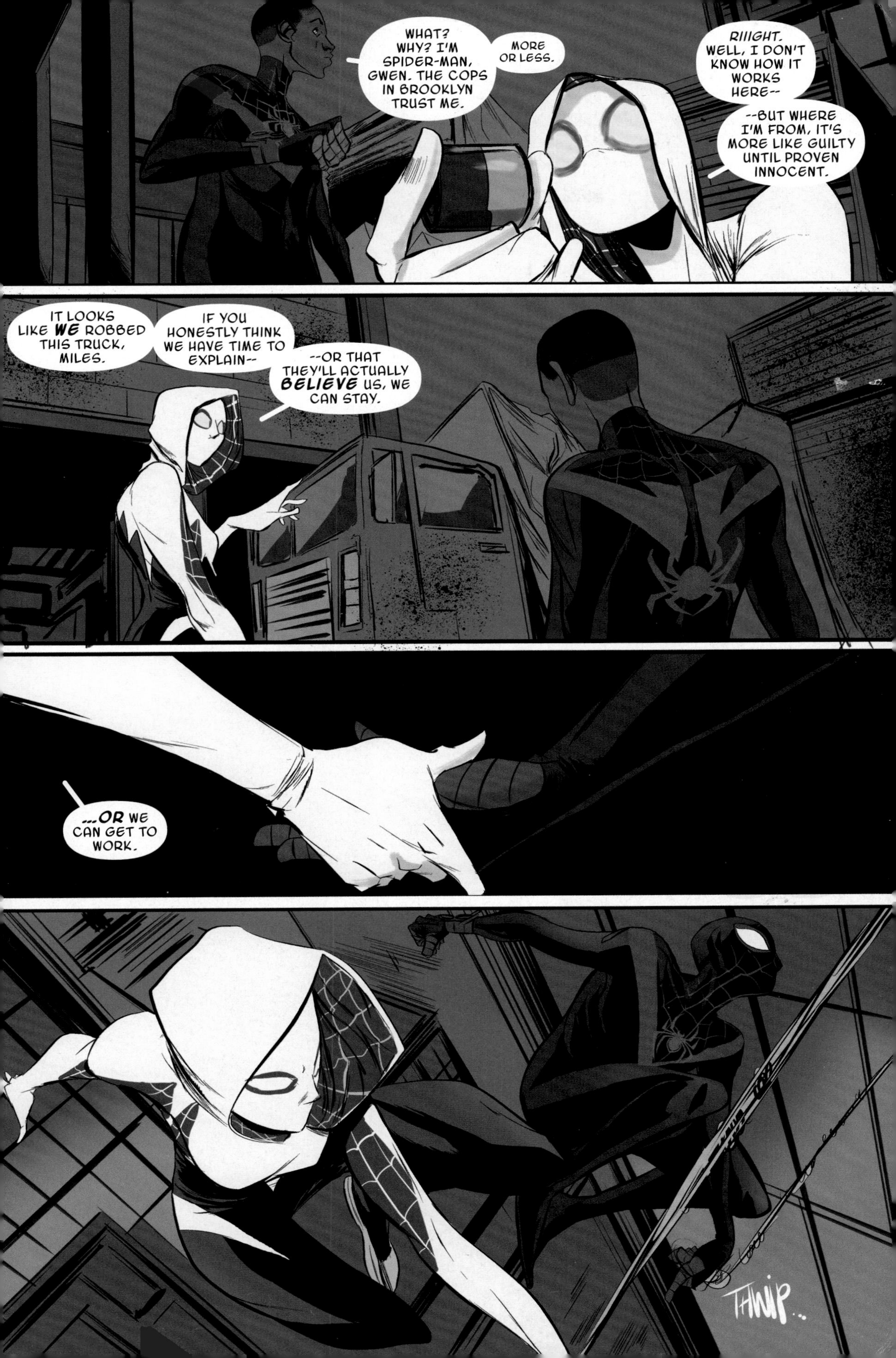

WHAT? WHY? I'M SPIDER-MAN, GWEN. THE COPS IN BROOKLYN TRUST ME.
MORE OR LESS.
RIIIGHT. WELL, I DON'T KNOW HOW IT WORKS HERE--
--BUT WHERE I'M FROM, IT'S MORE LIKE GUILTY UNTIL PROVEN INNOCENT.
IT LOOKS LIKE **WE** ROBBED THIS TRUCK, MILES.
IF YOU HONESTLY THINK WE HAVE TIME TO EXPLAIN--
--OR THAT THEY'LL ACTUALLY **BELIEVE** US, WE CAN STAY.
...**OR** WE CAN GET TO WORK.
THWIP...

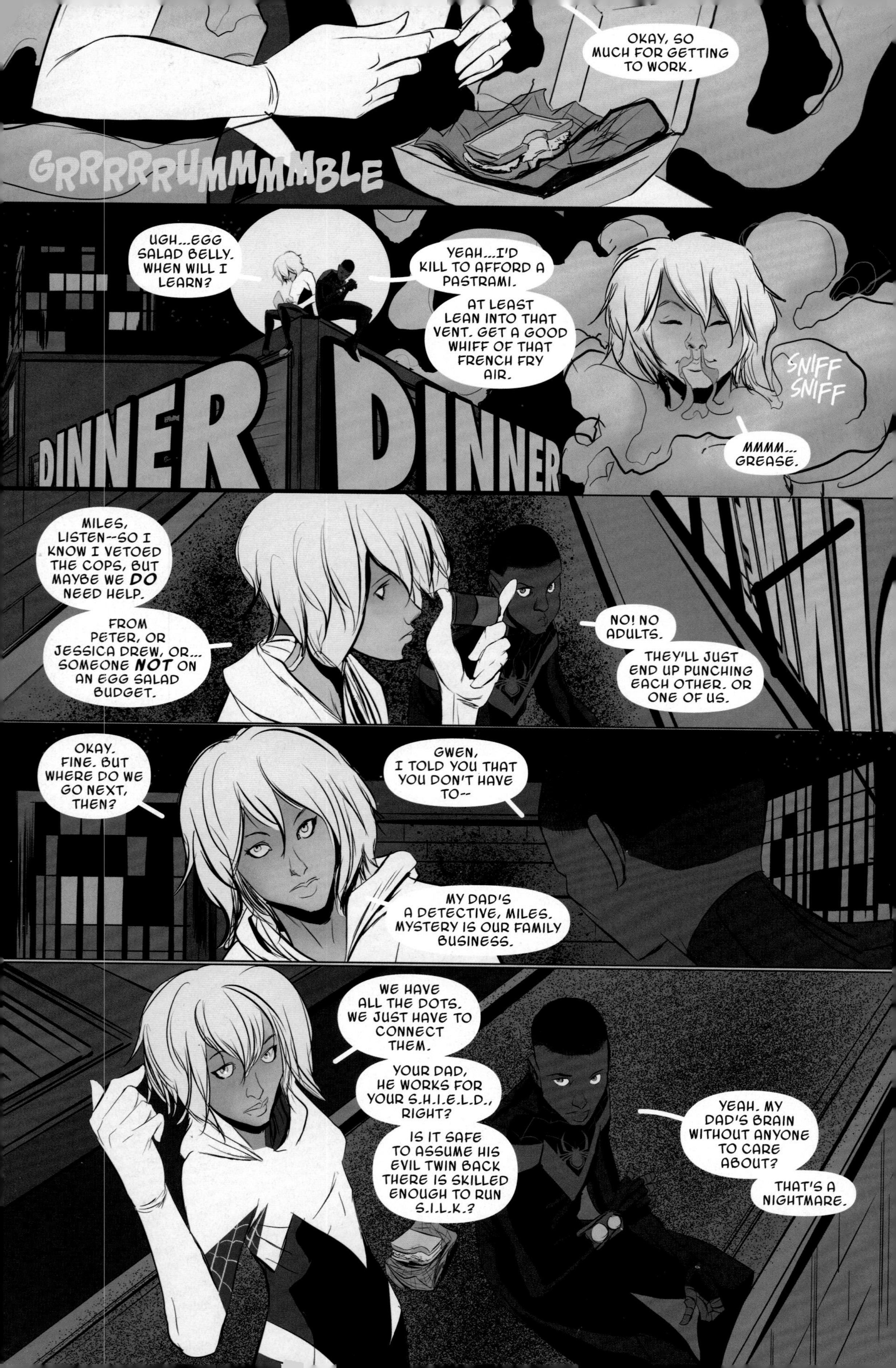
OKAY, SO MUCH FOR GETTING TO WORK.
GRRRRRUMMMMMBLE
UGH...EGG SALAD BELLY. WHEN WILL I LEARN?
YEAH...I'D KILL TO AFFORD A PASTRAMI.
AT LEAST LEAN INTO THAT VENT. GET A GOOD WHIFF OF THAT FRENCH FRY AIR.
DINNER
DINNER
SNIFF SNIFF
MMMM... GREASE.
MILES, LISTEN--SO I KNOW I VETOED THE COPS, BUT MAYBE WE DO NEED HELP.
FROM PETER, OR JESSICA DREW, OR... SOMEONE NOT ON AN EGG SALAD BUDGET.
NO! NO ADULTS.
THEY'LL JUST END UP PUNCHING EACH OTHER. OR ONE OF US.
OKAY. FINE. BUT WHERE DO WE GO NEXT, THEN?
GWEN, I TOLD YOU THAT YOU DON'T HAVE TO--
MY DAD'S A DETECTIVE, MILES. MYSTERY IS OUR FAMILY BUSINESS.
WE HAVE ALL THE DOTS. WE JUST HAVE TO CONNECT THEM.
YOUR DAD, HE WORKS FOR YOUR S.H.I.E.L.D., RIGHT?
IS IT SAFE TO ASSUME HIS EVIL TWIN BACK THERE IS SKILLED ENOUGH TO RUN S.I.L.K.?
YEAH. MY DAD'S BRAIN WITHOUT ANYONE TO CARE ABOUT?
THAT'S A NIGHTMARE.

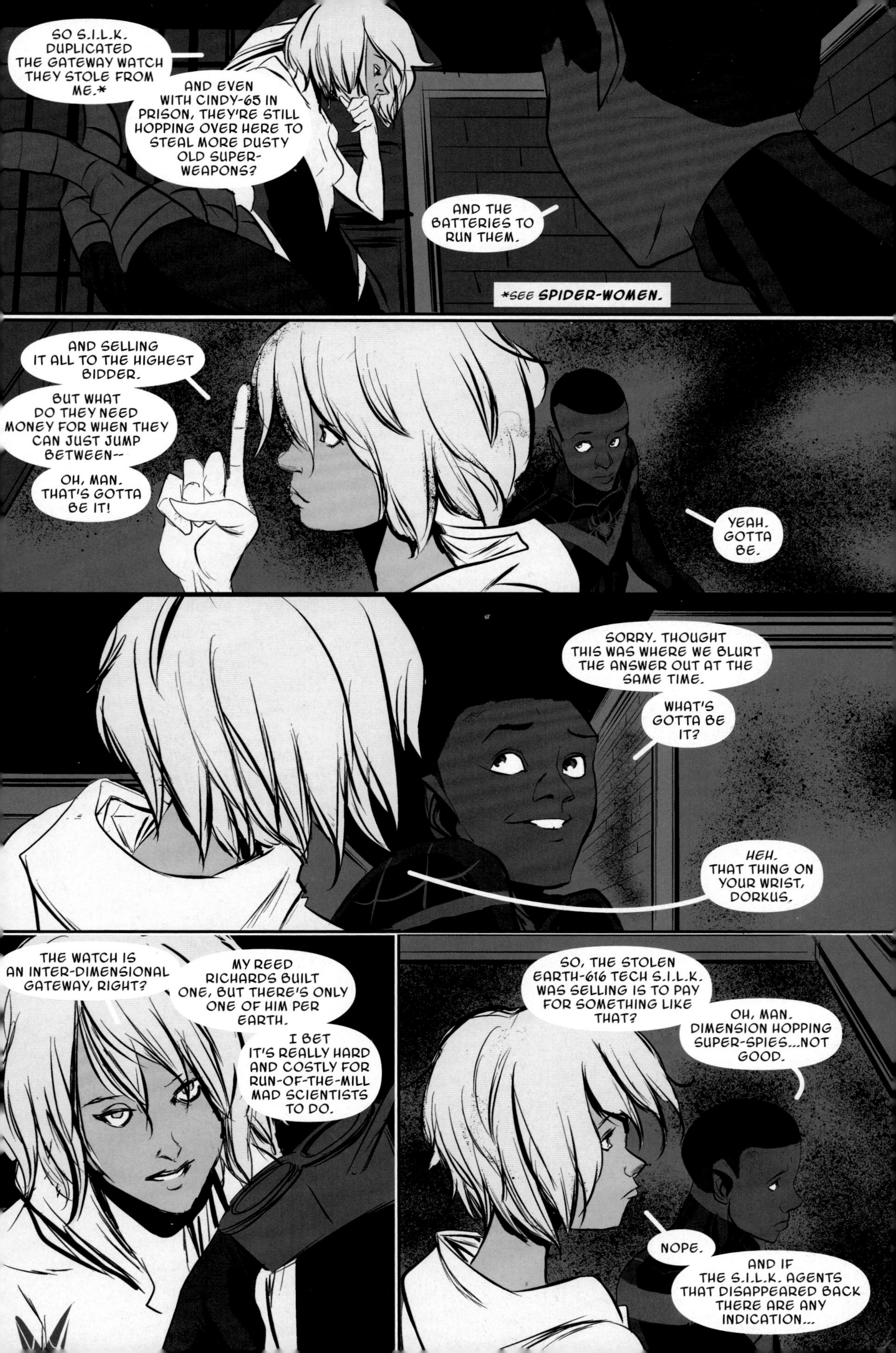
SO S.I.L.K. DUPLICATED THE GATEWAY WATCH THEY STOLE FROM ME.*
AND EVEN WITH CINDY-65 IN PRISON, THEY'RE STILL HOPPING OVER HERE TO STEAL MORE DUSTY OLD SUPER-WEAPONS?
AND THE BATTERIES TO RUN THEM.
*SEE SPIDER-WOMEN.
AND SELLING IT ALL TO THE HIGHEST BIDDER.
BUT WHAT DO THEY NEED MONEY FOR WHEN THEY CAN JUST JUMP BETWEEN--
OH, MAN. THAT'S GOTTA BE IT!
YEAH. GOTTA BE.
SORRY. THOUGHT THIS WAS WHERE WE BLURT THE ANSWER OUT AT THE SAME TIME.
WHAT'S GOTTA BE IT?
HEH. THAT THING ON YOUR WRIST, DORKUS.
THE WATCH IS AN INTER-DIMENSIONAL GATEWAY, RIGHT?
MY REED RICHARDS BUILT ONE, BUT THERE'S ONLY ONE OF HIM PER EARTH.
I BET IT'S REALLY HARD AND COSTLY FOR RUN-OF-THE-MILL MAD SCIENTISTS TO DO.
SO, THE STOLEN EARTH-616 TECH S.I.L.K. WAS SELLING IS TO PAY FOR SOMETHING LIKE THAT?
OH, MAN. DIMENSION HOPPING SUPER-SPIES...NOT GOOD.
NOPE.
AND IF THE S.I.L.K. AGENTS THAT DISAPPEARED BACK THERE ARE ANY INDICATION...

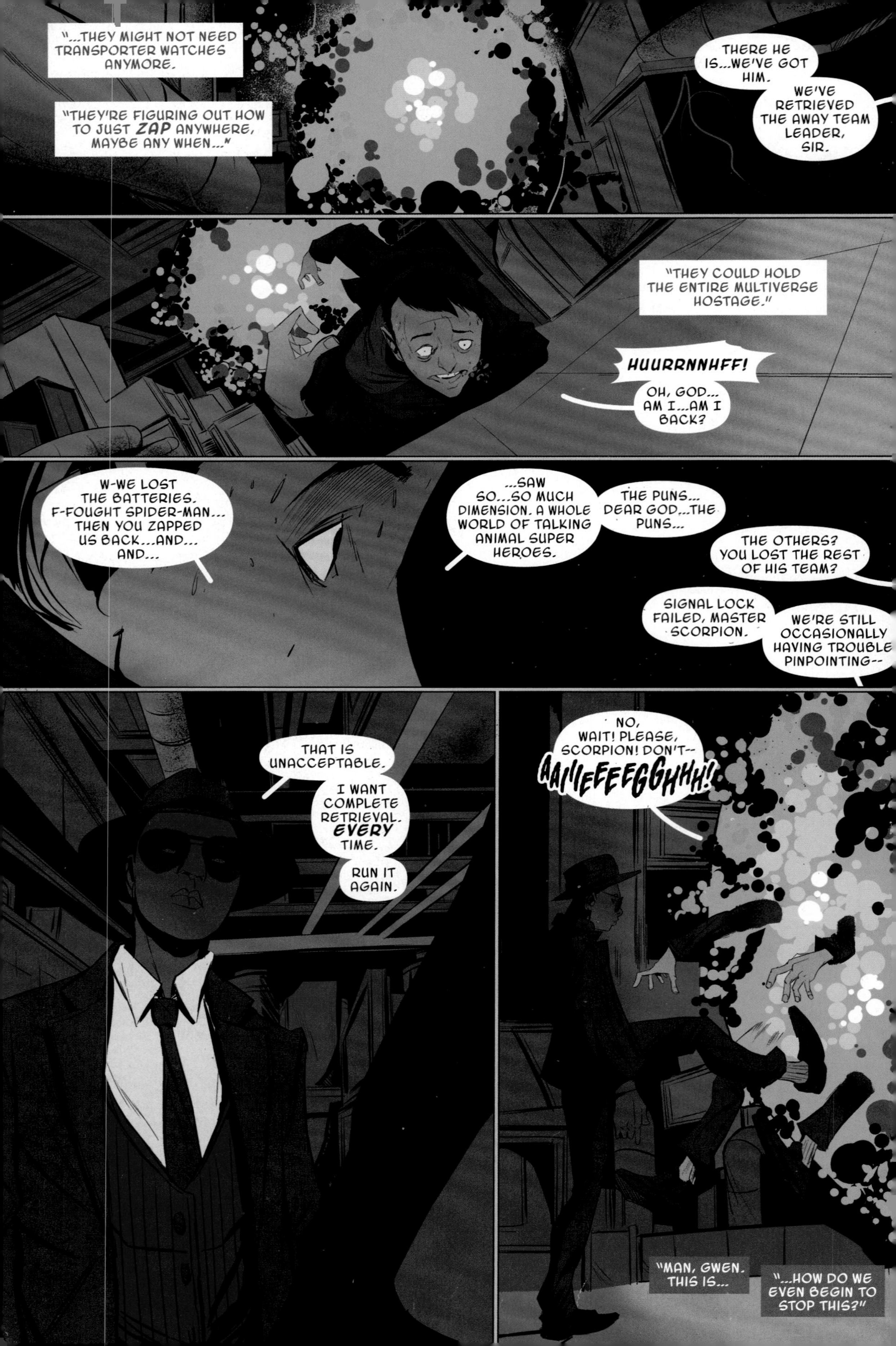
"...THEY MIGHT NOT NEED TRANSPORTER WATCHES ANYMORE.
"THEY'RE FIGURING OUT HOW TO JUST ZAP ANYWHERE, MAYBE ANY WHEN..."
THERE HE IS...WE'VE GOT HIM.
WE'VE RETRIEVED THE AWAY TEAM LEADER, SIR.
"THEY COULD HOLD THE ENTIRE MULTIVERSE HOSTAGE."
HUURRNNHFF!
OH, GOD... AM I...AM I BACK?
W-WE LOST THE BATTERIES. F-FOUGHT SPIDER-MAN... THEN YOU ZAPPED US BACK...AND... AND...
...SAW SO...SO MUCH DIMENSION. A WHOLE WORLD OF TALKING ANIMAL SUPER HEROES.
THE PUNS... DEAR GOD...THE PUNS...
THE OTHERS? YOU LOST THE REST OF HIS TEAM?
SIGNAL LOCK FAILED, MASTER SCORPION.
WE'RE STILL OCCASIONALLY HAVING TROUBLE PINPOINTING--
THAT IS UNACCEPTABLE.
I WANT COMPLETE RETRIEVAL. EVERY TIME.
RUN IT AGAIN.
NO, WAIT! PLEASE, SCORPION! DON'T--
AAIIIEEEEGGHHH!
"MAN, GWEN. THIS IS...
"...HOW DO WE EVEN BEGIN TO STOP THIS?"

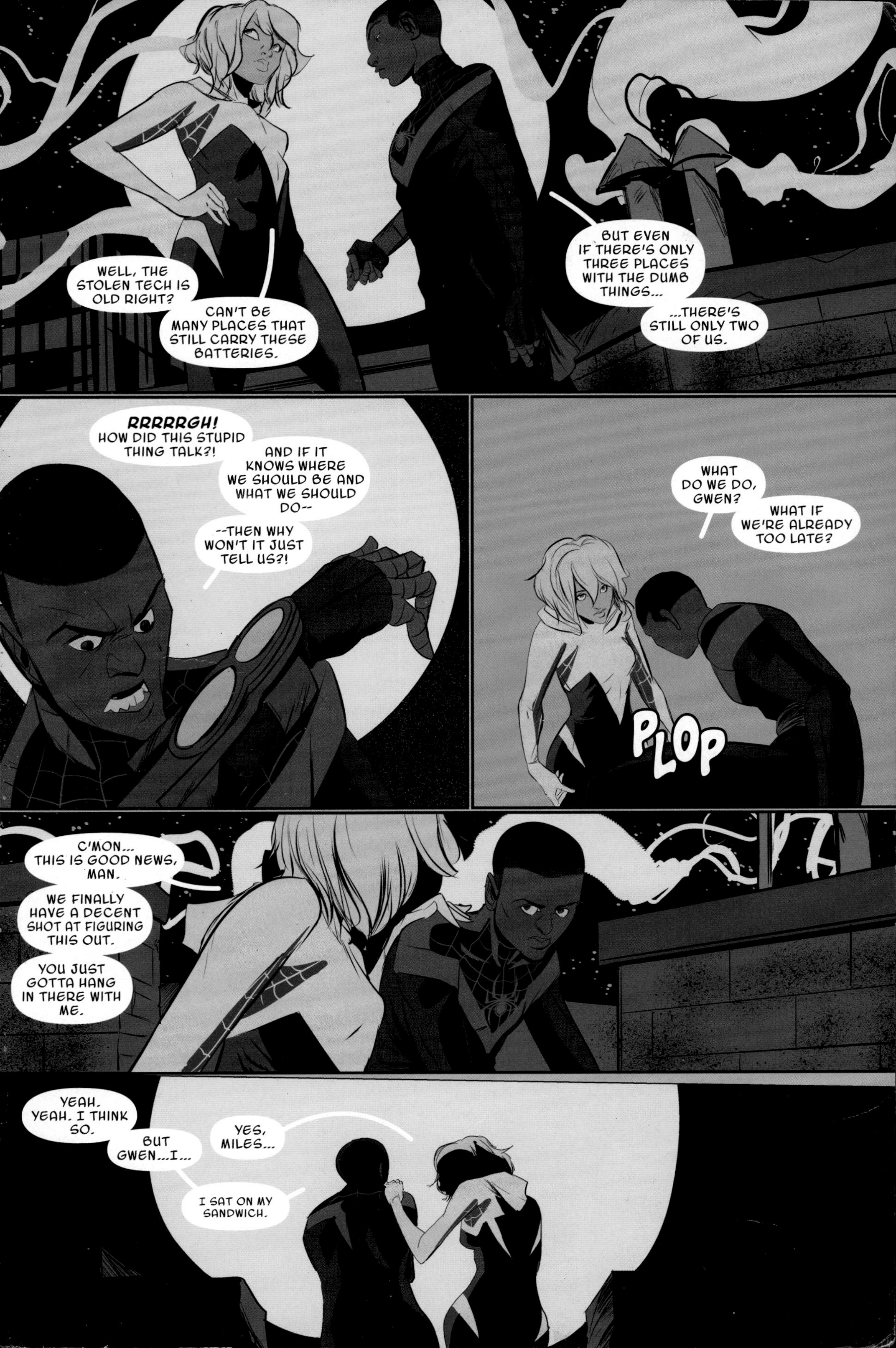
WELL, THE STOLEN TECH IS OLD RIGHT?
CAN'T BE MANY PLACES THAT STILL CARRY THESE BATTERIES.
BUT EVEN IF THERE'S ONLY THREE PLACES WITH THE DUMB THINGS...
...THERE'S STILL ONLY TWO OF US.
RRRRRGH! HOW DID THIS STUPID THING TALK?!
AND IF IT KNOWS WHERE WE SHOULD BE AND WHAT WE SHOULD DO--
--THEN WHY WON'T IT JUST TELL US?!
WHAT DO WE DO, GWEN?
WHAT IF WE'RE ALREADY TOO LATE?
PLOP
C'MON... THIS IS GOOD NEWS, MAN.
WE FINALLY HAVE A DECENT SHOT AT FIGURING THIS OUT.
YOU JUST GOTTA HANG IN THERE WITH ME.
YEAH. YEAH. I THINK SO.
BUT GWEN...I...
YES, MILES...
I SAT ON MY SANDWICH.

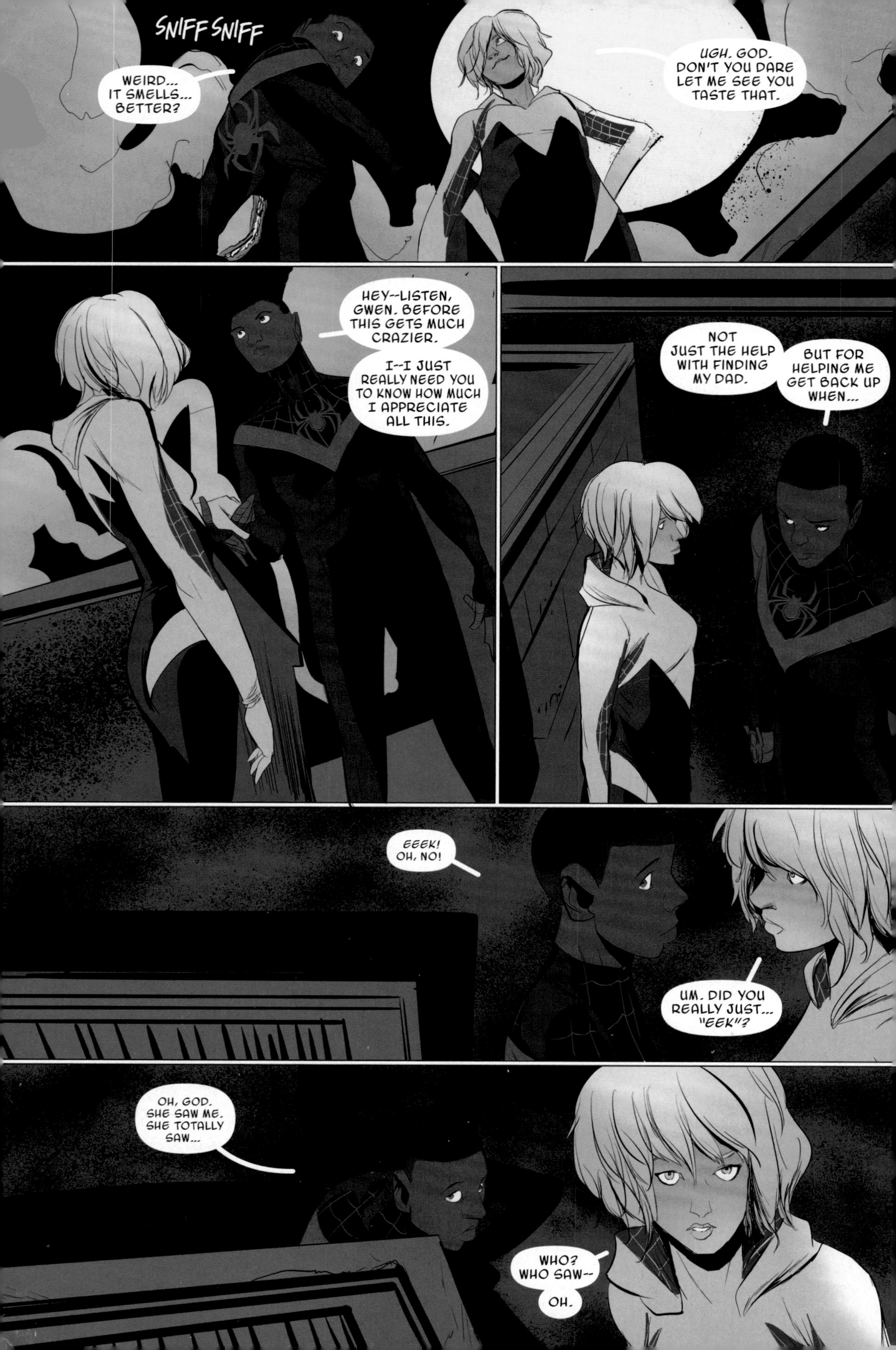
SNIFF SNIFF
WEIRD... IT SMELLS... BETTER?
UGH. GOD. DON'T YOU DARE LET ME SEE YOU TASTE THAT.
HEY--LISTEN, GWEN. BEFORE THIS GETS MUCH CRAZIER.
I--I JUST REALLY NEED YOU TO KNOW HOW MUCH I APPRECIATE ALL THIS.
NOT JUST THE HELP WITH FINDING MY DAD.
BUT FOR HELPING ME GET BACK UP WHEN...
EEEK! OH, NO!
UM. DID YOU REALLY JUST... "EEK"?
OH, GOD. SHE SAW ME. SHE TOTALLY SAW...
WHO? WHO SAW--
OH.

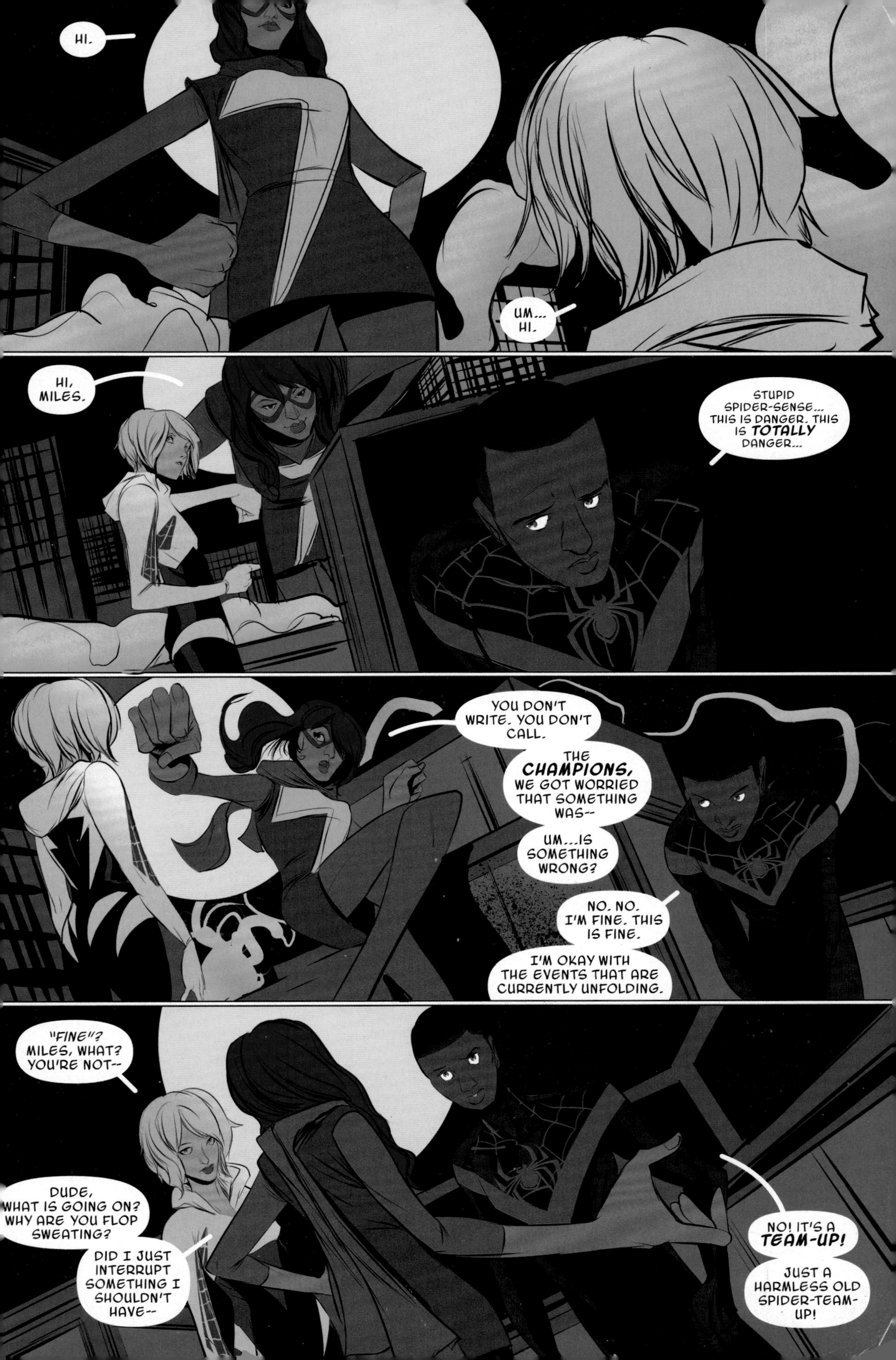
HI.
UM... HI.
HI, MILES.
STUPID SPIDER-SENSE... THIS IS DANGER. THIS IS TOTALLY DANGER...
YOU DON'T WRITE. YOU DON'T CALL.
THE CHAMPIONS, WE GOT WORRIED THAT SOMETHING WAS--
UM...IS SOMETHING WRONG?
NO. NO. I'M FINE. THIS IS FINE.
I'M OKAY WITH THE EVENTS THAT ARE CURRENTLY UNFOLDING.
"FINE"? MILES, WHAT? YOU'RE NOT--
DUDE, WHAT IS GOING ON? WHY ARE YOU FLOP SWEATING?
DID I JUST INTERRUPT SOMETHING I SHOULDN'T HAVE--
NO! IT'S A TEAM-UP!
JUST A HARMLESS OLD SPIDER-TEAM-UP!

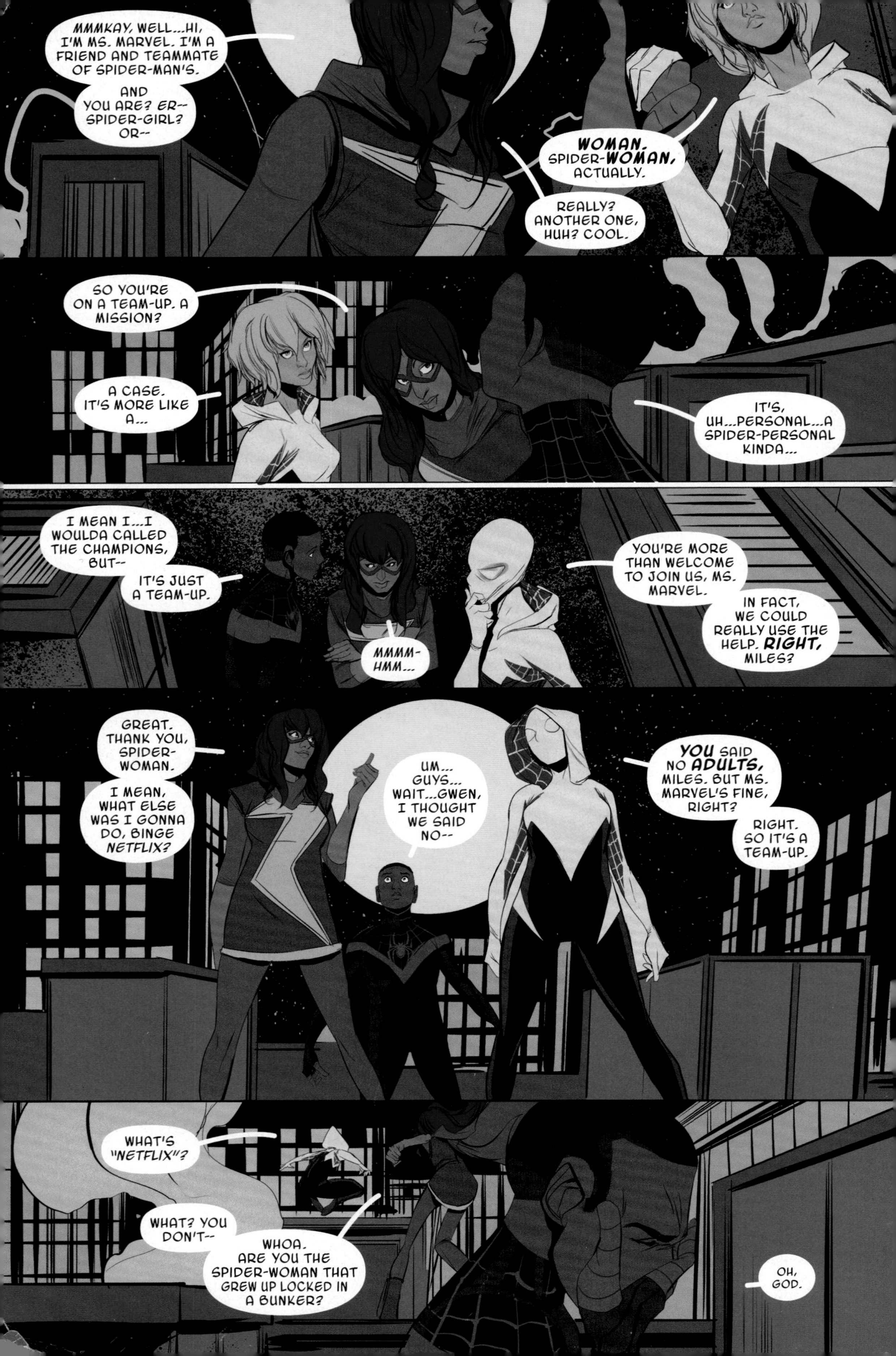

MMMKAY, WELL...HI, I'M MS. MARVEL. I'M A FRIEND AND TEAMMATE OF SPIDER-MAN'S.
AND YOU ARE? ER-- SPIDER-GIRL? OR--
WOMAN. SPIDER-**WOMAN,** ACTUALLY.
REALLY? ANOTHER ONE, HUH? COOL.
SO YOU'RE ON A TEAM-UP. A MISSION?
A CASE. IT'S MORE LIKE A...
IT'S, UH...PERSONAL...A SPIDER-PERSONAL KINDA...
I MEAN I...I WOULDA CALLED THE CHAMPIONS, BUT--
IT'S JUST A TEAM-UP.
MMMM-HMM...
YOU'RE MORE THAN WELCOME TO JOIN US, MS. MARVEL.
IN FACT, WE COULD REALLY USE THE HELP. **RIGHT,** MILES?
GREAT. THANK YOU, SPIDER-WOMAN.
I MEAN, WHAT ELSE WAS I GONNA DO, BINGE *NETFLIX*?
UM... GUYS... WAIT...GWEN, I THOUGHT WE SAID NO--
YOU SAID NO **ADULTS,** MILES. BUT MS. MARVEL'S FINE, RIGHT?
RIGHT. SO IT'S A TEAM-UP.
WHAT'S "*NETFLIX*"?
WHAT? YOU DON'T--
WHOA. ARE YOU THE SPIDER-WOMAN THAT GREW UP LOCKED IN A BUNKER?
OH, GOD.

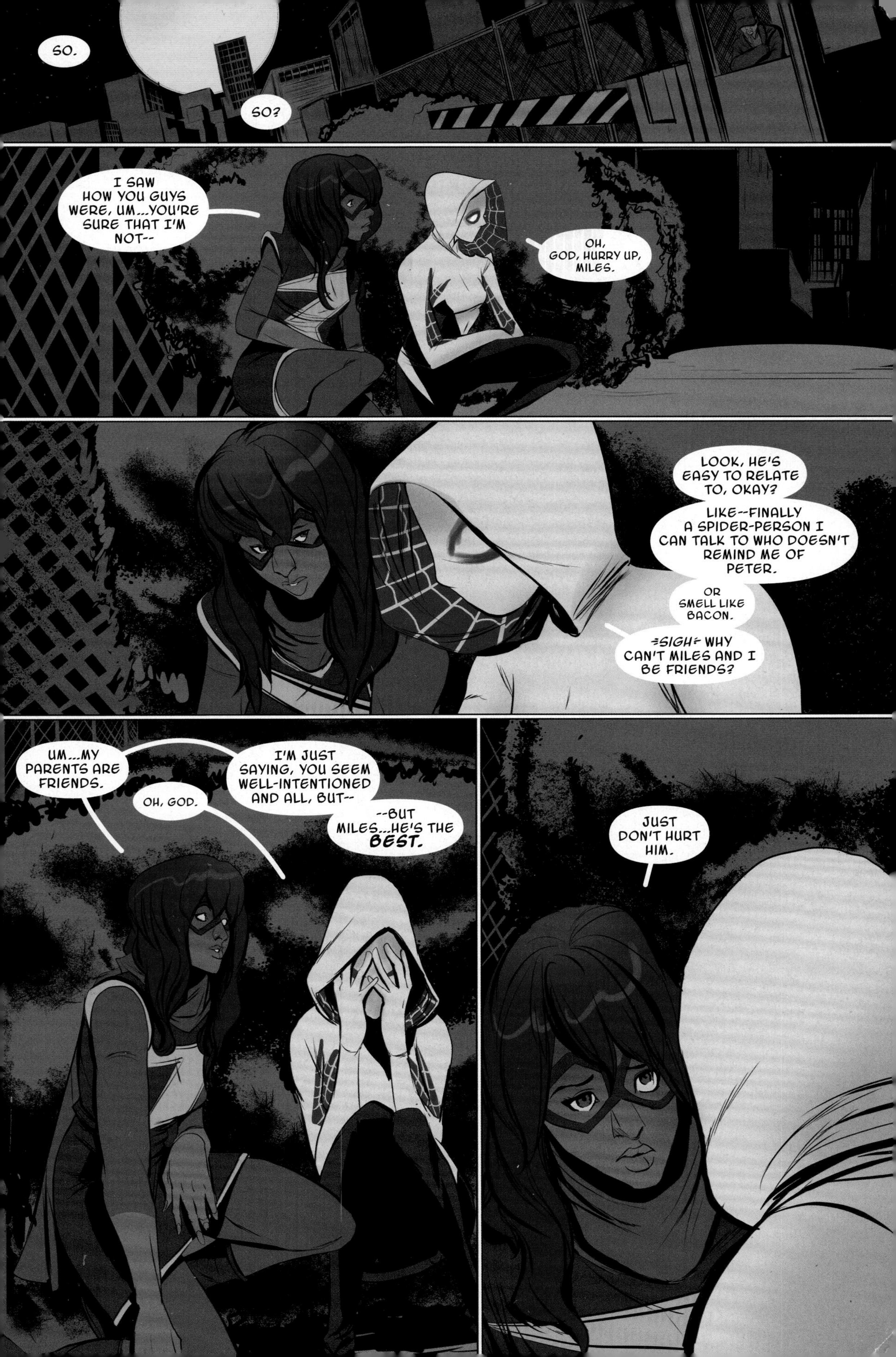
SO.
SO?
I SAW HOW YOU GUYS WERE, UM...YOU'RE SURE THAT I'M NOT--
OH, GOD, HURRY UP, MILES.
LOOK, HE'S EASY TO RELATE TO, OKAY?
LIKE--FINALLY A SPIDER-PERSON I CAN TALK TO WHO DOESN'T REMIND ME OF PETER.
OR SMELL LIKE BACON.
=SIGH= WHY CAN'T MILES AND I BE FRIENDS?
UM...MY PARENTS ARE FRIENDS.
I'M JUST SAYING, YOU SEEM WELL-INTENTIONED AND ALL, BUT--
OH, GOD.
--BUT MILES...HE'S THE BEST.
JUST DON'T HURT HIM.

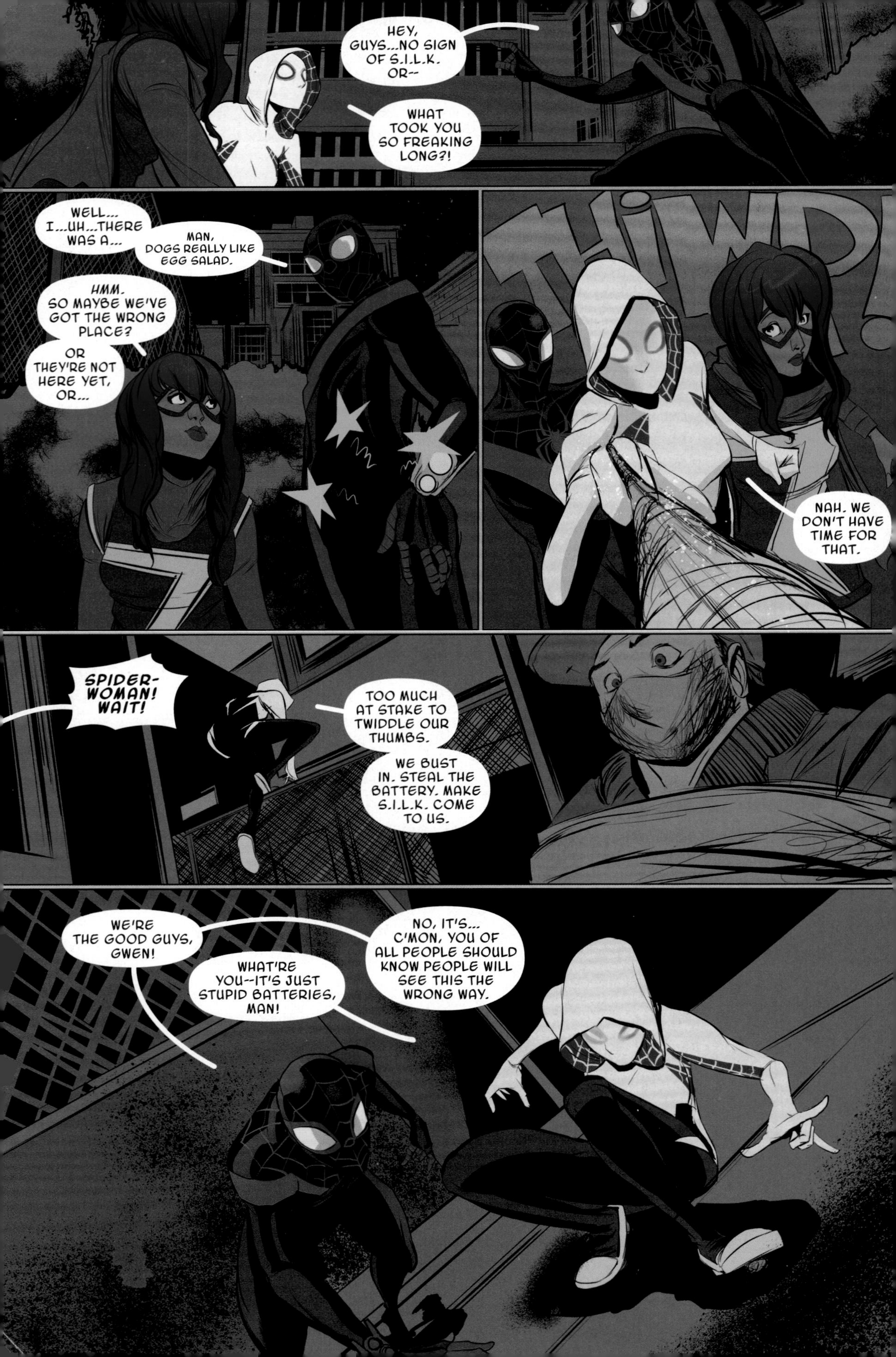
HEY, GUYS...NO SIGN OF S.I.L.K. OR--
WHAT TOOK YOU SO FREAKING LONG?!
WELL... I...UH...THERE WAS A...
MAN, DOGS REALLY LIKE EGG SALAD.
HMM. SO MAYBE WE'VE GOT THE WRONG PLACE?
OR THEY'RE NOT HERE YET, OR...
THWIP!
NAH. WE DON'T HAVE TIME FOR THAT.
SPIDER-WOMAN! WAIT!
TOO MUCH AT STAKE TO TWIDDLE OUR THUMBS.
WE BUST IN. STEAL THE BATTERY. MAKE S.I.L.K. COME TO US.
WE'RE THE GOOD GUYS, GWEN!
WHAT'RE YOU--IT'S JUST STUPID BATTERIES, MAN!
NO, IT'S... C'MON, YOU OF ALL PEOPLE SHOULD KNOW PEOPLE WILL SEE THIS THE WRONG WAY.

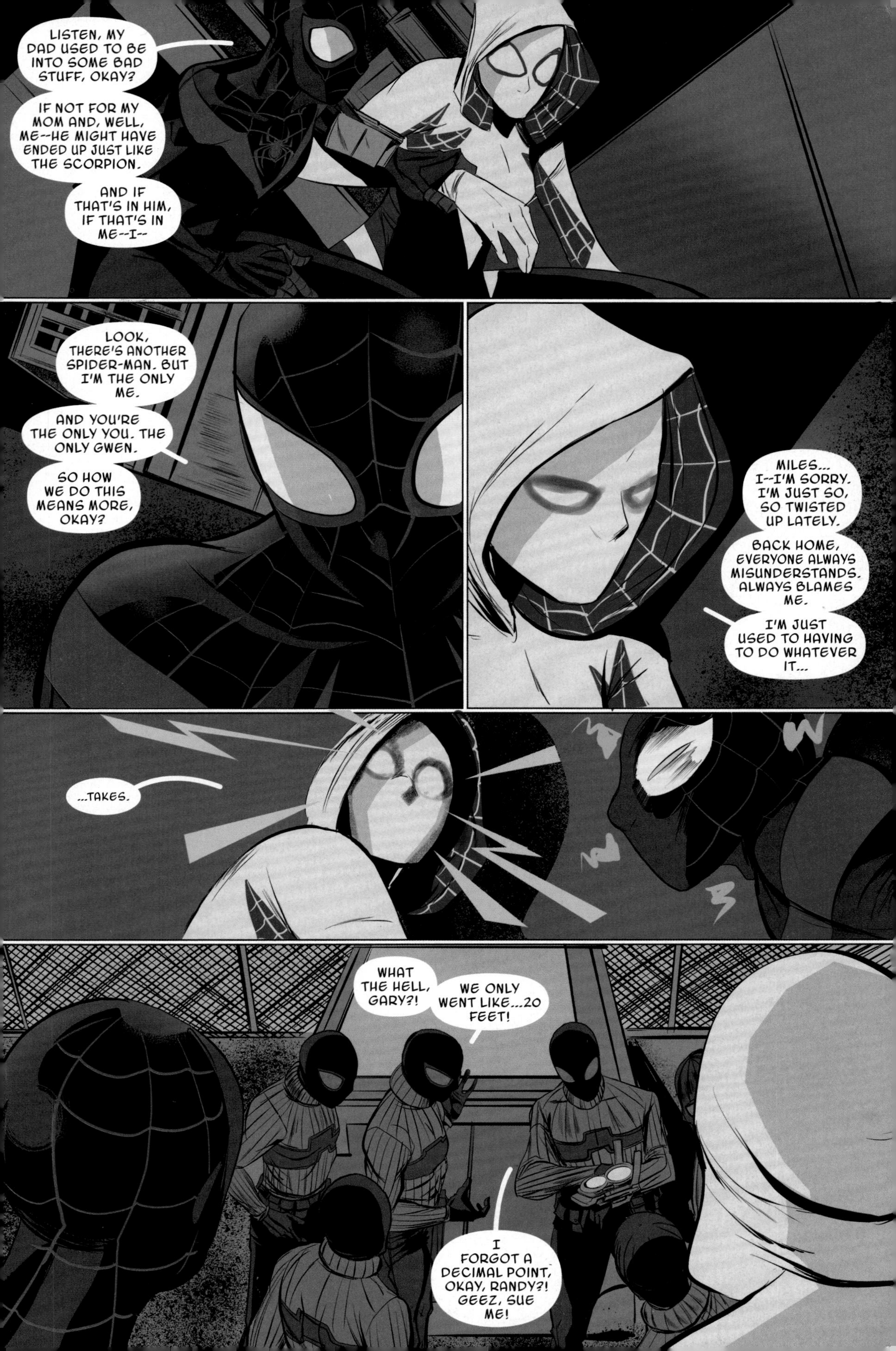
LISTEN, MY DAD USED TO BE INTO SOME BAD STUFF, OKAY?
IF NOT FOR MY MOM AND, WELL, ME--HE MIGHT HAVE ENDED UP JUST LIKE THE SCORPION.
AND IF THAT'S IN HIM, IF THAT'S IN ME--I--
LOOK, THERE'S ANOTHER SPIDER-MAN. BUT I'M THE ONLY ME.
AND YOU'RE THE ONLY YOU. THE ONLY GWEN.
SO HOW WE DO THIS MEANS MORE, OKAY?
MILES... I--I'M SORRY. I'M JUST SO, SO TWISTED UP LATELY.
BACK HOME, EVERYONE ALWAYS MISUNDERSTANDS. ALWAYS BLAMES ME.
I'M JUST USED TO HAVING TO DO WHATEVER IT...
...TAKES.
WHAT THE HELL, GARY?!
WE ONLY WENT LIKE...20 FEET!
I FORGOT A DECIMAL POINT, OKAY, RANDY?! GEEZ, SUE ME!

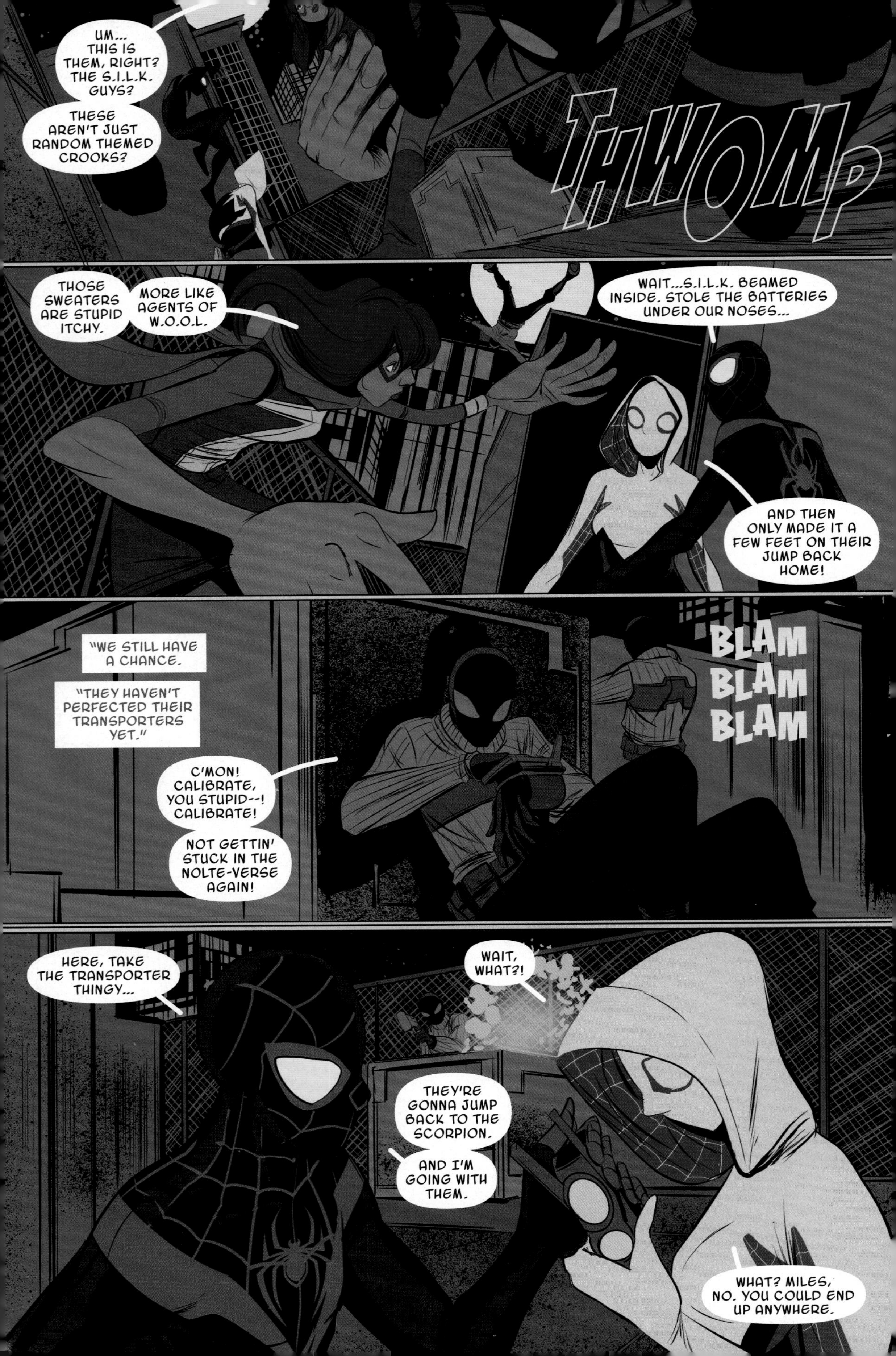
UM... THIS IS THEM, RIGHT? THE S.I.L.K. GUYS?
THESE AREN'T JUST RANDOM THEMED CROOKS?
THWOMP
THOSE SWEATERS ARE STUPID ITCHY.
MORE LIKE AGENTS OF W.O.O.L.
WAIT...S.I.L.K. BEAMED INSIDE. STOLE THE BATTERIES UNDER OUR NOSES...
AND THEN ONLY MADE IT A FEW FEET ON THEIR JUMP BACK HOME!
"WE STILL HAVE A CHANCE.
"THEY HAVEN'T PERFECTED THEIR TRANSPORTERS YET."
BLAM BLAM BLAM
C'MON! CALIBRATE, YOU STUPID--! CALIBRATE!
NOT GETTIN' STUCK IN THE NOLTE-VERSE AGAIN!
HERE, TAKE THE TRANSPORTER THINGY...
WAIT, WHAT?!
THEY'RE GONNA JUMP BACK TO THE SCORPION.
AND I'M GOING WITH THEM.
WHAT? MILES, NO. YOU COULD END UP ANYWHERE.

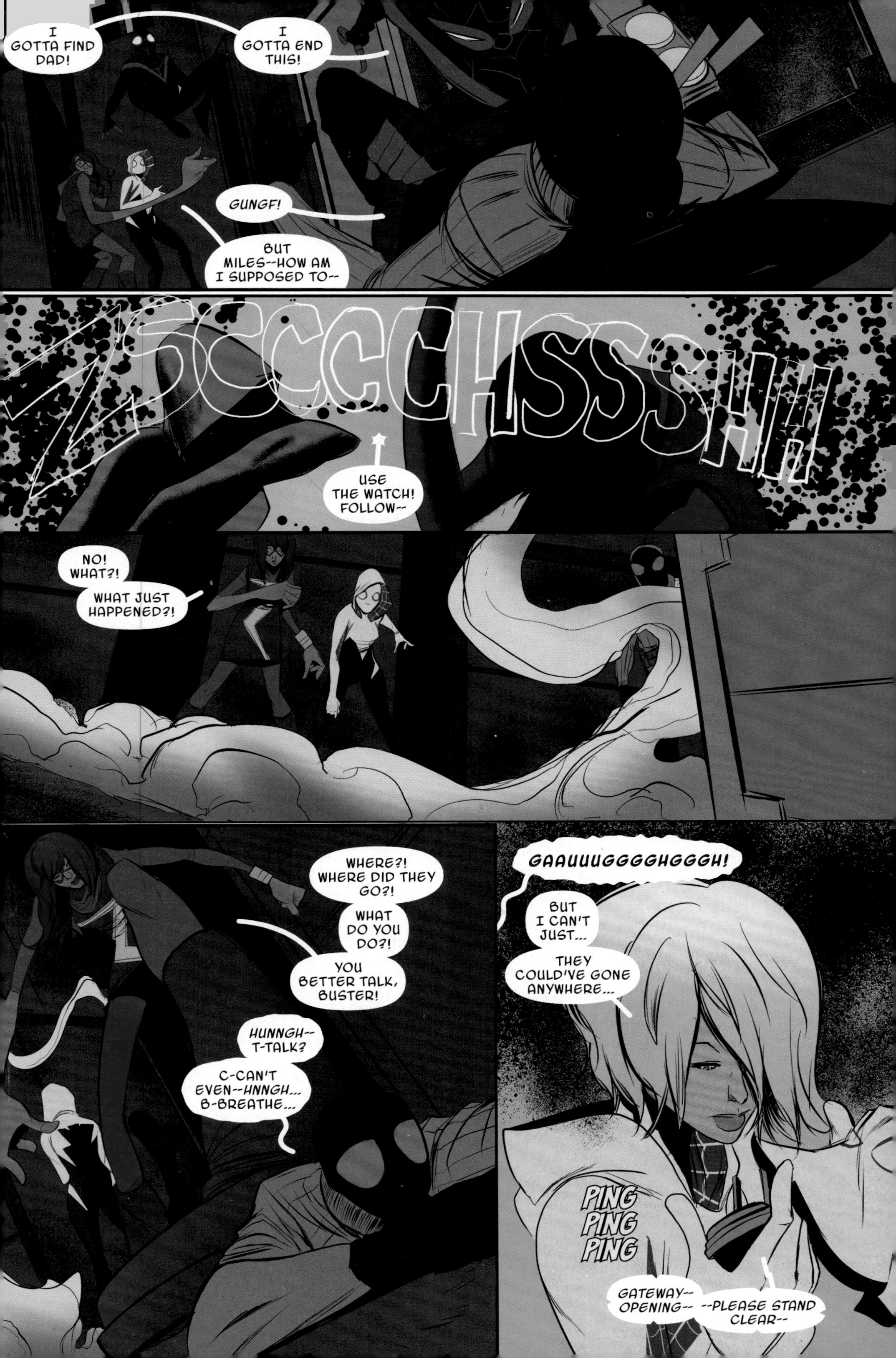
I GOTTA FIND DAD!
I GOTTA END THIS!
GUNGF!
BUT MILES--HOW AM I SUPPOSED TO--
SCCCCHSSSSHH
USE THE WATCH! FOLLOW--
NO! WHAT?!
WHAT JUST HAPPENED?!
WHERE?! WHERE DID THEY GO?!
WHAT DO YOU DO?!
YOU BETTER TALK, BUSTER!
HUNNGH-- T-TALK?
C-CAN'T EVEN--HNNGH... B-BREATHE...
GAAUUUGGGGHGGGH!
BUT I CAN'T JUST...
THEY COULD'VE GONE ANYWHERE...
PING PING PING
GATEWAY-- OPENING--
--PLEASE STAND CLEAR--

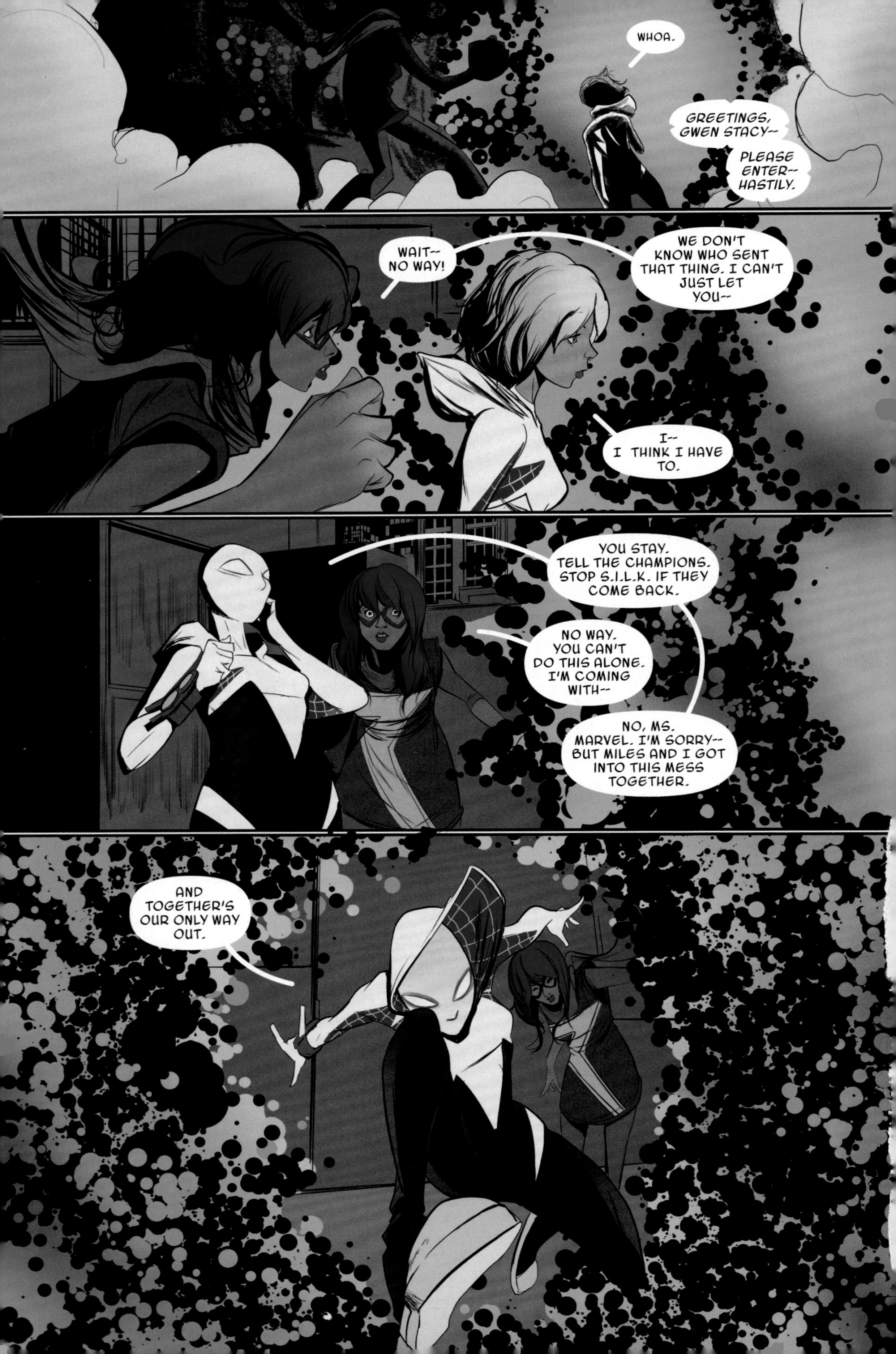
WHOA.
GREETINGS, GWEN STACY--
PLEASE ENTER-- HASTILY.
WAIT-- NO WAY!
WE DON'T KNOW WHO SENT THAT THING. I CAN'T JUST LET YOU--
I-- I THINK I HAVE TO.
YOU STAY. TELL THE CHAMPIONS. STOP S.I.L.K. IF THEY COME BACK.
NO WAY. YOU CAN'T DO THIS ALONE. I'M COMING WITH--
NO, MS. MARVEL. I'M SORRY-- BUT MILES AND I GOT INTO THIS MESS TOGETHER.
AND TOGETHER'S OUR ONLY WAY OUT.

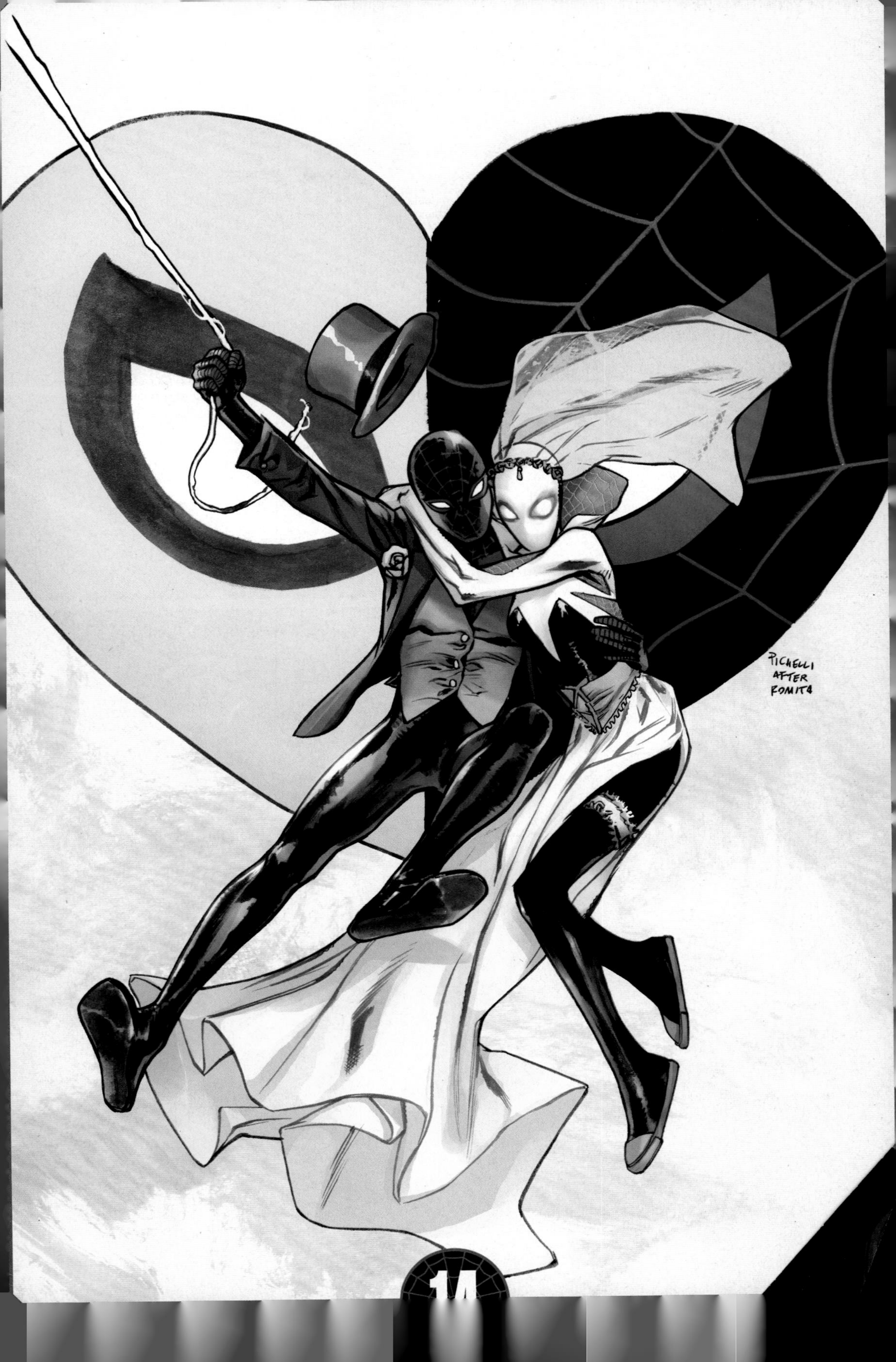
PICHELLI
AFTER
ROMITA

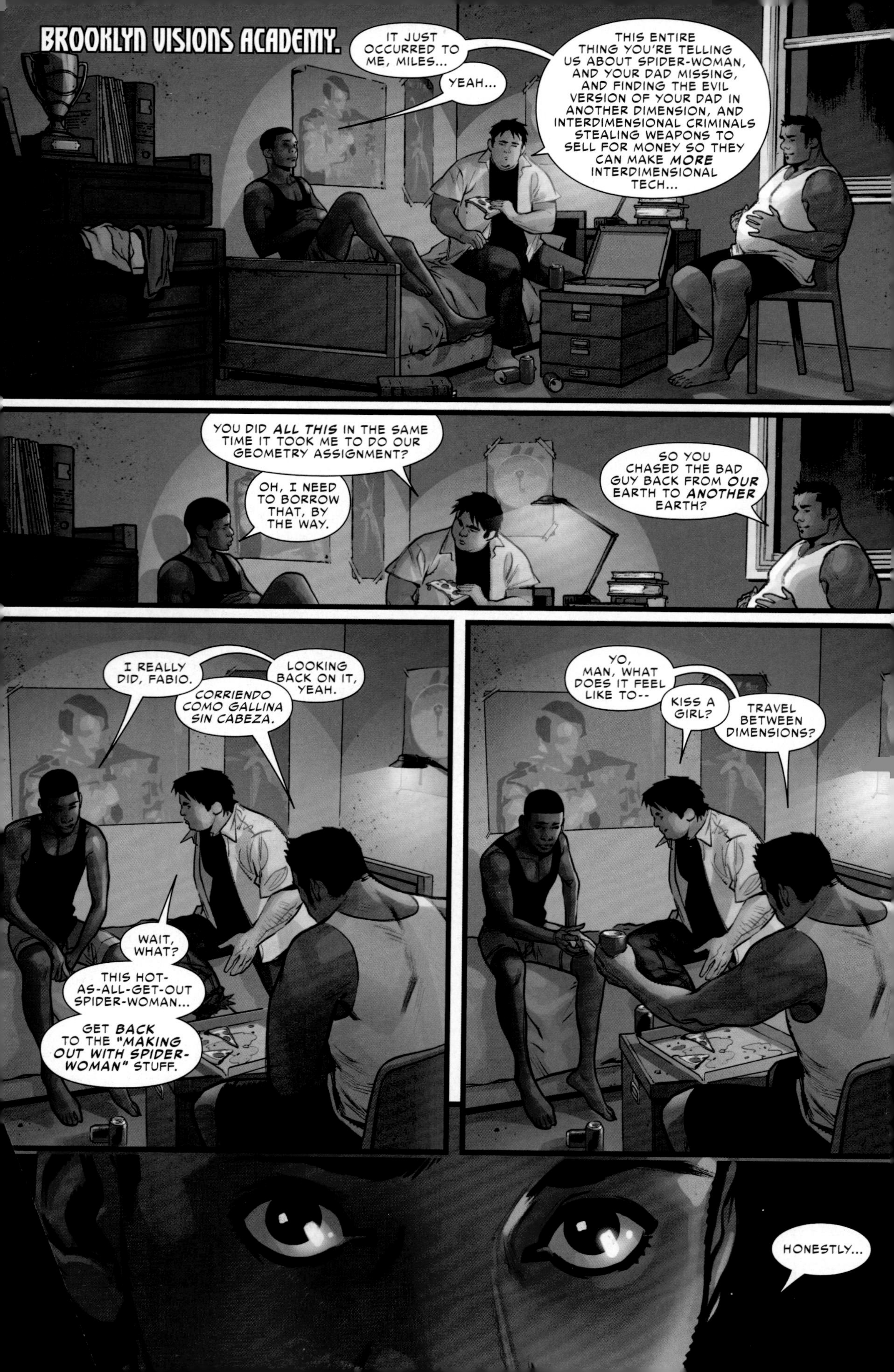
BROOKLYN VISIONS ACADEMY.
IT JUST OCCURRED TO ME, MILES...
YEAH...
THIS ENTIRE THING YOU'RE TELLING US ABOUT SPIDER-WOMAN, AND YOUR DAD MISSING, AND FINDING THE EVIL VERSION OF YOUR DAD IN ANOTHER DIMENSION, AND INTERDIMENSIONAL CRIMINALS STEALING WEAPONS TO SELL FOR MONEY SO THEY CAN MAKE *MORE* INTERDIMENSIONAL TECH...
YOU DID *ALL THIS* IN THE SAME TIME IT TOOK ME TO DO OUR GEOMETRY ASSIGNMENT?
OH, I NEED TO BORROW THAT, BY THE WAY.
SO YOU CHASED THE BAD GUY BACK FROM *OUR* EARTH TO *ANOTHER* EARTH?
I REALLY DID, FABIO.
LOOKING BACK ON IT, YEAH.
CORRIENDO COMO GALLINA SIN CABEZA.
WAIT, WHAT?
THIS HOT-AS-ALL-GET-OUT SPIDER-WOMAN...
GET *BACK* TO THE *"MAKING OUT WITH SPIDER-WOMAN"* STUFF.
YO, MAN, WHAT DOES IT FEEL LIKE TO--
KISS A GIRL?
TRAVEL BETWEEN DIMENSIONS?
HONESTLY...

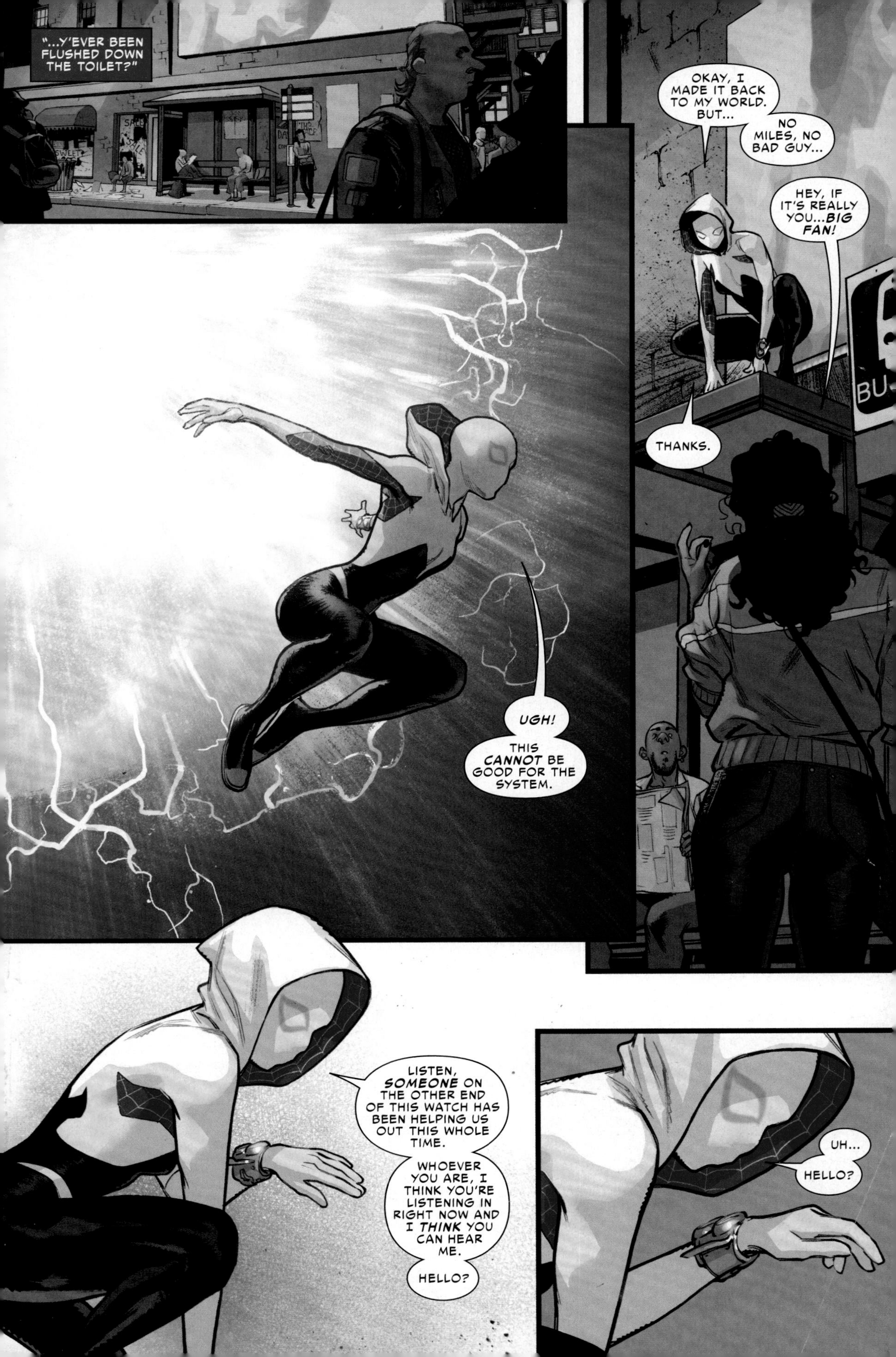
"...Y'EVER BEEN FLUSHED DOWN THE TOILET?"
UGH!
THIS CANNOT BE GOOD FOR THE SYSTEM.
OKAY, I MADE IT BACK TO MY WORLD. BUT...
NO MILES, NO BAD GUY...
HEY, IF IT'S REALLY YOU...BIG FAN!
THANKS.
BU
LISTEN, SOMEONE ON THE OTHER END OF THIS WATCH HAS BEEN HELPING US OUT THIS WHOLE TIME.
WHOEVER YOU ARE, I THINK YOU'RE LISTENING IN RIGHT NOW AND I THINK YOU CAN HEAR ME.
HELLO?
UH...
HELLO?

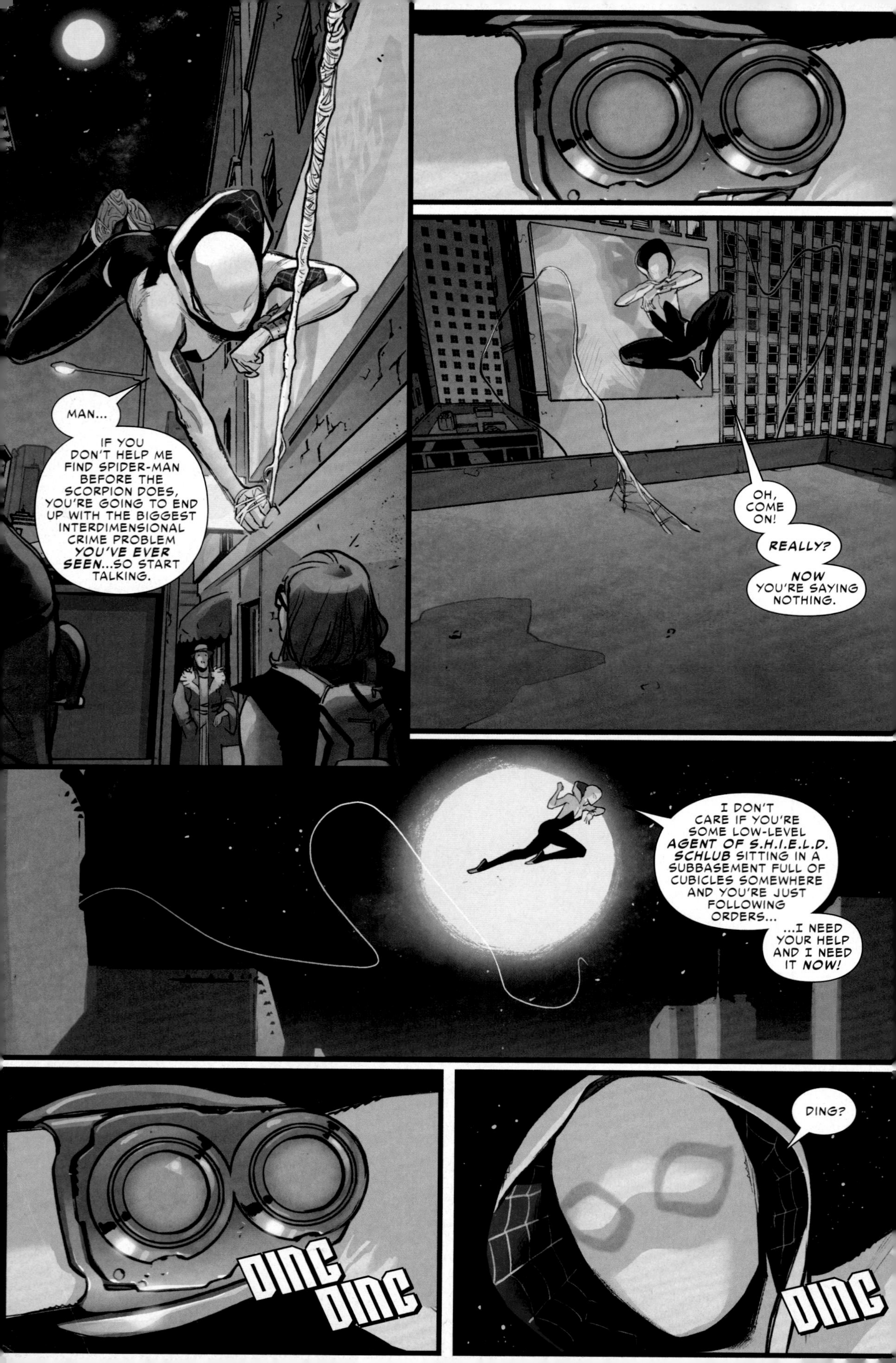
MAN...
IF YOU DON'T HELP ME FIND SPIDER-MAN BEFORE THE SCORPION DOES, YOU'RE GOING TO END UP WITH THE BIGGEST INTERDIMENSIONAL CRIME PROBLEM YOU'VE EVER SEEN...SO START TALKING.
OH, COME ON!
REALLY?
NOW YOU'RE SAYING NOTHING.
I DON'T CARE IF YOU'RE SOME LOW-LEVEL AGENT OF S.H.I.E.L.D. SCHLUB SITTING IN A SUBBASEMENT FULL OF CUBICLES SOMEWHERE AND YOU'RE JUST FOLLOWING ORDERS...
...I NEED YOUR HELP AND I NEED IT NOW!
DING DING
DING?
DING

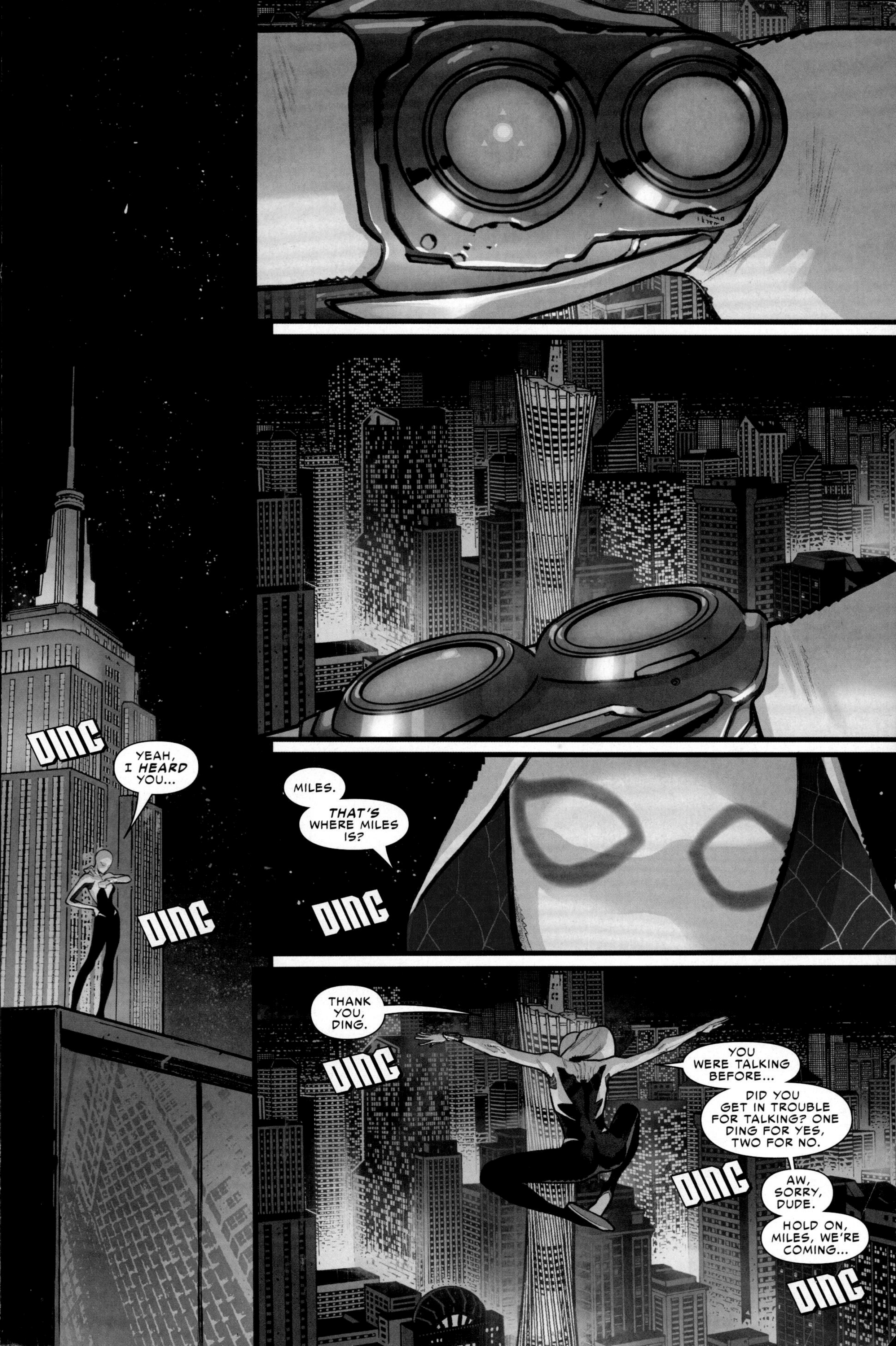

DING
YEAH, I HEARD YOU...
DING
MILES.
THAT'S WHERE MILES IS?
DING
THANK YOU, DING.
DING
YOU WERE TALKING BEFORE...
DID YOU GET IN TROUBLE FOR TALKING? ONE DING FOR YES, TWO FOR NO.
DING
AW, SORRY, DUDE.
HOLD ON, MILES, WE'RE COMING...
DING

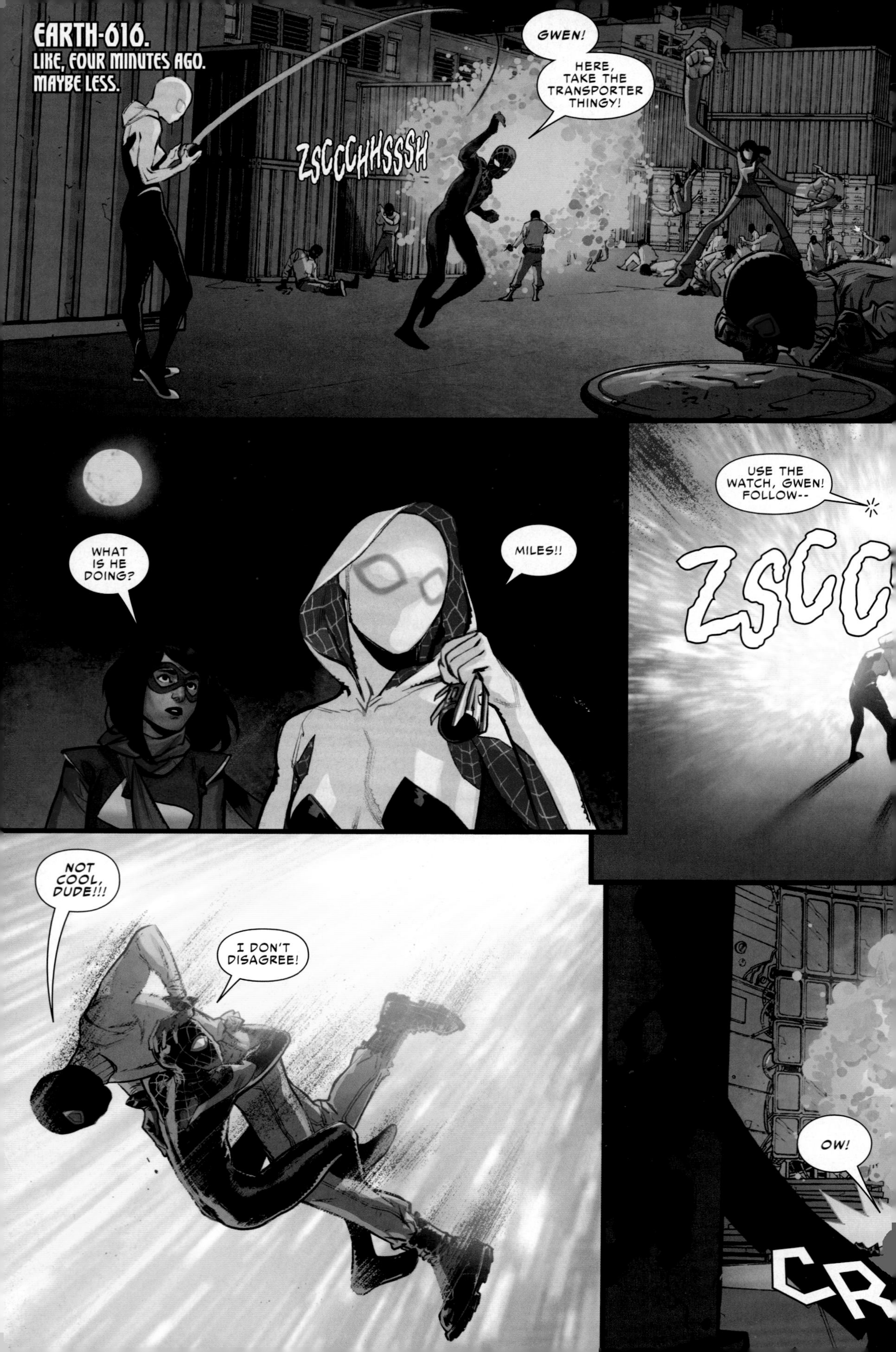
EARTH-616.
LIKE, FOUR MINUTES AGO. MAYBE LESS.
GWEN!
HERE, TAKE THE TRANSPORTER THINGY!
ZSCCCHHSSSH
WHAT IS HE DOING?
MILES!!
USE THE WATCH, GWEN! FOLLOW--
ZSCC
NOT COOL, DUDE!!!
I DON'T DISAGREE!
OW!
CR

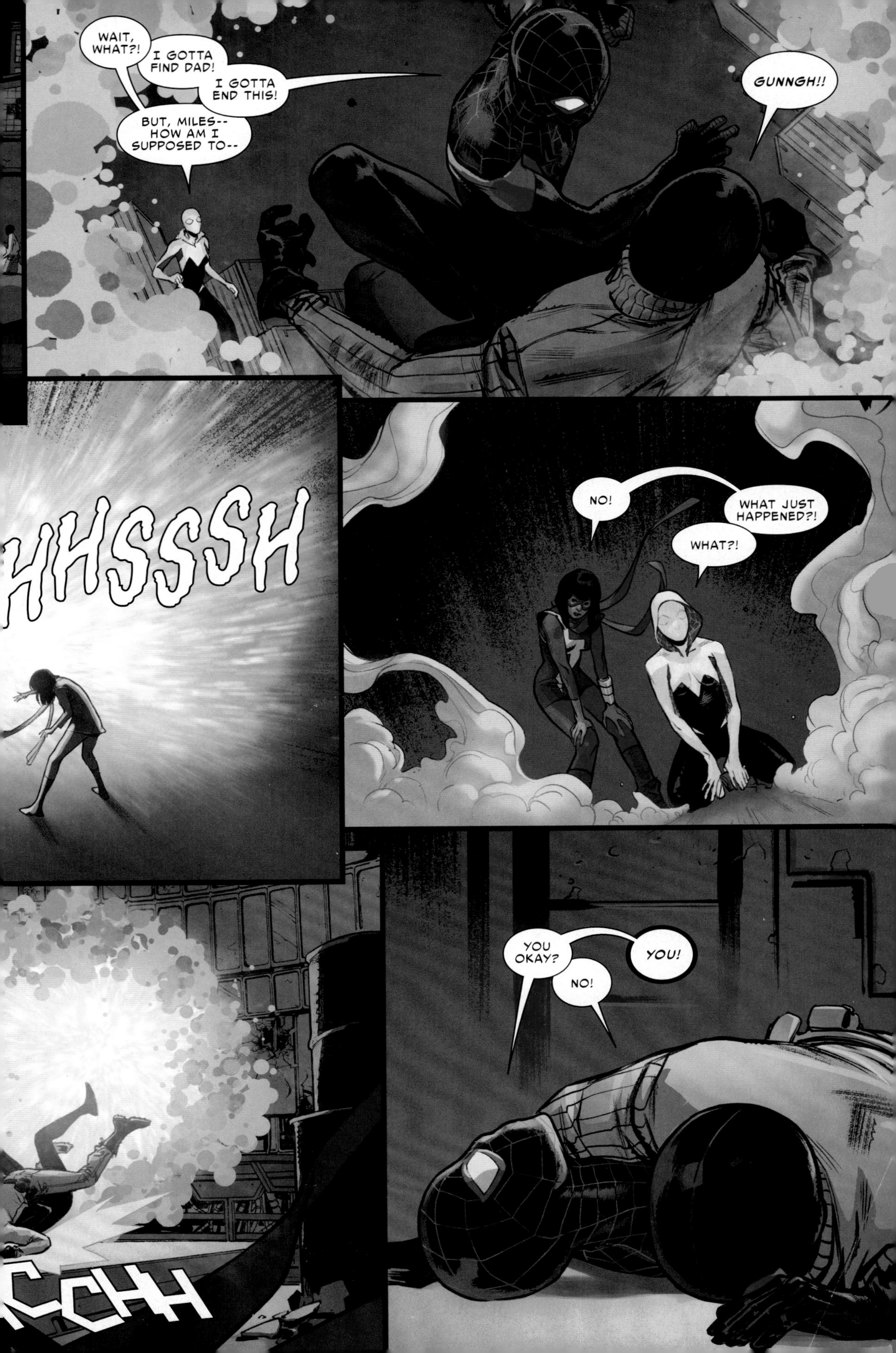
WAIT, WHAT?!
I GOTTA FIND DAD!
I GOTTA END THIS!
BUT, MILES-- HOW AM I SUPPOSED TO--
GUNNGH!!
HHSSSH
NO!
WHAT JUST HAPPENED?!
WHAT?!
CCHH
YOU OKAY?
YOU!
NO!

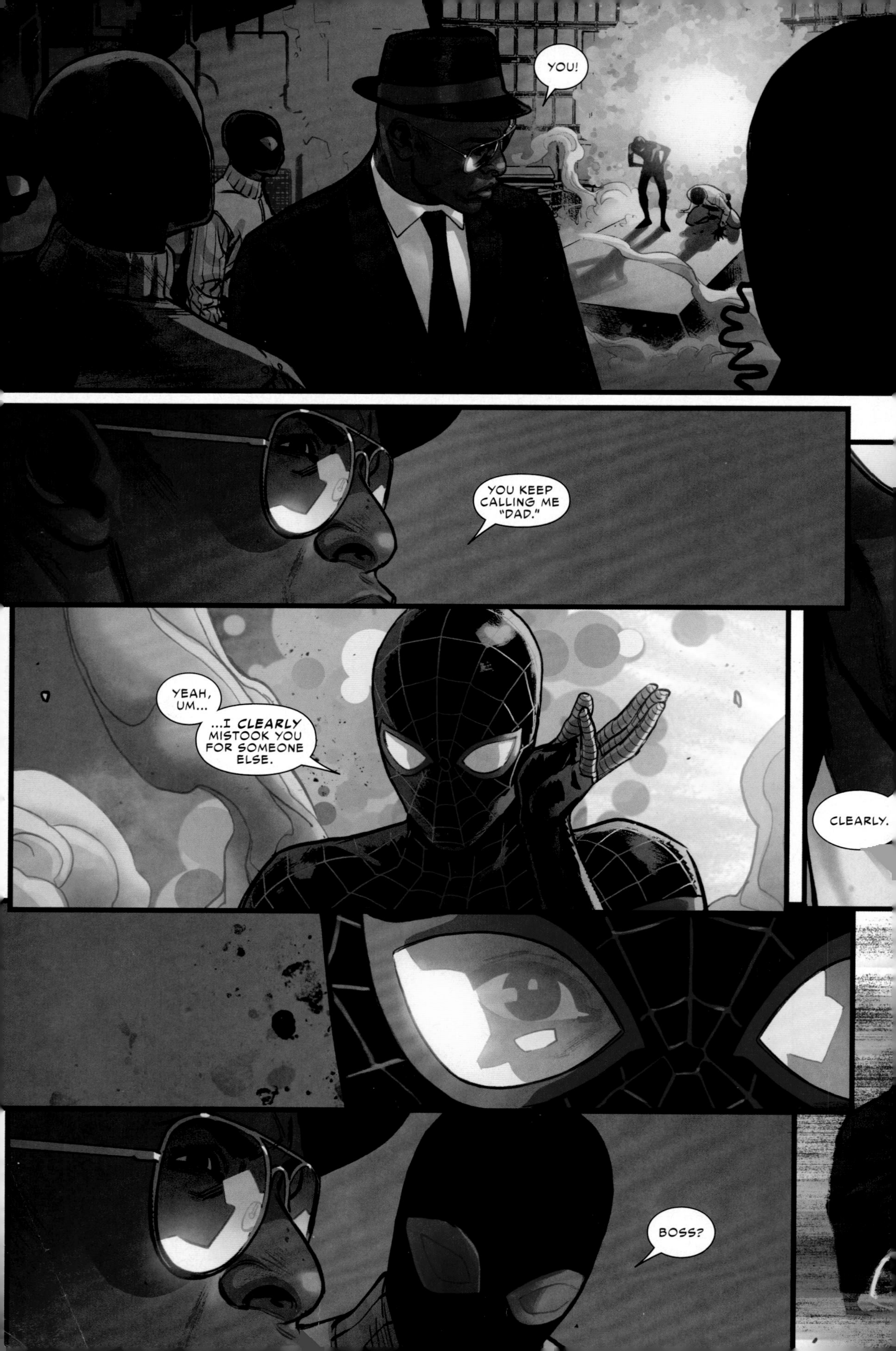
YOU!
YOU KEEP CALLING ME "DAD."
YEAH, UM...
...I CLEARLY MISTOOK YOU FOR SOMEONE ELSE.
CLEARLY.
BOSS?

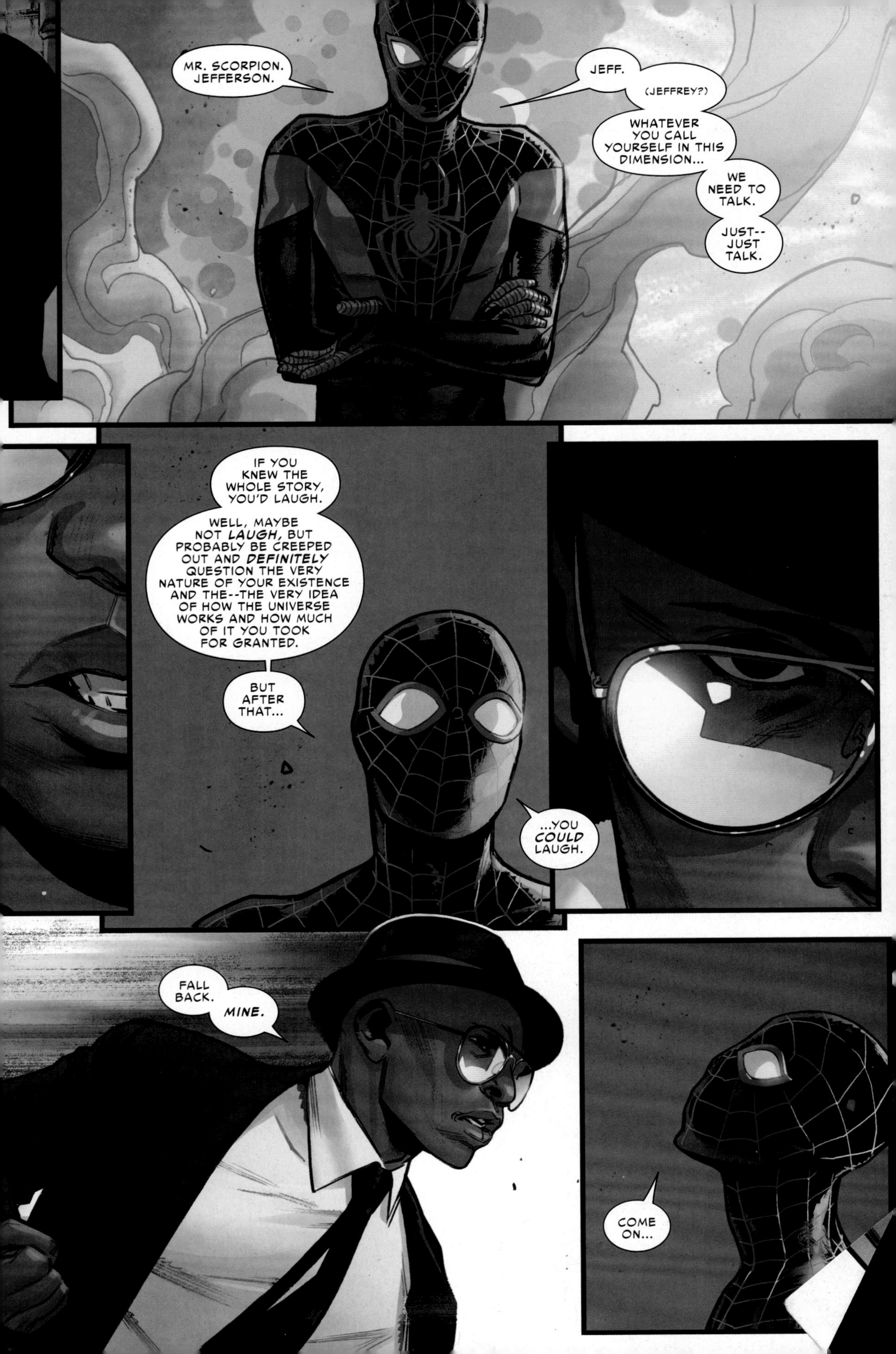
MR. SCORPION. JEFFERSON.
JEFF.
(JEFFREY?)
WHATEVER YOU CALL YOURSELF IN THIS DIMENSION...
WE NEED TO TALK.
JUST-- JUST TALK.
IF YOU KNEW THE WHOLE STORY, YOU'D LAUGH.
WELL, MAYBE NOT *LAUGH,* BUT PROBABLY BE CREEPED OUT AND *DEFINITELY* QUESTION THE VERY NATURE OF YOUR EXISTENCE AND THE--THE VERY IDEA OF HOW THE UNIVERSE WORKS AND HOW MUCH OF IT YOU TOOK FOR GRANTED.
BUT AFTER THAT...
...YOU *COULD* LAUGH.
FALL BACK. *MINE.*
COME ON...

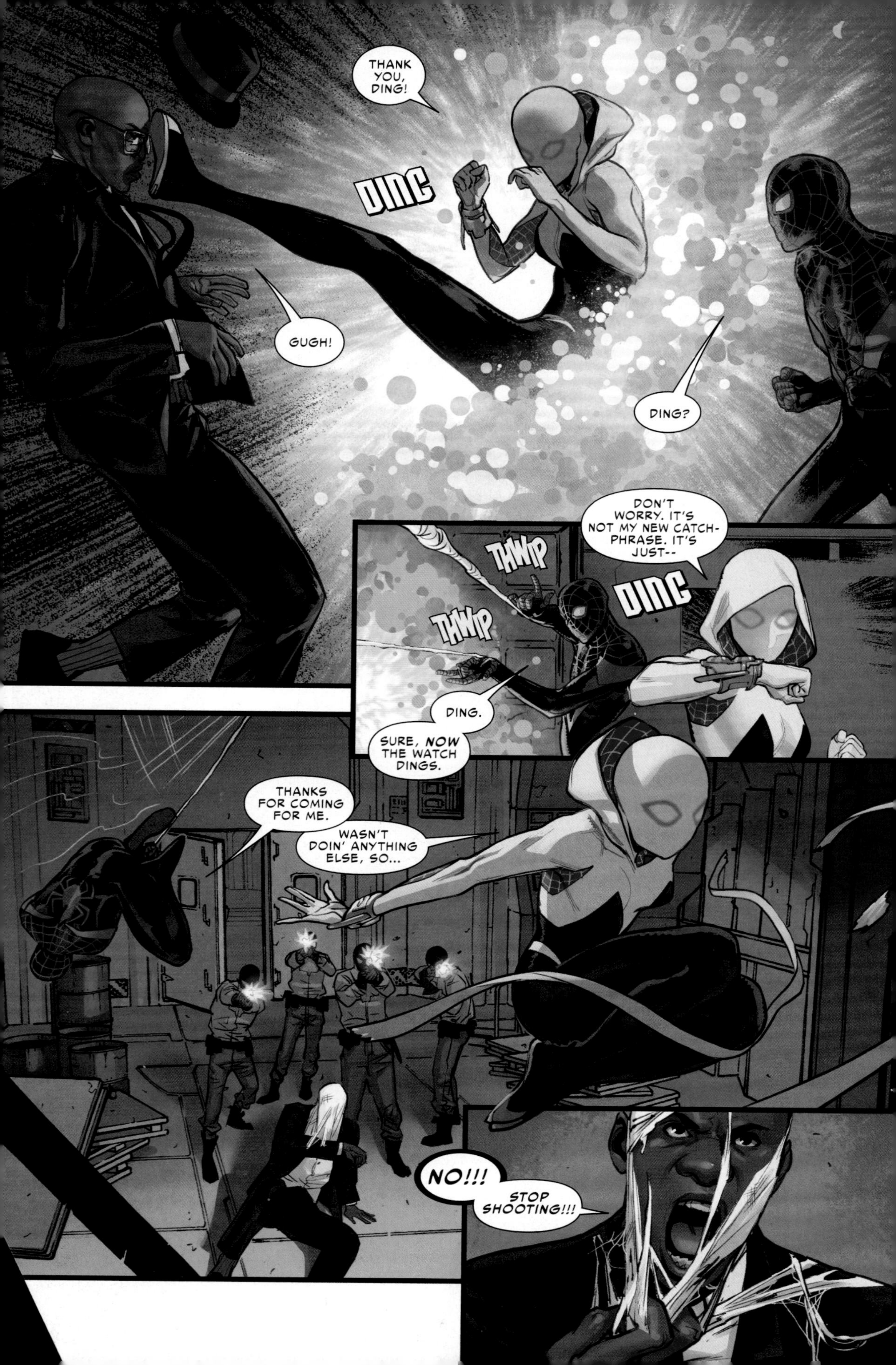
THANK YOU, DING!
DING
GUGH!
DING?
DON'T WORRY. IT'S NOT MY NEW CATCH-PHRASE. IT'S JUST--
THWIP
THWIP
DING
DING.
SURE, NOW THE WATCH DINGS.
THANKS FOR COMING FOR ME.
WASN'T DOIN' ANYTHING ELSE, SO...
NO!!!
STOP SHOOTING!!!

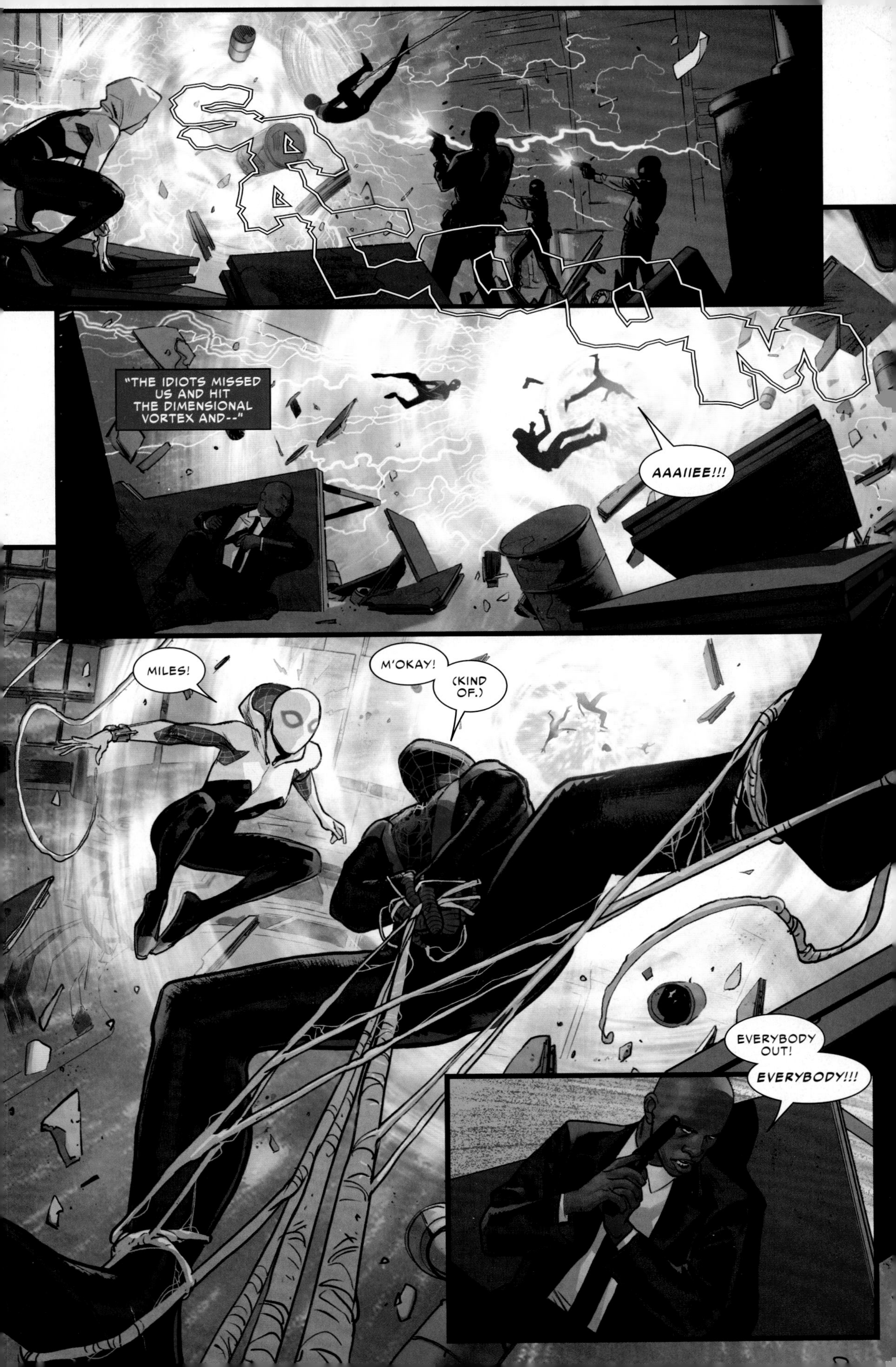
"THE IDIOTS MISSED US AND HIT THE DIMENSIONAL VORTEX AND--"
AAAIIEE!!!
MILES!
M'OKAY!
(KIND OF.)
EVERYBODY OUT!
EVERYBODY!!!

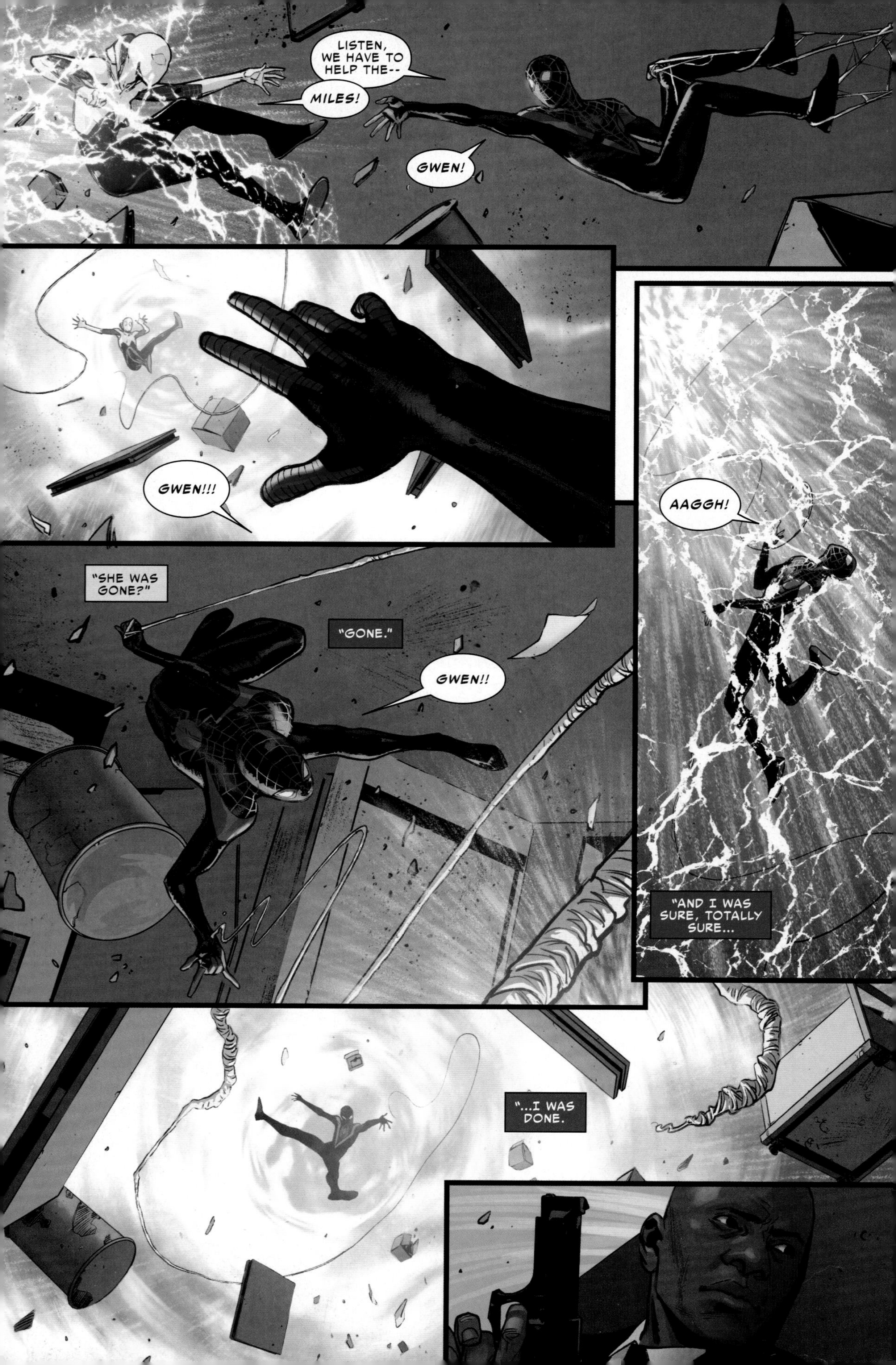
LISTEN, WE HAVE TO HELP THE--
MILES!
GWEN!
GWEN!!!
AAGGH!
"SHE WAS GONE?"
"GONE."
GWEN!!
"AND I WAS SURE, TOTALLY SURE...
"...I WAS DONE.

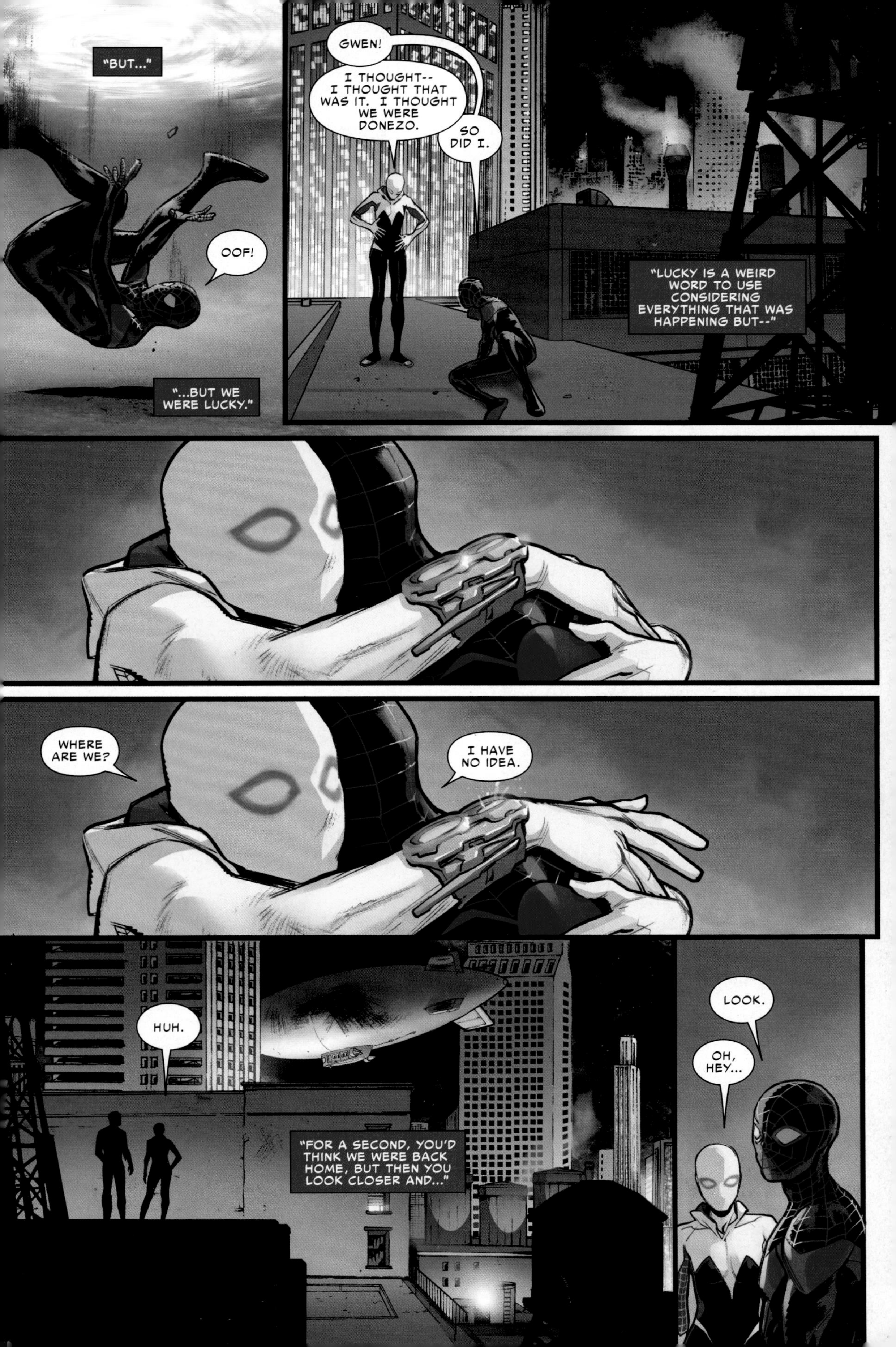
"BUT..."
OOF!
"...BUT WE WERE LUCKY."
GWEN!
I THOUGHT-- I THOUGHT THAT WAS IT. I THOUGHT WE WERE DONEZO.
SO DID I.
"LUCKY IS A WEIRD WORD TO USE CONSIDERING EVERYTHING THAT WAS HAPPENING BUT--"
WHERE ARE WE?
I HAVE NO IDEA.
HUH.
"FOR A SECOND, YOU'D THINK WE WERE BACK HOME, BUT THEN YOU LOOK CLOSER AND..."
LOOK.
OH, HEY...

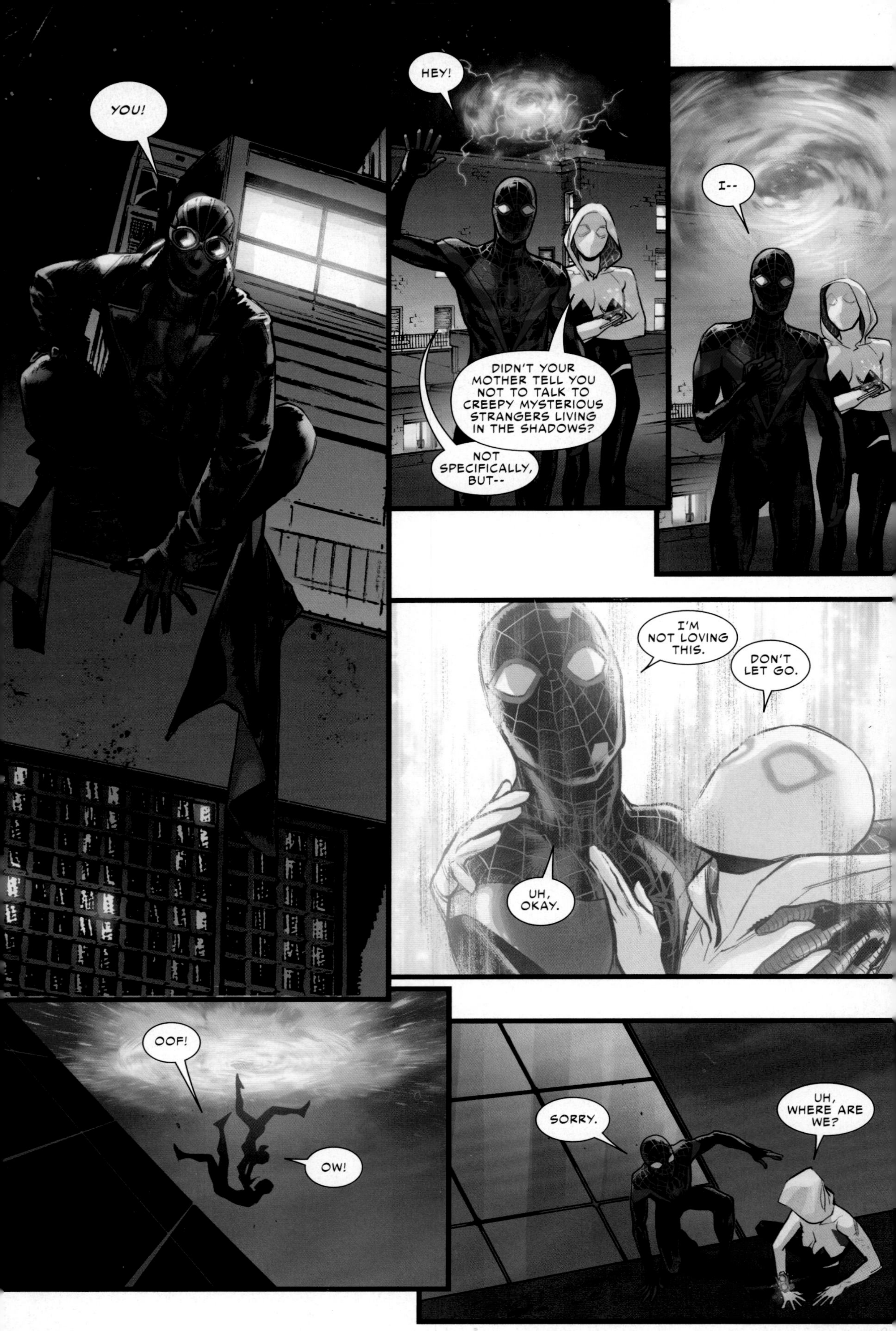
YOU!
HEY!
DIDN'T YOUR MOTHER TELL YOU NOT TO TALK TO CREEPY MYSTERIOUS STRANGERS LIVING IN THE SHADOWS?
NOT SPECIFICALLY, BUT--
I--
I'M NOT LOVING THIS.
DON'T LET GO.
UH, OKAY.
OOF!
OW!
SORRY.
UH, WHERE ARE WE?

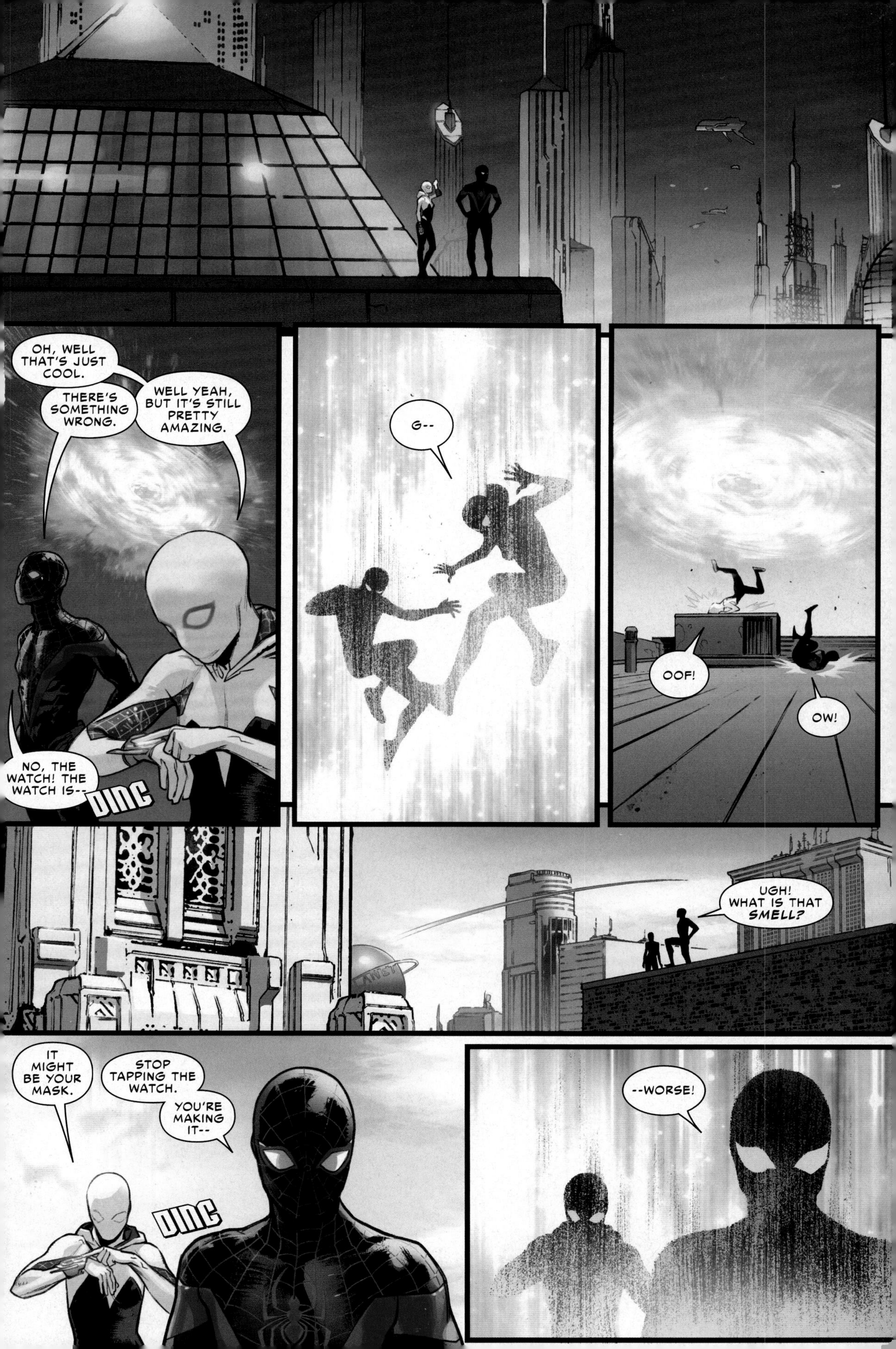
OH, WELL THAT'S JUST COOL.
THERE'S SOMETHING WRONG.
WELL YEAH, BUT IT'S STILL PRETTY AMAZING.
NO, THE WATCH! THE WATCH IS--
DING
G--
OOF!
OW!
UGH! WHAT IS THAT SMELL?
IT MIGHT BE YOUR MASK.
STOP TAPPING THE WATCH.
YOU'RE MAKING IT--
DING
--WORSE!

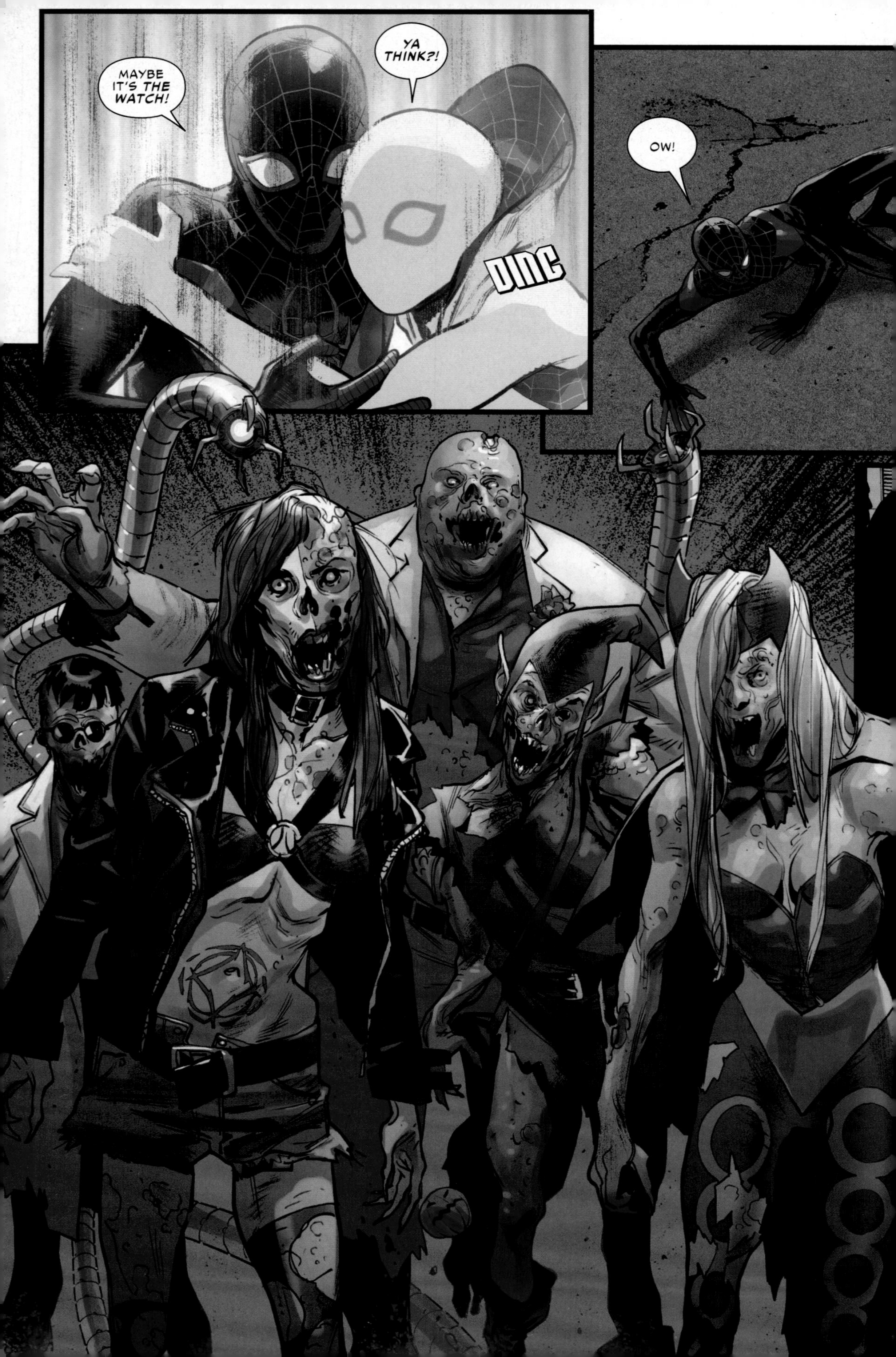
MAYBE IT'S THE WATCH!
YA THINK?!
DING
OW!

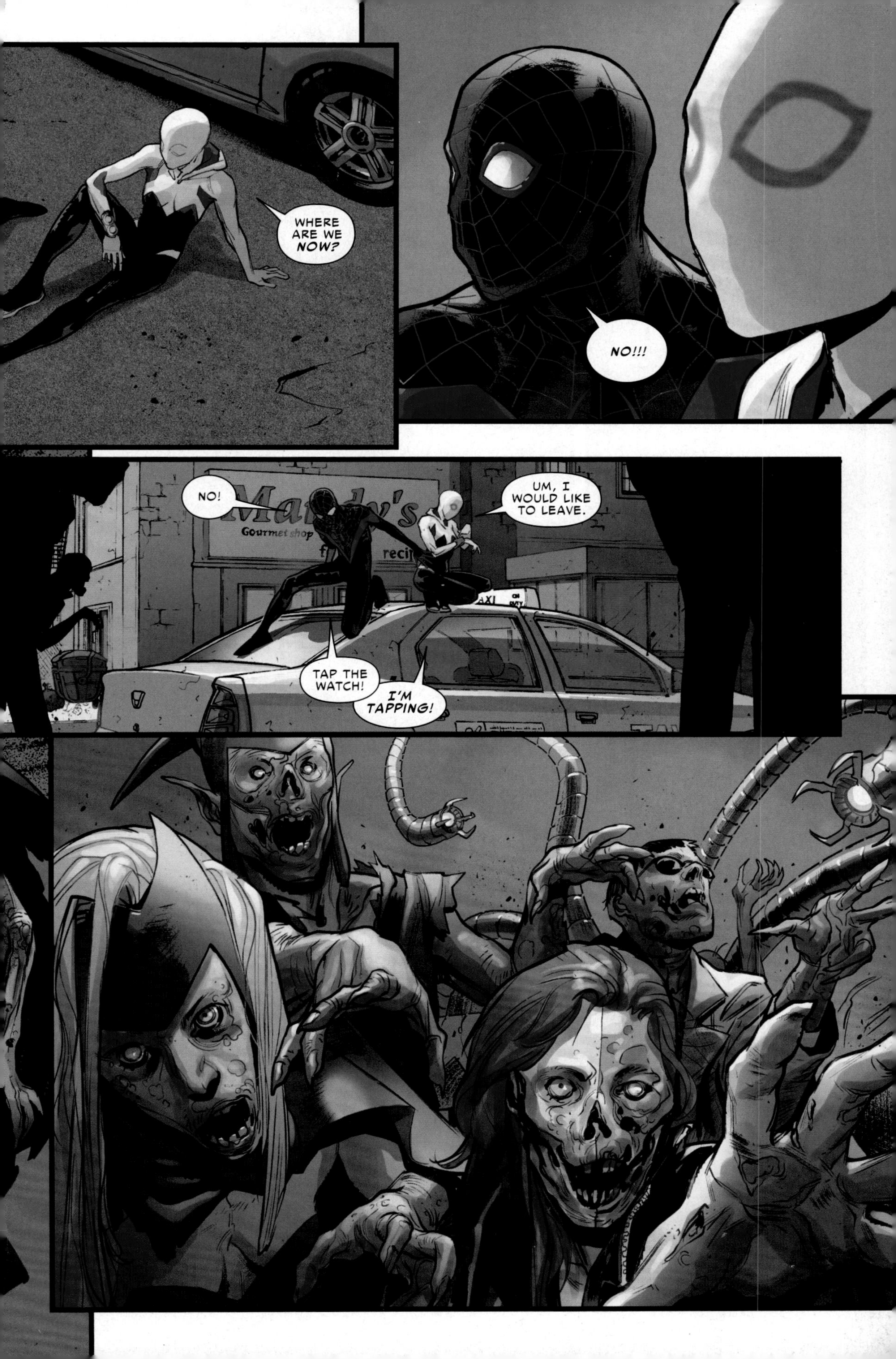
WHERE ARE WE NOW?
NO!!!
NO!
UM, I WOULD LIKE TO LEAVE.
TAP THE WATCH!
I'M TAPPING!

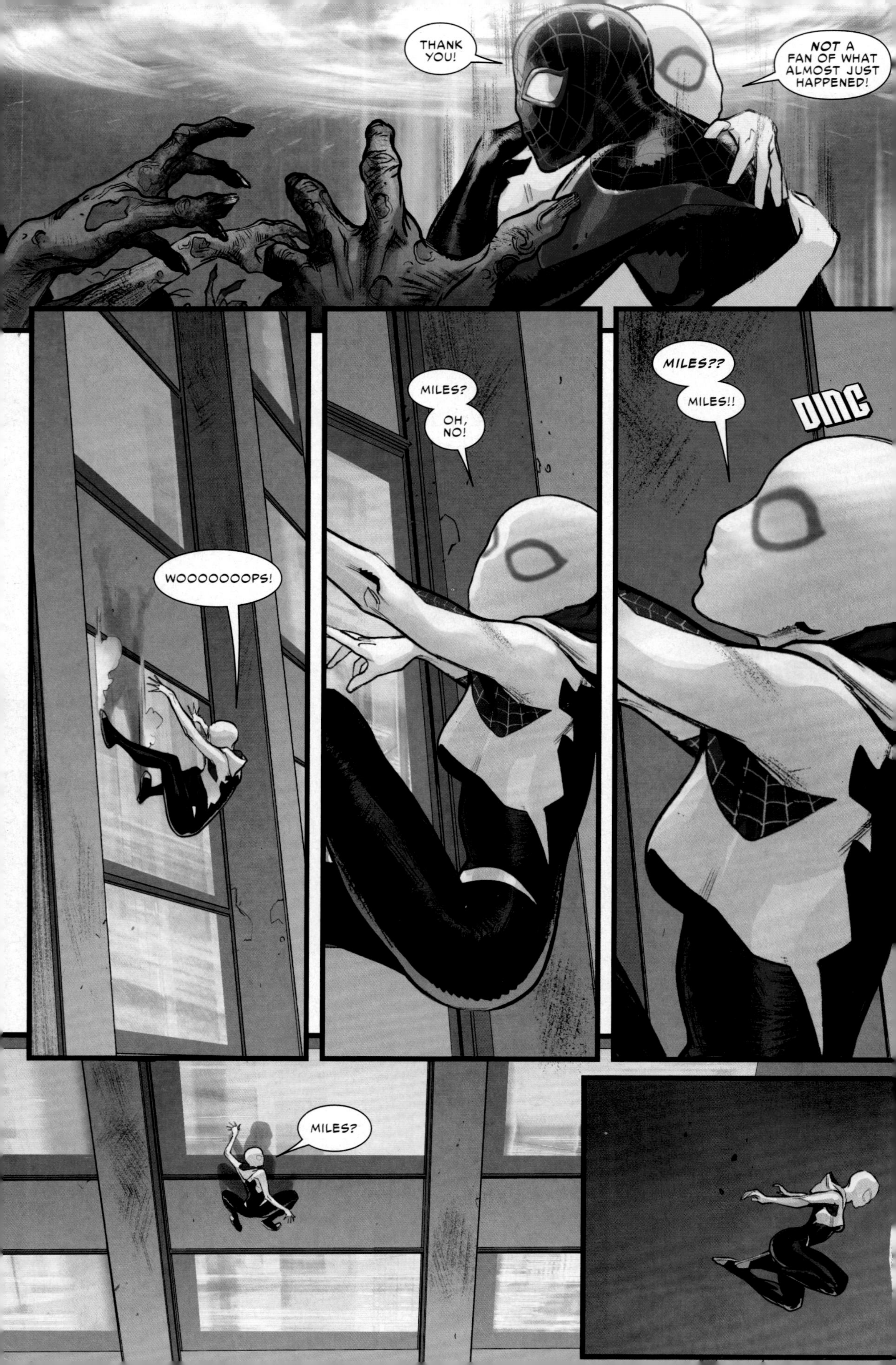
THANK YOU!
NOT A FAN OF WHAT ALMOST JUST HAPPENED!
WOOOOOOOPS!
MILES?
OH, NO!
MILES??
MILES!!
DINC
MILES?

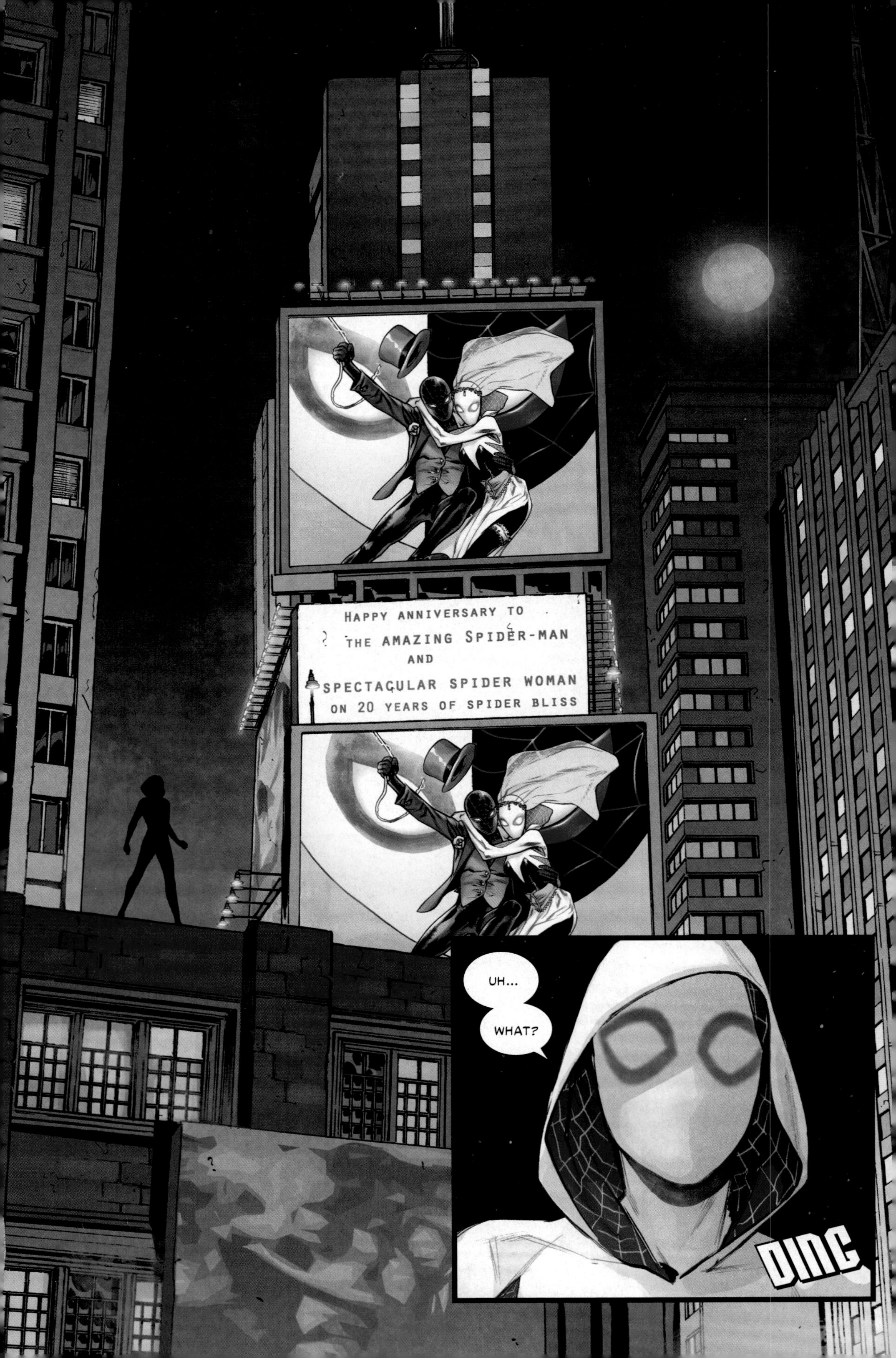

HAPPY ANNIVERSARY TO
THE AMAZING SPIDER-MAN
AND
SPECTACULAR SPIDER WOMAN
ON 20 YEARS OF SPIDER BLISS
UH...
WHAT?
DING

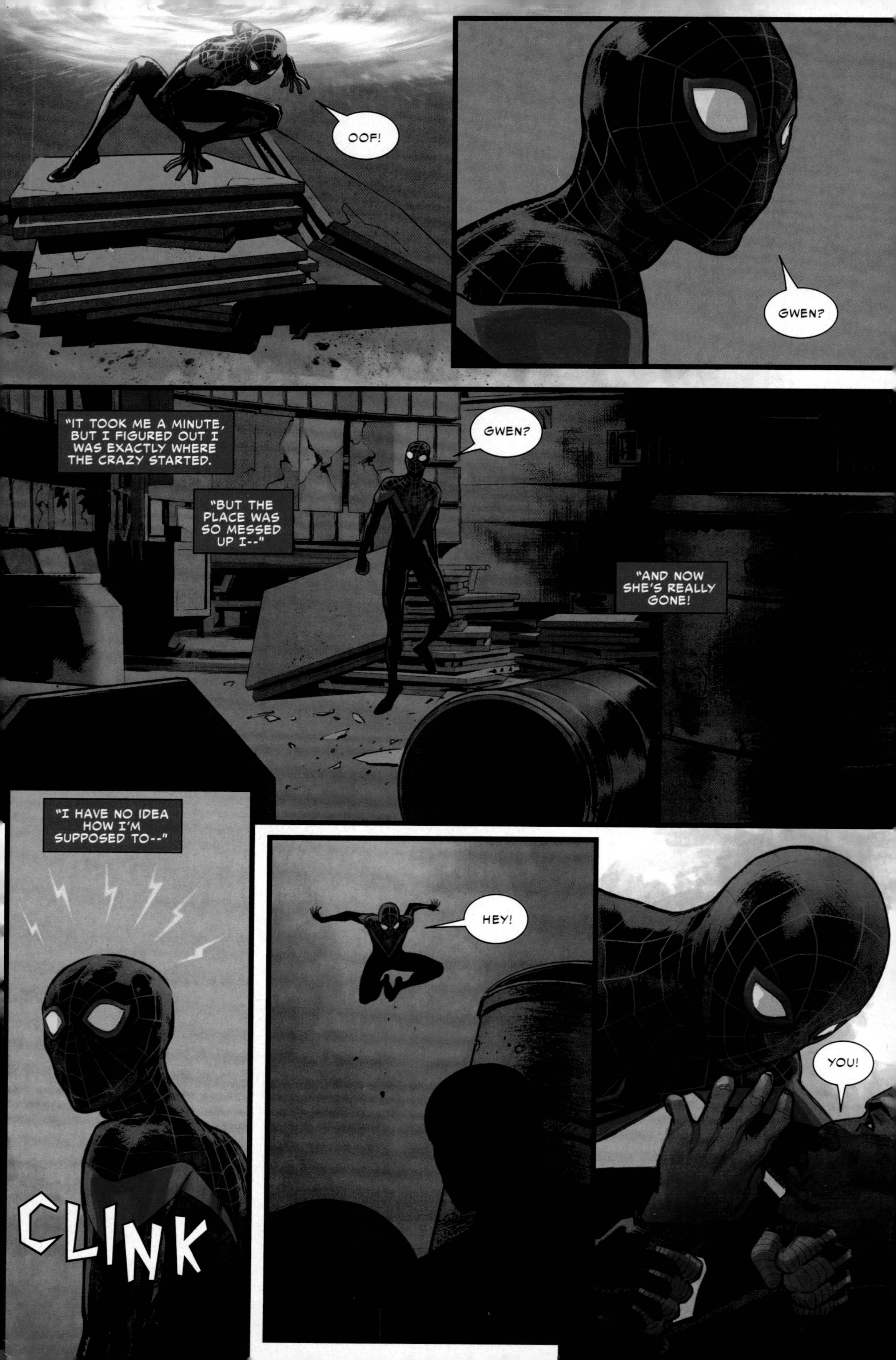

OOF!
GWEN?
"IT TOOK ME A MINUTE, BUT I FIGURED OUT I WAS EXACTLY WHERE THE CRAZY STARTED.
GWEN?
"BUT THE PLACE WAS SO MESSED UP I--"
"AND NOW SHE'S REALLY GONE!
"I HAVE NO IDEA HOW I'M SUPPOSED TO--"
CLINK
HEY!
YOU!

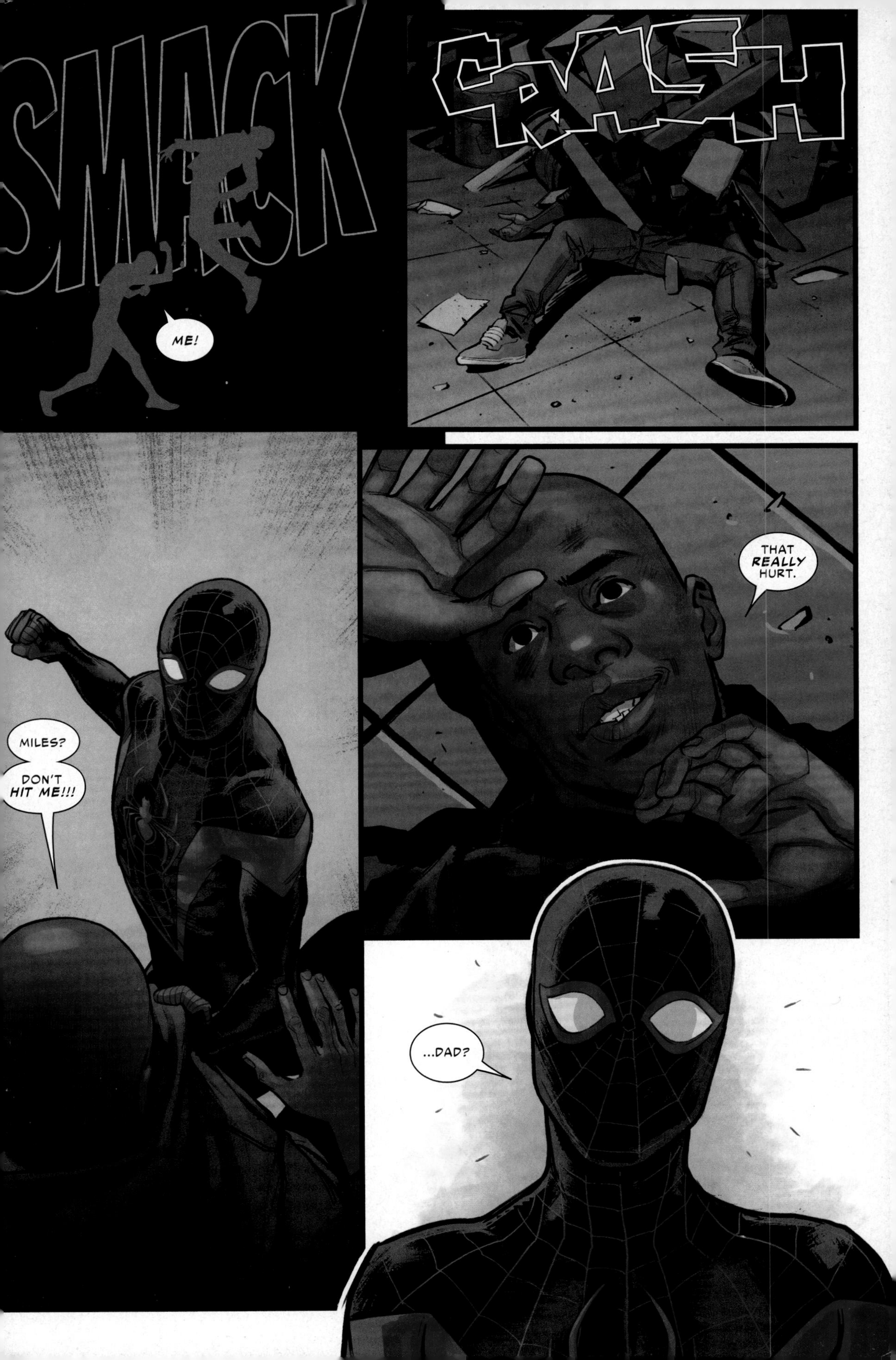
SMACK
ME!
CRASH
MILES?
DON'T HIT ME!!!
THAT REALLY HURT.
...DAD?

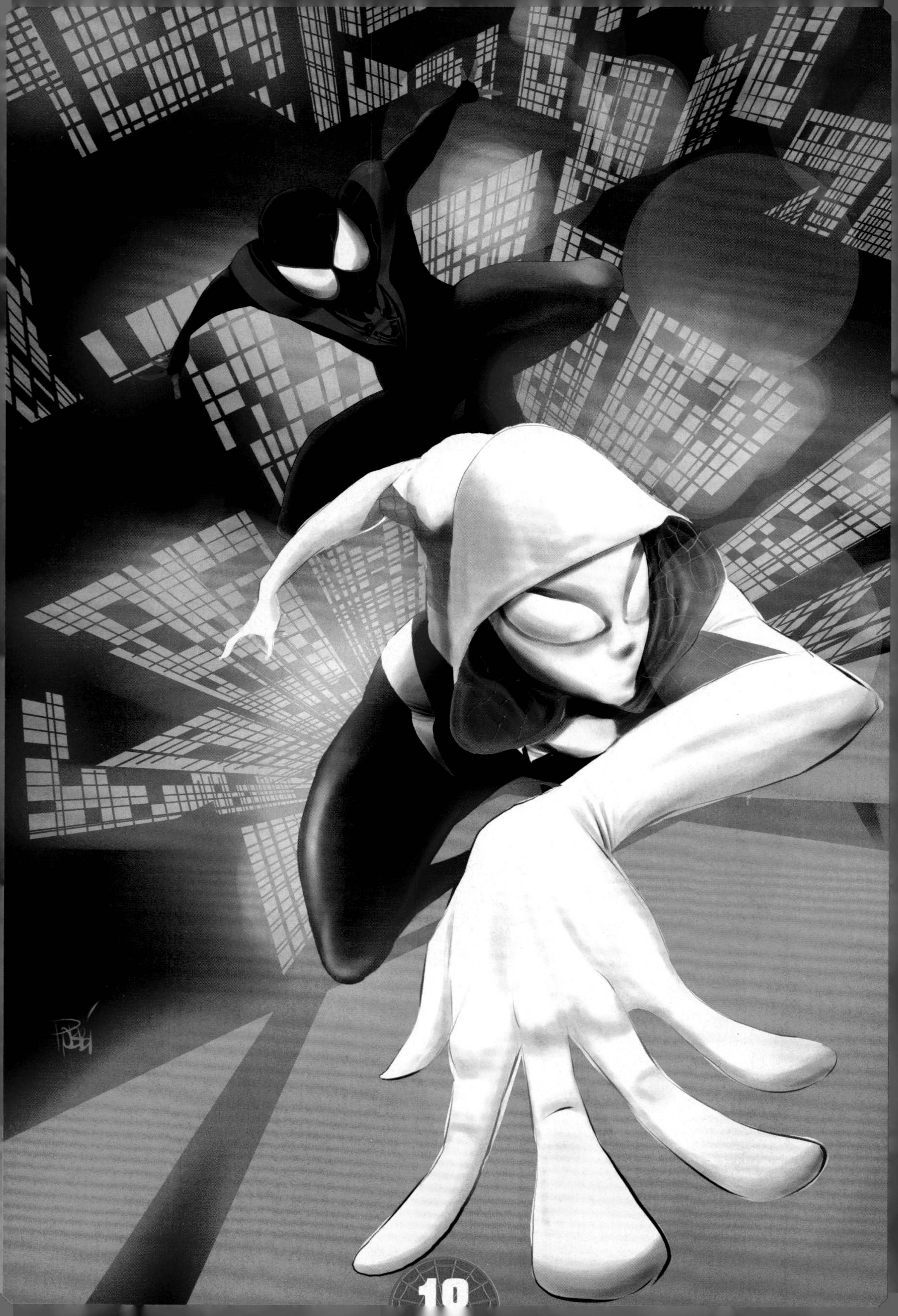
10

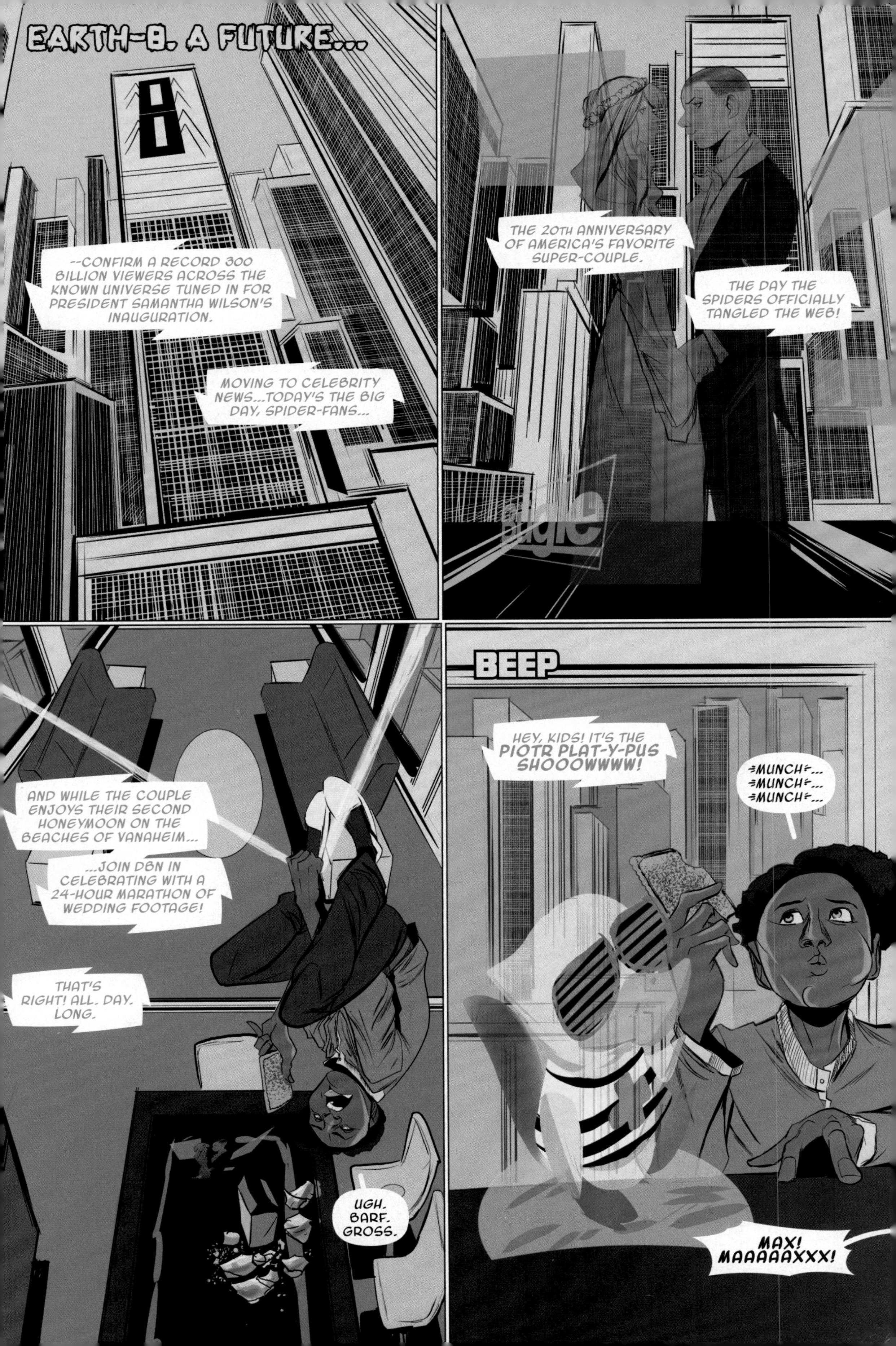
EARTH-8. A FUTURE...
--CONFIRM A RECORD 300 BILLION VIEWERS ACROSS THE KNOWN UNIVERSE TUNED IN FOR PRESIDENT SAMANTHA WILSON'S INAUGURATION.
MOVING TO CELEBRITY NEWS...TODAY'S THE BIG DAY, SPIDER-FANS...
THE 20TH ANNIVERSARY OF AMERICA'S FAVORITE SUPER-COUPLE.
THE DAY THE SPIDERS OFFICIALLY TANGLED THE WEB!
AND WHILE THE COUPLE ENJOYS THEIR SECOND HONEYMOON ON THE BEACHES OF VANAHEIM...
...JOIN DBN IN CELEBRATING WITH A 24-HOUR MARATHON OF WEDDING FOOTAGE!
THAT'S RIGHT! ALL. DAY. LONG.
UGH. BARF. GROSS.
BEEP
HEY, KIDS! IT'S THE PIOTR PLAT-Y-PUS SHOOOWWWW!
=MUNCH=... =MUNCH=... =MUNCH=...
MAX! MAAAAAXXX!

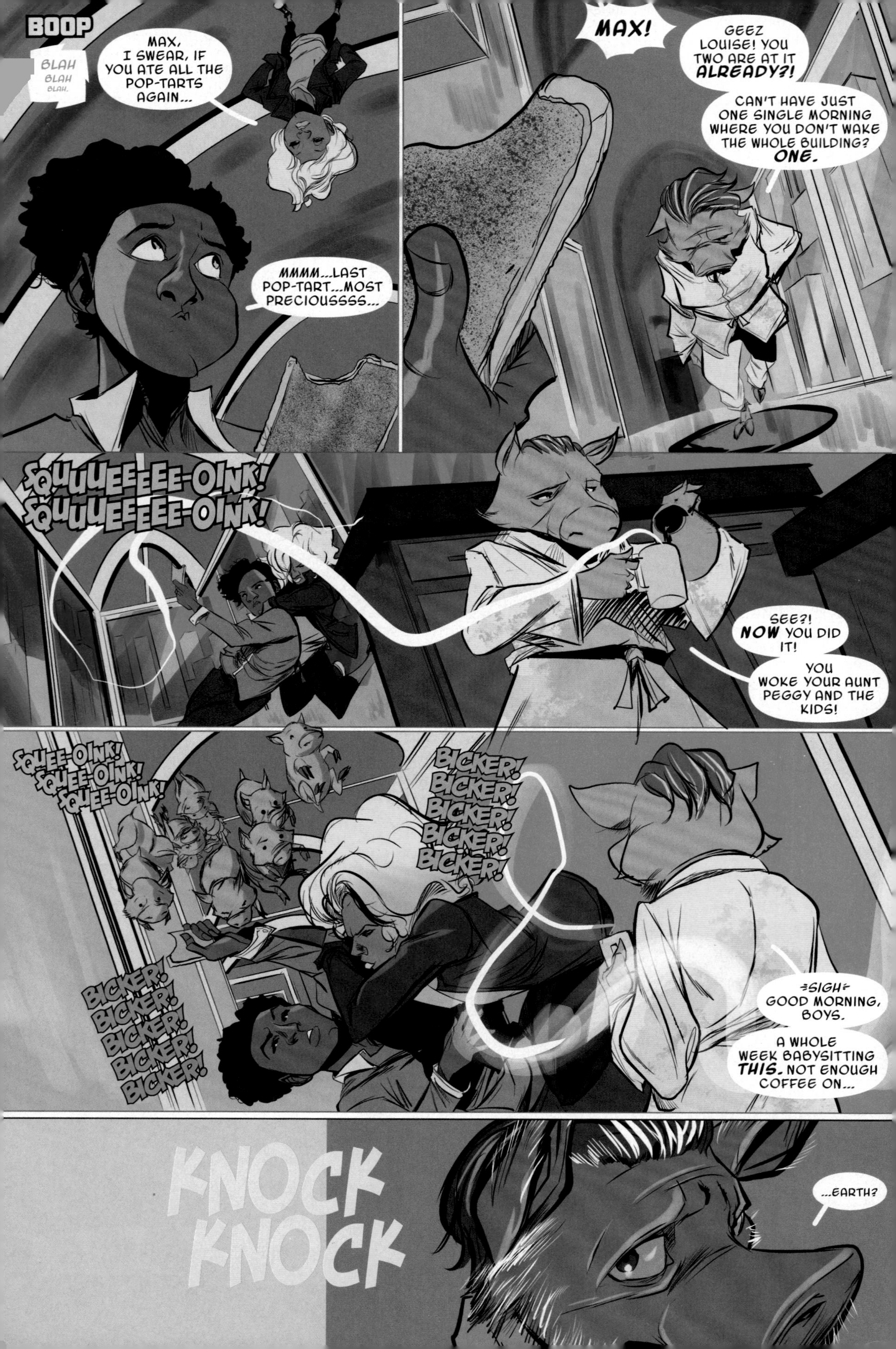
BOOP
BLAH BLAH BLAH.
MAX, I SWEAR, IF YOU ATE ALL THE POP-TARTS AGAIN...
MMMM...LAST POP-TART...MOST PRECIOUSSSS...
MAX!
GEEZ LOUISE! YOU TWO ARE AT IT ALREADY?!
CAN'T HAVE JUST ONE SINGLE MORNING WHERE YOU DON'T WAKE THE WHOLE BUILDING? ONE.
SQUUUEEEEE-OINK! SQUUUEEEEE-OINK!
SEE?! NOW YOU DID IT!
YOU WOKE YOUR AUNT PEGGY AND THE KIDS!
SQUEE-OINK! SQUEE-OINK! SQUEE-OINK!
BICKER! BICKER! BICKER! BICKER! BICKER!
BICKER! BICKER! BICKER! BICKER! BICKER!
=SIGH= GOOD MORNING, BOYS.
A WHOLE WEEK BABYSITTING THIS. NOT ENOUGH COFFEE ON...
KNOCK KNOCK
...EARTH?

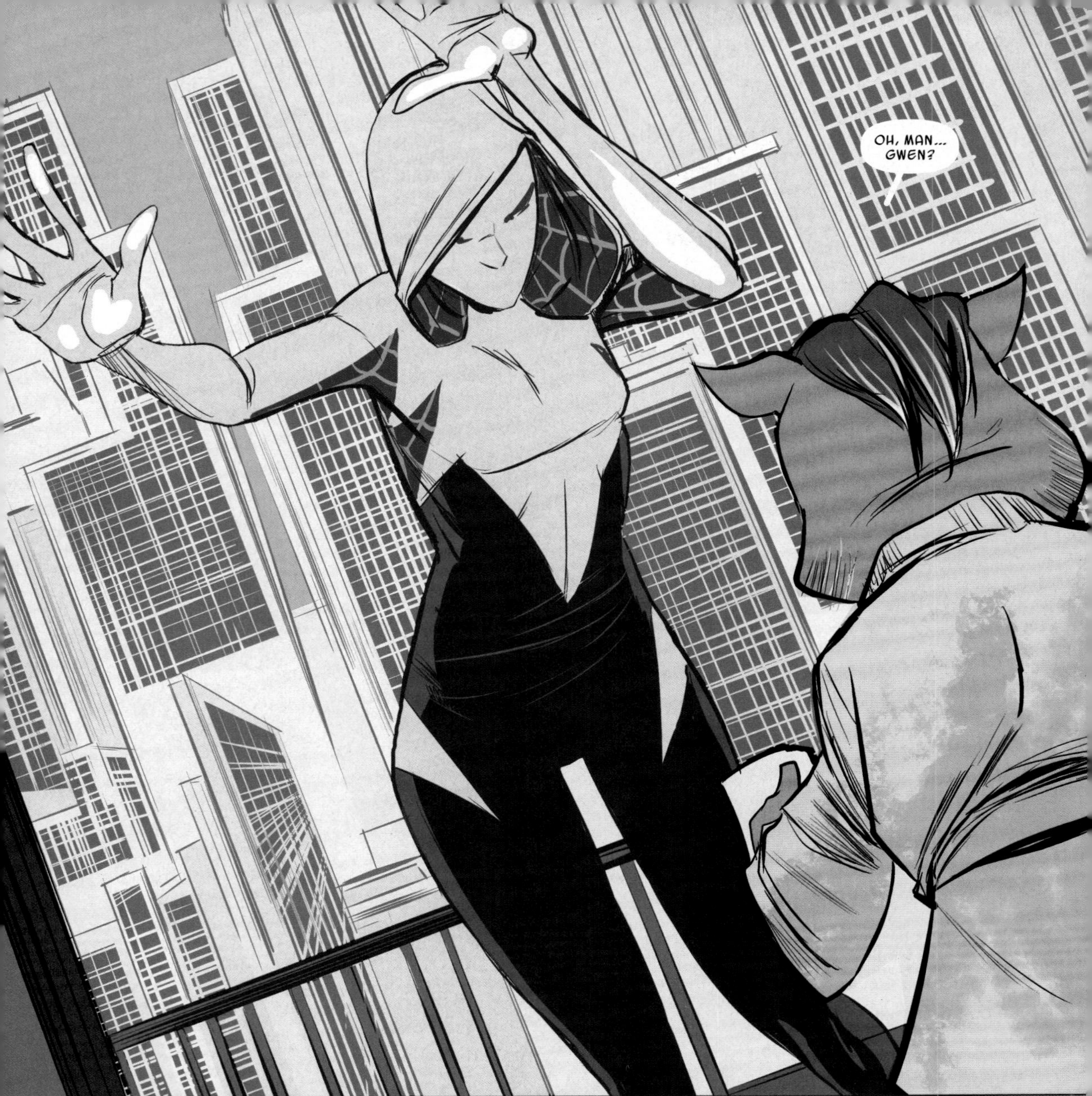
OH, MAN...
GWEN?

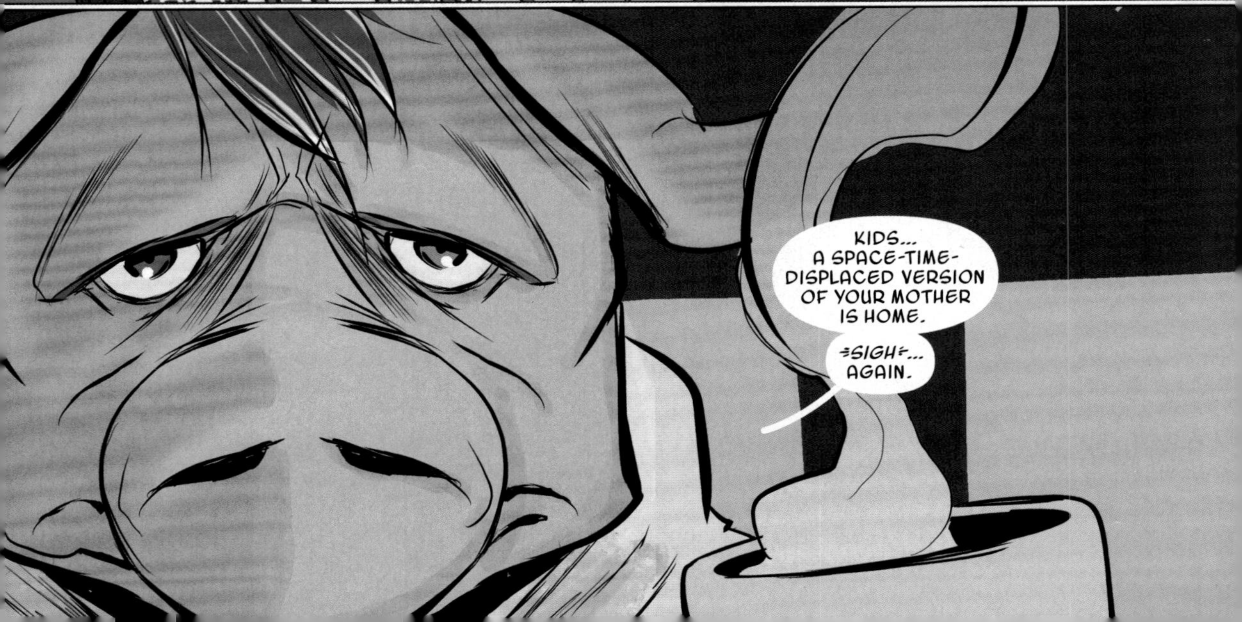
KIDS...
A SPACE-TIME-DISPLACED VERSION OF YOUR MOTHER IS HOME.
=SIGH=...
AGAIN.

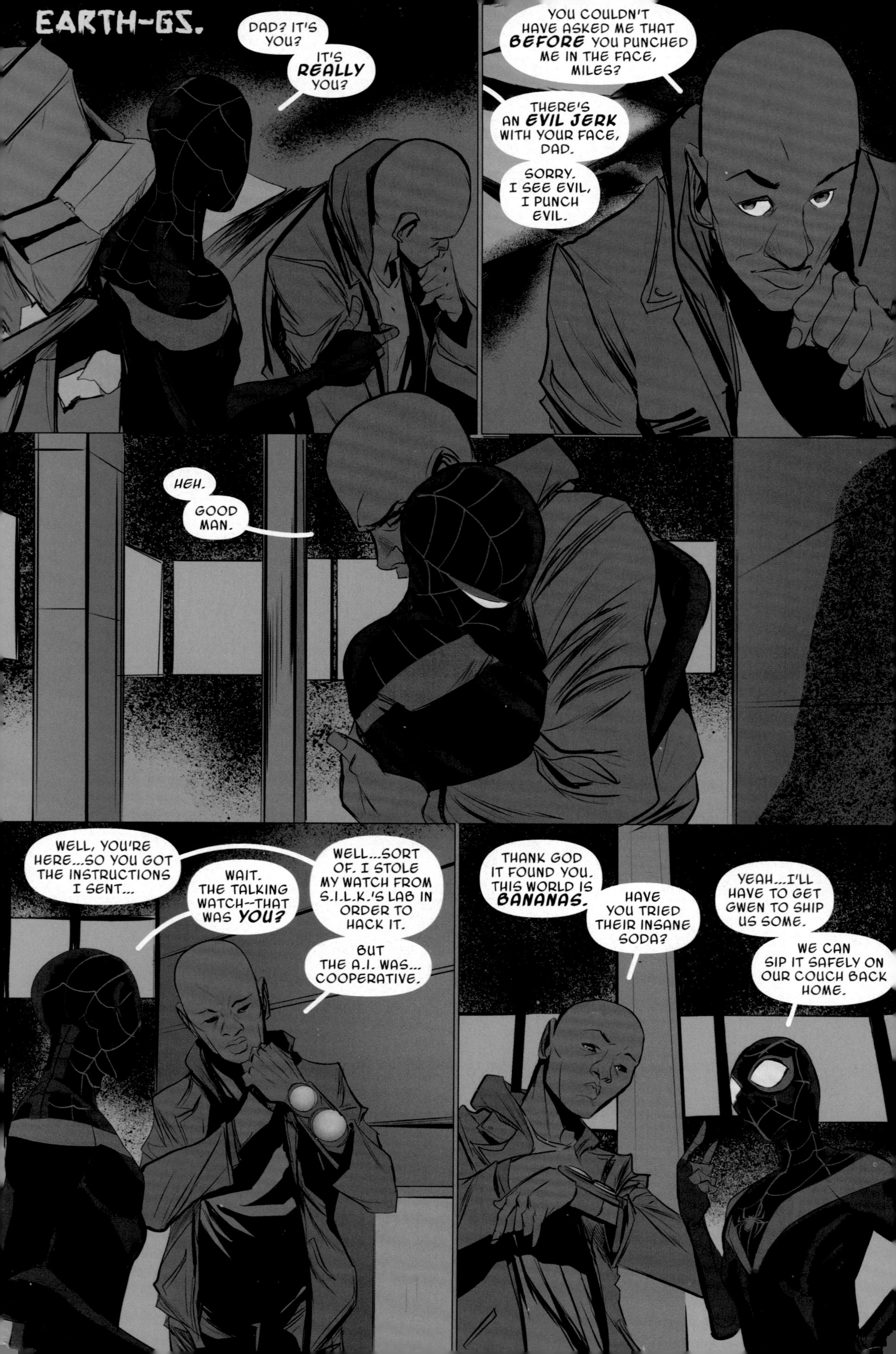
EARTH-65.
DAD? IT'S YOU?
IT'S REALLY YOU?
YOU COULDN'T HAVE ASKED ME THAT BEFORE YOU PUNCHED ME IN THE FACE, MILES?
THERE'S AN EVIL JERK WITH YOUR FACE, DAD.
SORRY. I SEE EVIL, I PUNCH EVIL.
HEH.
GOOD MAN.
WELL, YOU'RE HERE...SO YOU GOT THE INSTRUCTIONS I SENT...
WAIT. THE TALKING WATCH--THAT WAS YOU?
WELL...SORT OF. I STOLE MY WATCH FROM S.I.L.K.'S LAB IN ORDER TO HACK IT.
BUT THE A.I. WAS... COOPERATIVE.
THANK GOD IT FOUND YOU. THIS WORLD IS BANANAS.
HAVE YOU TRIED THEIR INSANE SODA?
YEAH...I'LL HAVE TO GET GWEN TO SHIP US SOME.
WE CAN SIP IT SAFELY ON OUR COUCH BACK HOME.

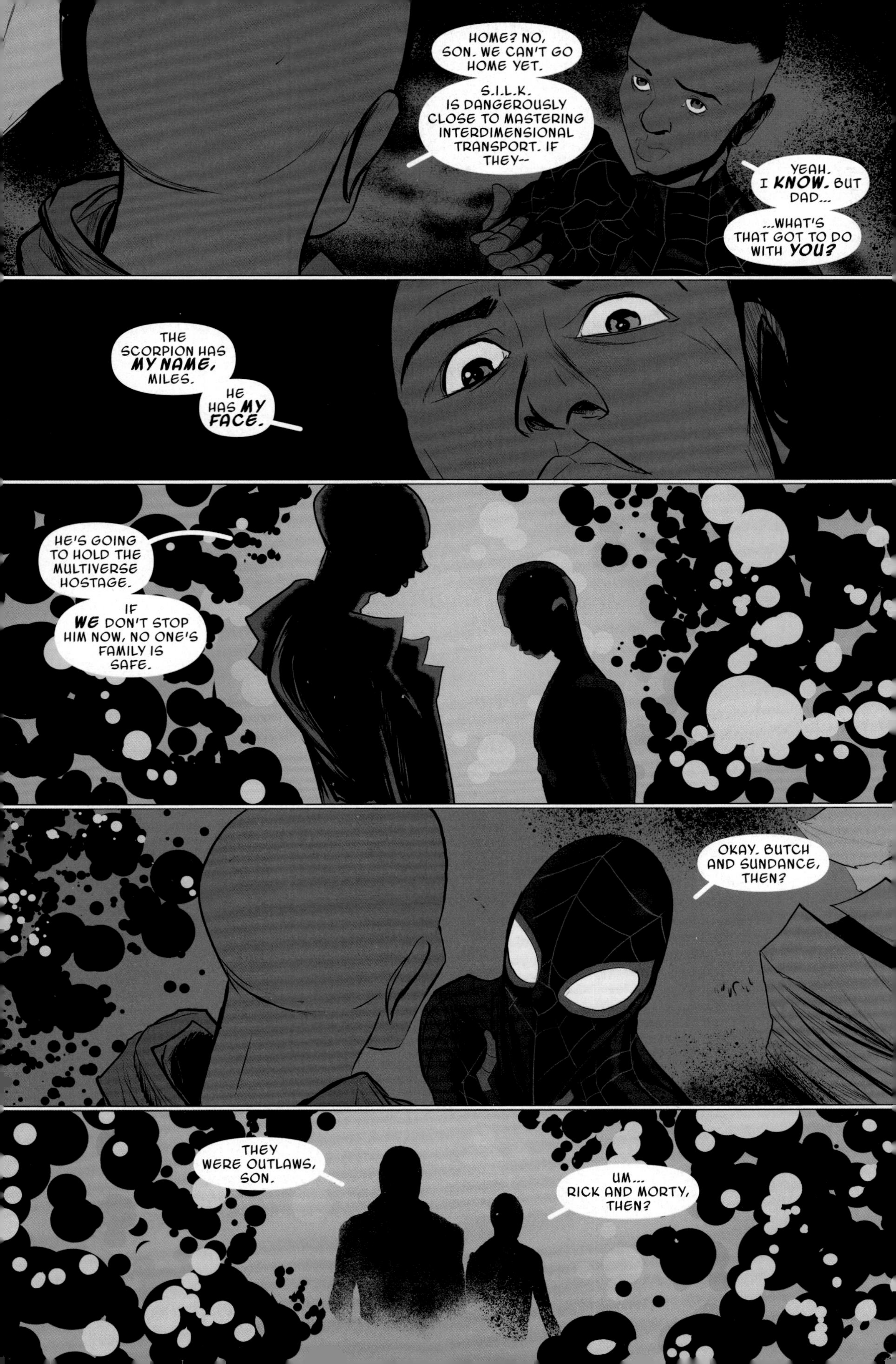
HOME? NO, SON. WE CAN'T GO HOME YET.
S.I.L.K. IS DANGEROUSLY CLOSE TO MASTERING INTERDIMENSIONAL TRANSPORT. IF THEY--
YEAH. I KNOW. BUT DAD...
...WHAT'S THAT GOT TO DO WITH YOU?
THE SCORPION HAS MY NAME, MILES.
HE HAS MY FACE.
HE'S GOING TO HOLD THE MULTIVERSE HOSTAGE.
IF WE DON'T STOP HIM NOW, NO ONE'S FAMILY IS SAFE.
OKAY. BUTCH AND SUNDANCE, THEN?
THEY WERE OUTLAWS, SON.
UM... RICK AND MORTY, THEN?

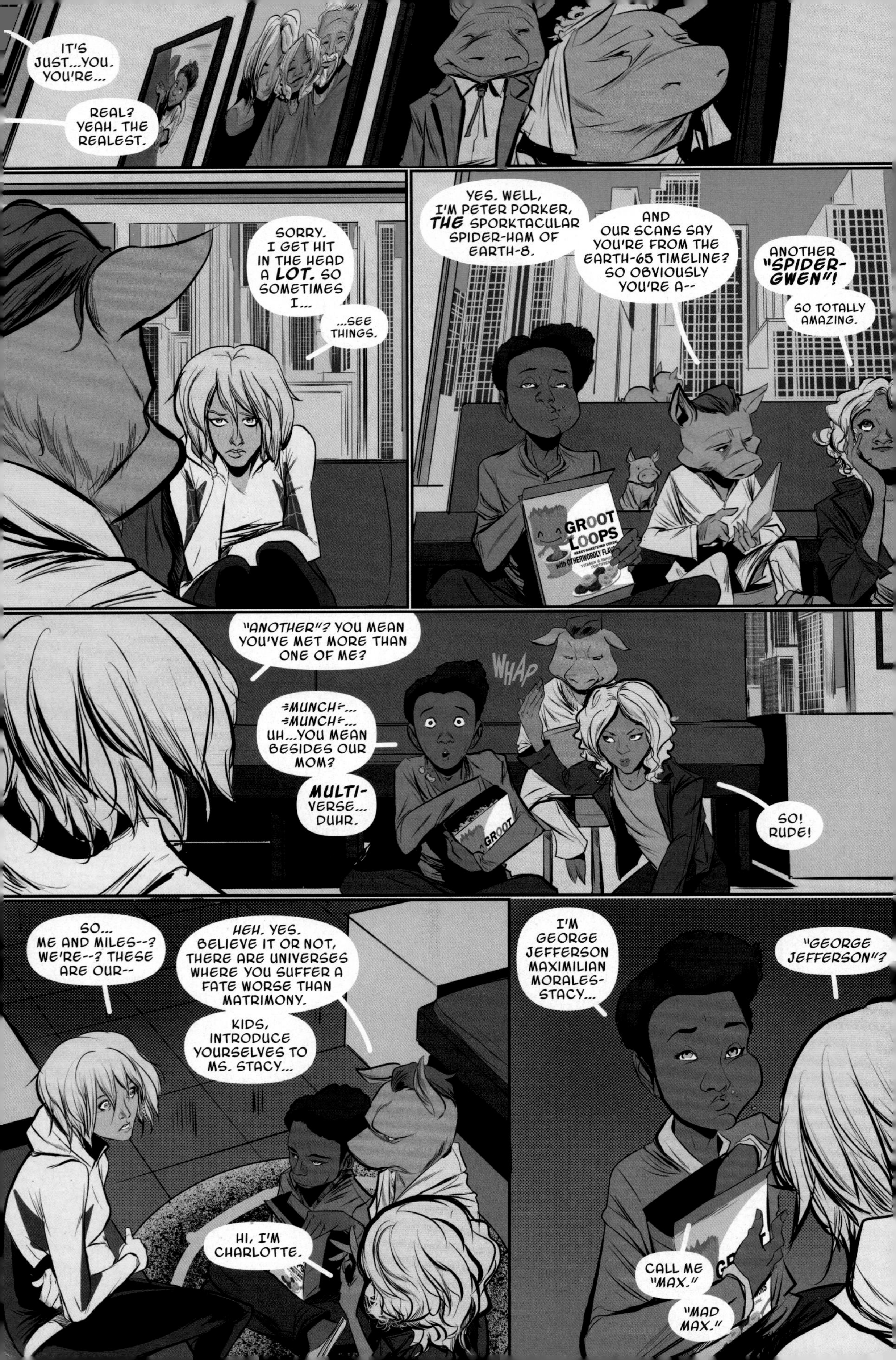
IT'S JUST...YOU. YOU'RE...
REAL? YEAH. THE REALEST.
SORRY. I GET HIT IN THE HEAD A LOT. SO SOMETIMES I...
...SEE THINGS.
YES. WELL, I'M PETER PORKER, THE SPORKTACULAR SPIDER-HAM OF EARTH-8.
AND OUR SCANS SAY YOU'RE FROM THE EARTH-65 TIMELINE? SO OBVIOUSLY YOU'RE A--
ANOTHER "SPIDER-GWEN"!
SO TOTALLY AMAZING.
GROOT LOOPS
"ANOTHER"? YOU MEAN YOU'VE MET MORE THAN ONE OF ME?
WHAP
=MUNCH=... =MUNCH=... UH...YOU MEAN BESIDES OUR MOM?
MULTI-VERSE... DUHR.
SO! RUDE!
SO... ME AND MILES--? WE'RE--? THESE ARE OUR--
HEH. YES. BELIEVE IT OR NOT, THERE ARE UNIVERSES WHERE YOU SUFFER A FATE WORSE THAN MATRIMONY.
KIDS, INTRODUCE YOURSELVES TO MS. STACY...
HI, I'M CHARLOTTE.
I'M GEORGE JEFFERSON MAXIMILIAN MORALES-STACY...
"GEORGE JEFFERSON"?
CALL ME "MAX."
"MAD MAX."

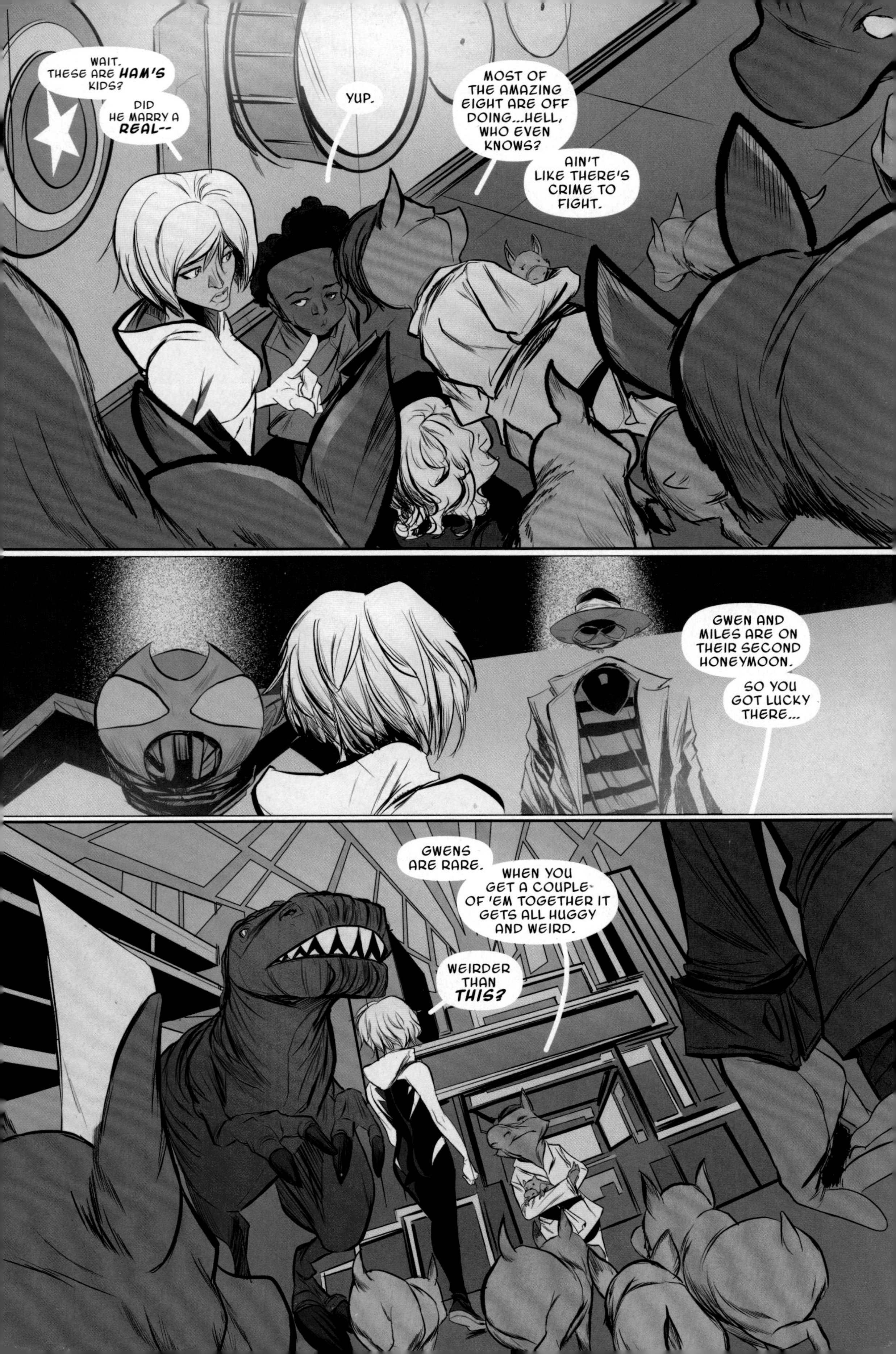
WAIT. THESE ARE HAM'S KIDS?
DID HE MARRY A REAL--
YUP.
MOST OF THE AMAZING EIGHT ARE OFF DOING...HELL, WHO EVEN KNOWS?
AIN'T LIKE THERE'S CRIME TO FIGHT.
GWEN AND MILES ARE ON THEIR SECOND HONEYMOON.
SO YOU GOT LUCKY THERE...
GWENS ARE RARE.
WHEN YOU GET A COUPLE OF 'EM TOGETHER IT GETS ALL HUGGY AND WEIRD.
WEIRDER THAN THIS?

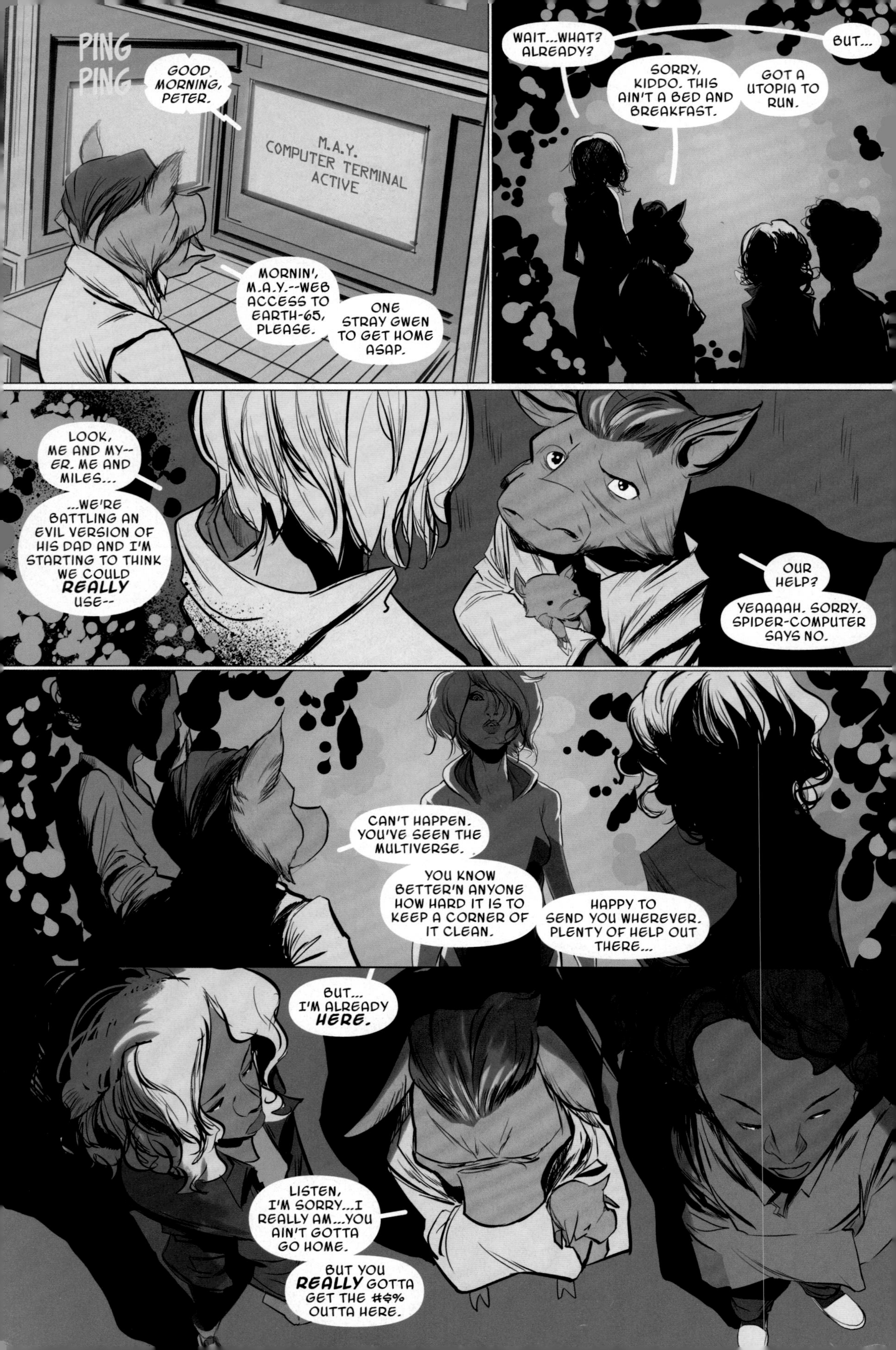
PING
PING
GOOD MORNING, PETER.
M.A.Y. COMPUTER TERMINAL ACTIVE
MORNIN', M.A.Y.--WEB ACCESS TO EARTH-65, PLEASE.
ONE STRAY GWEN TO GET HOME ASAP.
WAIT...WHAT? ALREADY?
BUT...
SORRY, KIDDO. THIS AIN'T A BED AND BREAKFAST.
GOT A UTOPIA TO RUN.
LOOK, ME AND MY-- ER. ME AND MILES...
...WE'RE BATTLING AN EVIL VERSION OF HIS DAD AND I'M STARTING TO THINK WE COULD **REALLY** USE--
OUR HELP?
YEAAAAH. SORRY. SPIDER-COMPUTER SAYS NO.
CAN'T HAPPEN. YOU'VE SEEN THE MULTIVERSE.
YOU KNOW BETTER'N ANYONE HOW HARD IT IS TO KEEP A CORNER OF IT CLEAN.
HAPPY TO SEND YOU WHEREVER. PLENTY OF HELP OUT THERE...
BUT... I'M ALREADY **HERE.**
LISTEN, I'M SORRY...I REALLY AM...YOU AIN'T GOTTA GO HOME.
BUT YOU **REALLY** GOTTA GET THE #$% OUTTA HERE.

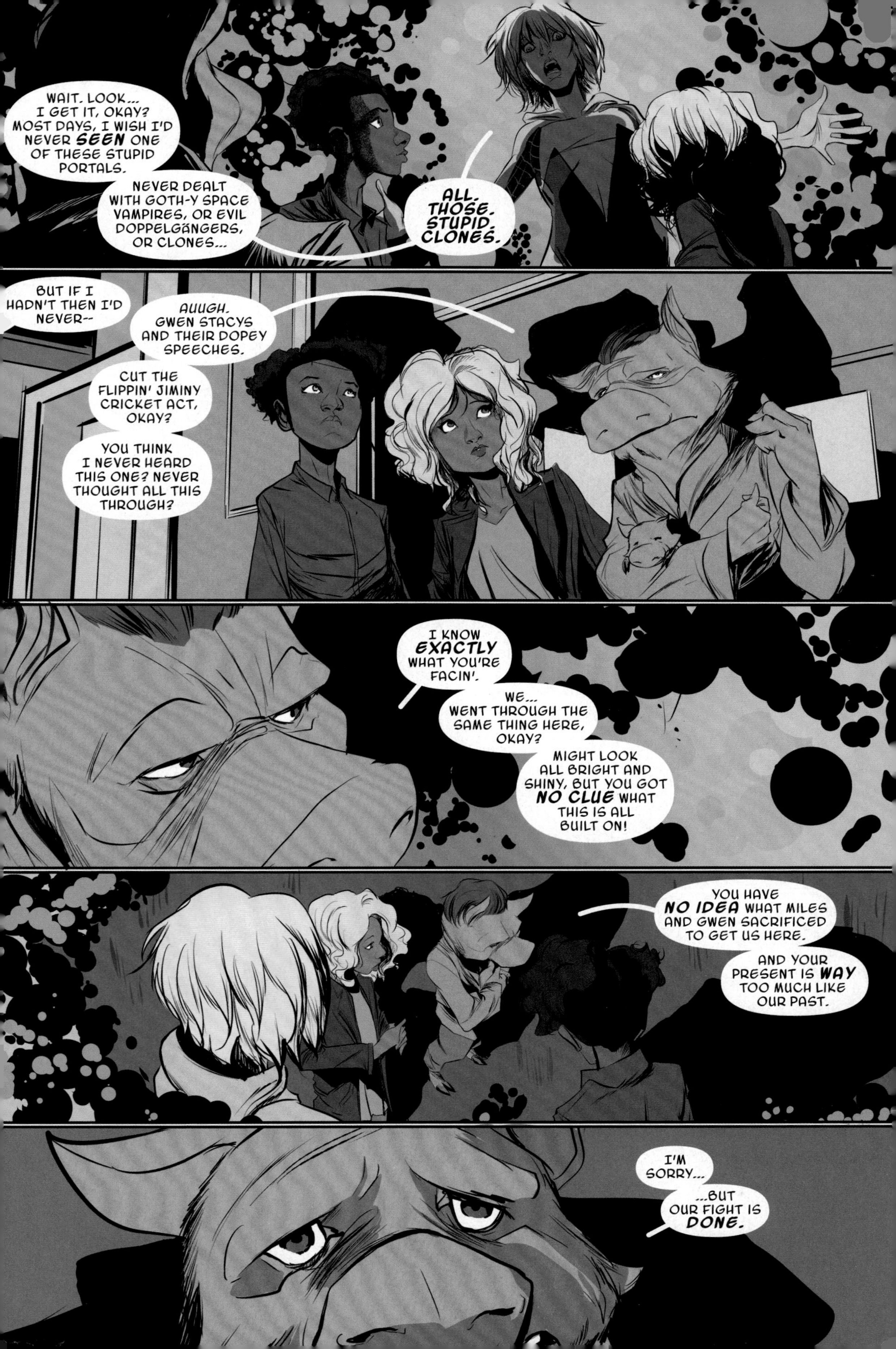
WAIT. LOOK... I GET IT, OKAY? MOST DAYS, I WISH I'D NEVER SEEN ONE OF THESE STUPID PORTALS.
NEVER DEALT WITH GOTH-Y SPACE VAMPIRES, OR EVIL DOPPELGÄNGERS, OR CLONES...
ALL. THOSE. STUPID. CLONES.
BUT IF I HADN'T THEN I'D NEVER--
AUUGH. GWEN STACYS AND THEIR DOPEY SPEECHES.
CUT THE FLIPPIN' JIMINY CRICKET ACT, OKAY?
YOU THINK I NEVER HEARD THIS ONE? NEVER THOUGHT ALL THIS THROUGH?
I KNOW EXACTLY WHAT YOU'RE FACIN'.
WE... WENT THROUGH THE SAME THING HERE, OKAY?
MIGHT LOOK ALL BRIGHT AND SHINY, BUT YOU GOT NO CLUE WHAT THIS IS ALL BUILT ON!
YOU HAVE NO IDEA WHAT MILES AND GWEN SACRIFICED TO GET US HERE.
AND YOUR PRESENT IS WAY TOO MUCH LIKE OUR PAST.
I'M SORRY...
...BUT OUR FIGHT IS DONE.

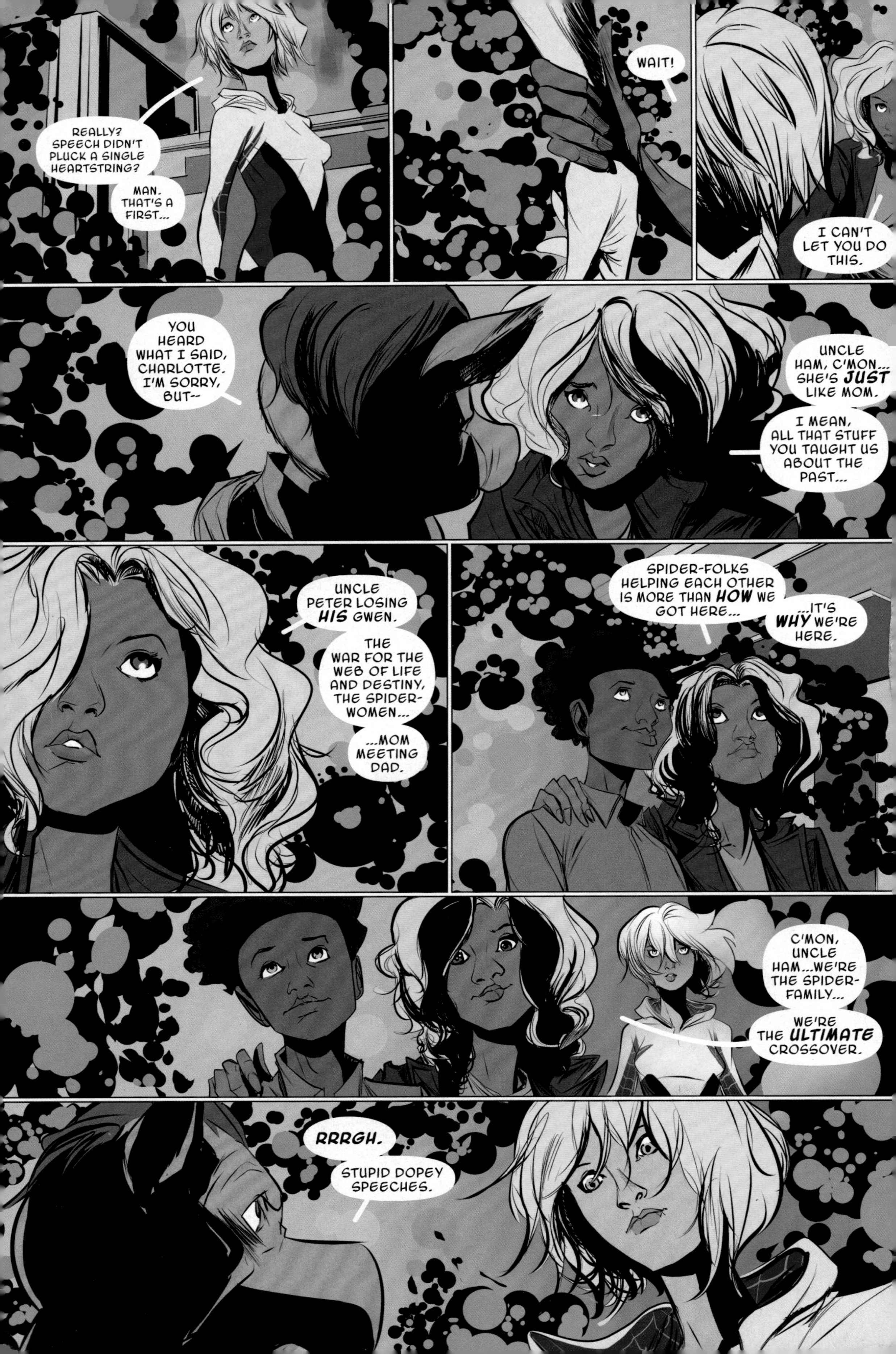
REALLY? SPEECH DIDN'T PLUCK A SINGLE HEARTSTRING?
MAN. THAT'S A FIRST...
WAIT!
I CAN'T LET YOU DO THIS.
YOU HEARD WHAT I SAID, CHARLOTTE. I'M SORRY, BUT--
UNCLE HAM, C'MON... SHE'S JUST LIKE MOM.
I MEAN, ALL THAT STUFF YOU TAUGHT US ABOUT THE PAST...
UNCLE PETER LOSING HIS GWEN.
THE WAR FOR THE WEB OF LIFE AND DESTINY, THE SPIDER-WOMEN...
...MOM MEETING DAD.
SPIDER-FOLKS HELPING EACH OTHER IS MORE THAN HOW WE GOT HERE...
...IT'S WHY WE'RE HERE.
C'MON, UNCLE HAM...WE'RE THE SPIDER-FAMILY...
WE'RE THE ULTIMATE CROSSOVER.
RRRGH.
STUPID DOPEY SPEECHES.

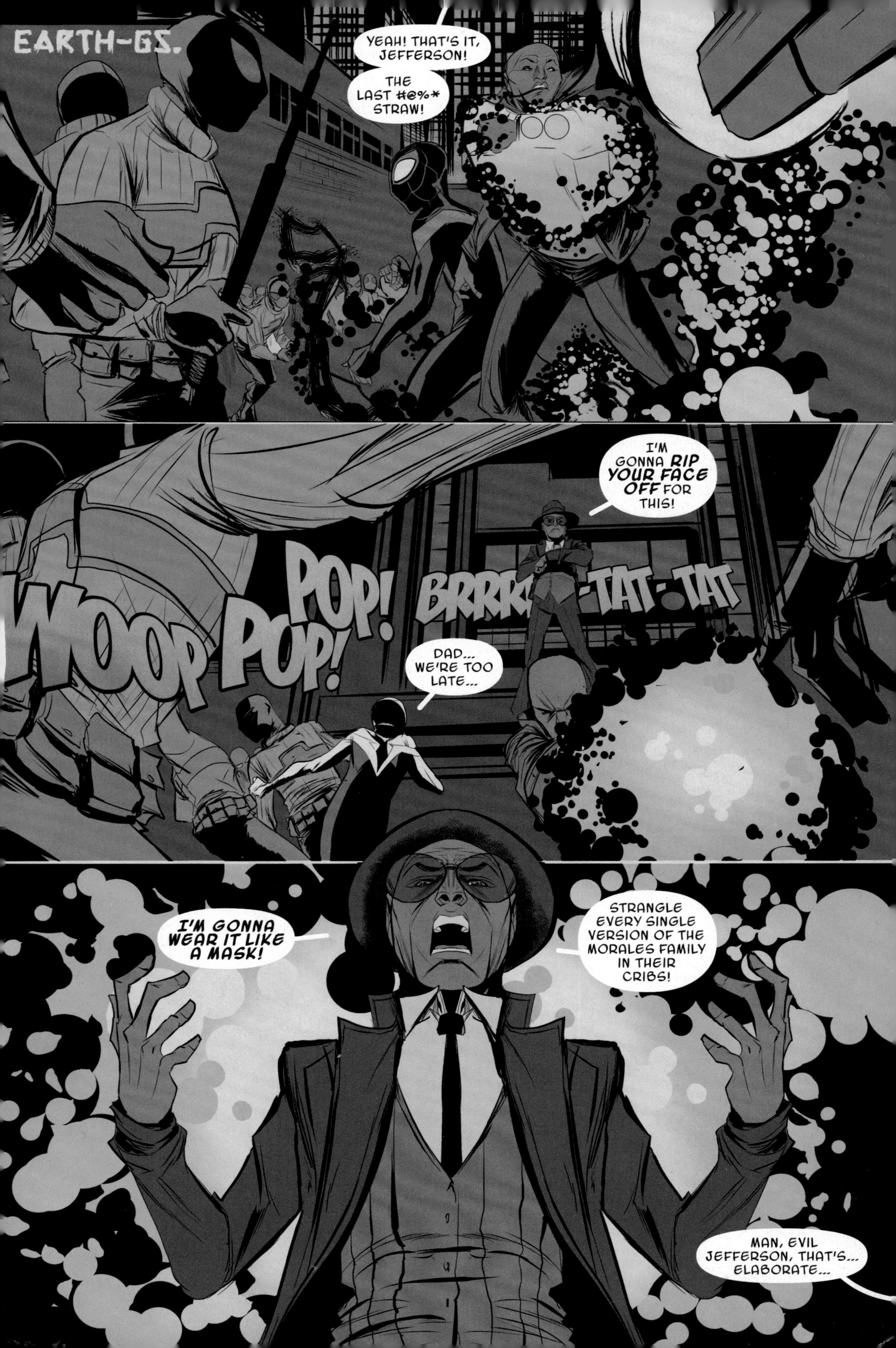
EARTH-GS.
YEAH! THAT'S IT, JEFFERSON!
THE LAST #@%* STRAW!
I'M GONNA RIP YOUR FACE OFF FOR THIS!
WOOP POP! POP! BRRRR-TAT-TAT
DAD... WE'RE TOO LATE...
I'M GONNA WEAR IT LIKE A MASK!
STRANGLE EVERY SINGLE VERSION OF THE MORALES FAMILY IN THEIR CRIBS!
MAN, EVIL JEFFERSON, THAT'S... ELABORATE...

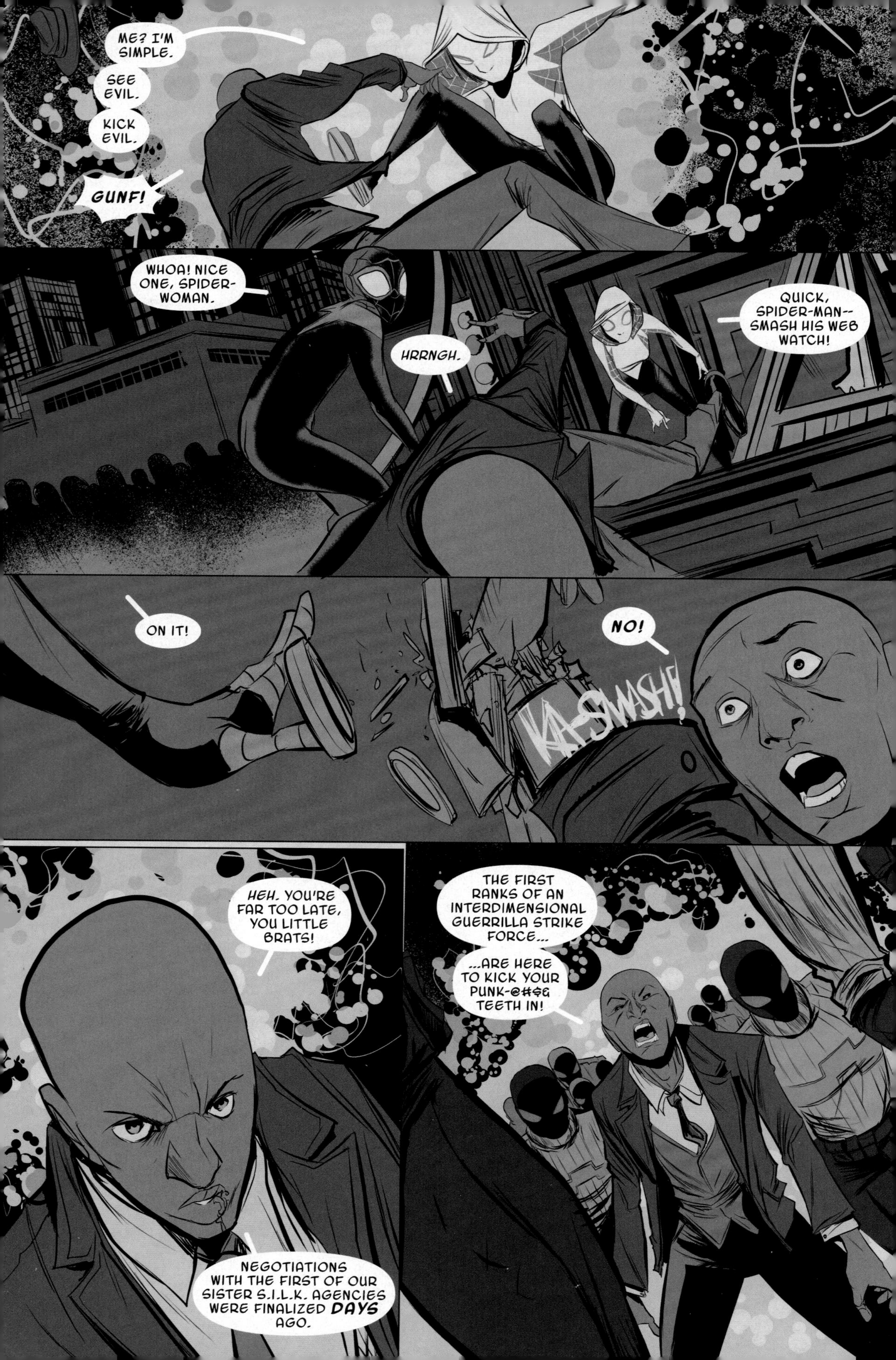
ME? I'M SIMPLE.
SEE EVIL.
KICK EVIL.
GUNF!
WHOA! NICE ONE, SPIDER-WOMAN.
HRRNGH.
QUICK, SPIDER-MAN-- SMASH HIS WEB WATCH!
ON IT!
NO!
KA-SWASH!
HEH. YOU'RE FAR TOO LATE, YOU LITTLE BRATS!
NEGOTIATIONS WITH THE FIRST OF OUR SISTER S.I.L.K. AGENCIES WERE FINALIZED DAYS AGO.
THE FIRST RANKS OF AN INTERDIMENSIONAL GUERRILLA STRIKE FORCE...
...ARE HERE TO KICK YOUR PUNK-@#$& TEETH IN!

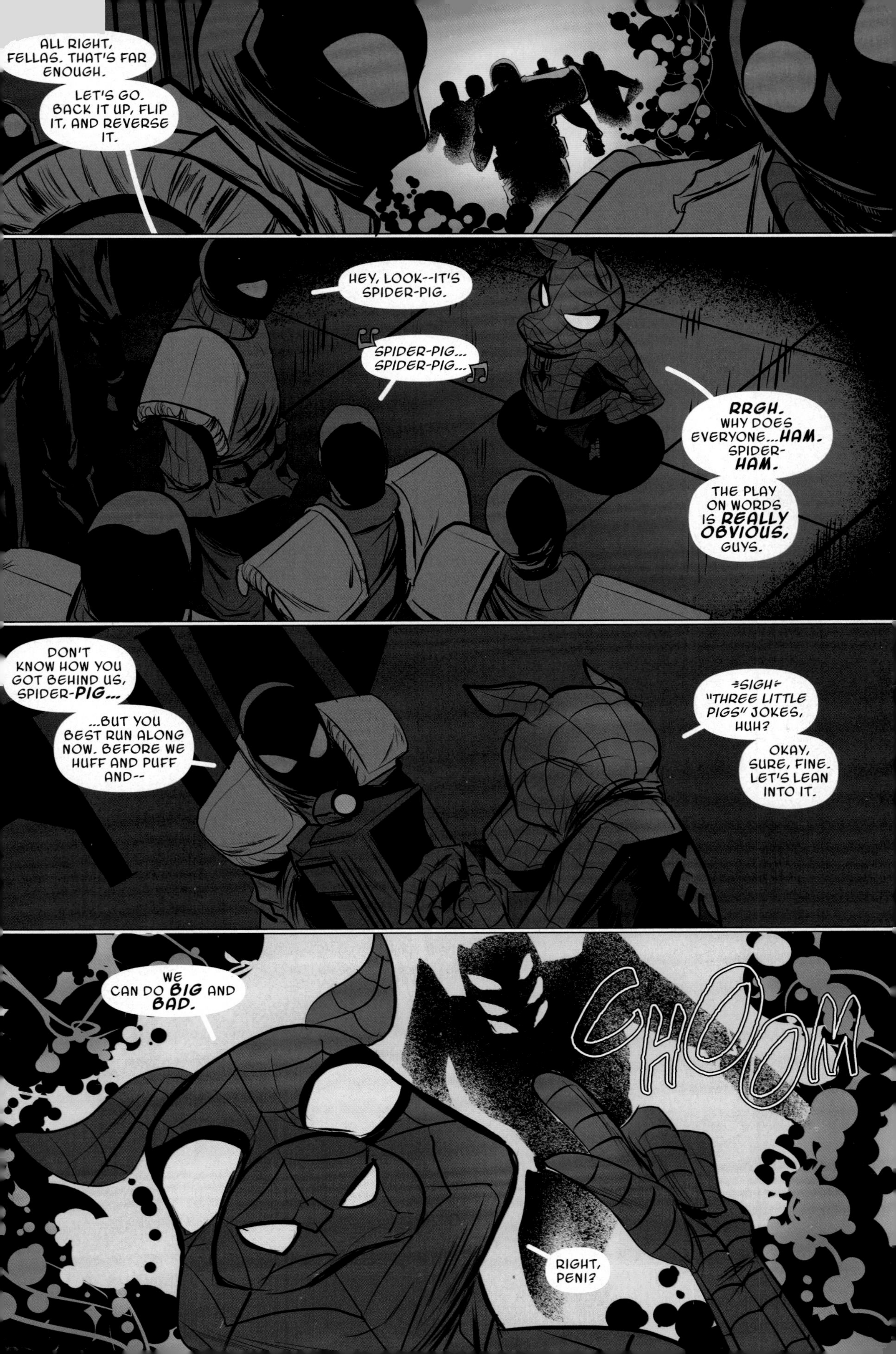

ALL RIGHT, FELLAS. THAT'S FAR ENOUGH.
LET'S GO. BACK IT UP, FLIP IT, AND REVERSE IT.
HEY, LOOK--IT'S SPIDER-PIG.
SPIDER-PIG... SPIDER-PIG...
RRGH. WHY DOES EVERYONE... HAM. SPIDER-HAM.
THE PLAY ON WORDS IS REALLY OBVIOUS, GUYS.
DON'T KNOW HOW YOU GOT BEHIND US, SPIDER-PIG...
...BUT YOU BEST RUN ALONG NOW. BEFORE WE HUFF AND PUFF AND--
=SIGH= "THREE LITTLE PIGS" JOKES, HUH?
OKAY, SURE, FINE. LET'S LEAN INTO IT.
WE CAN DO BIG AND BAD.
CHOOM
RIGHT, PENI?

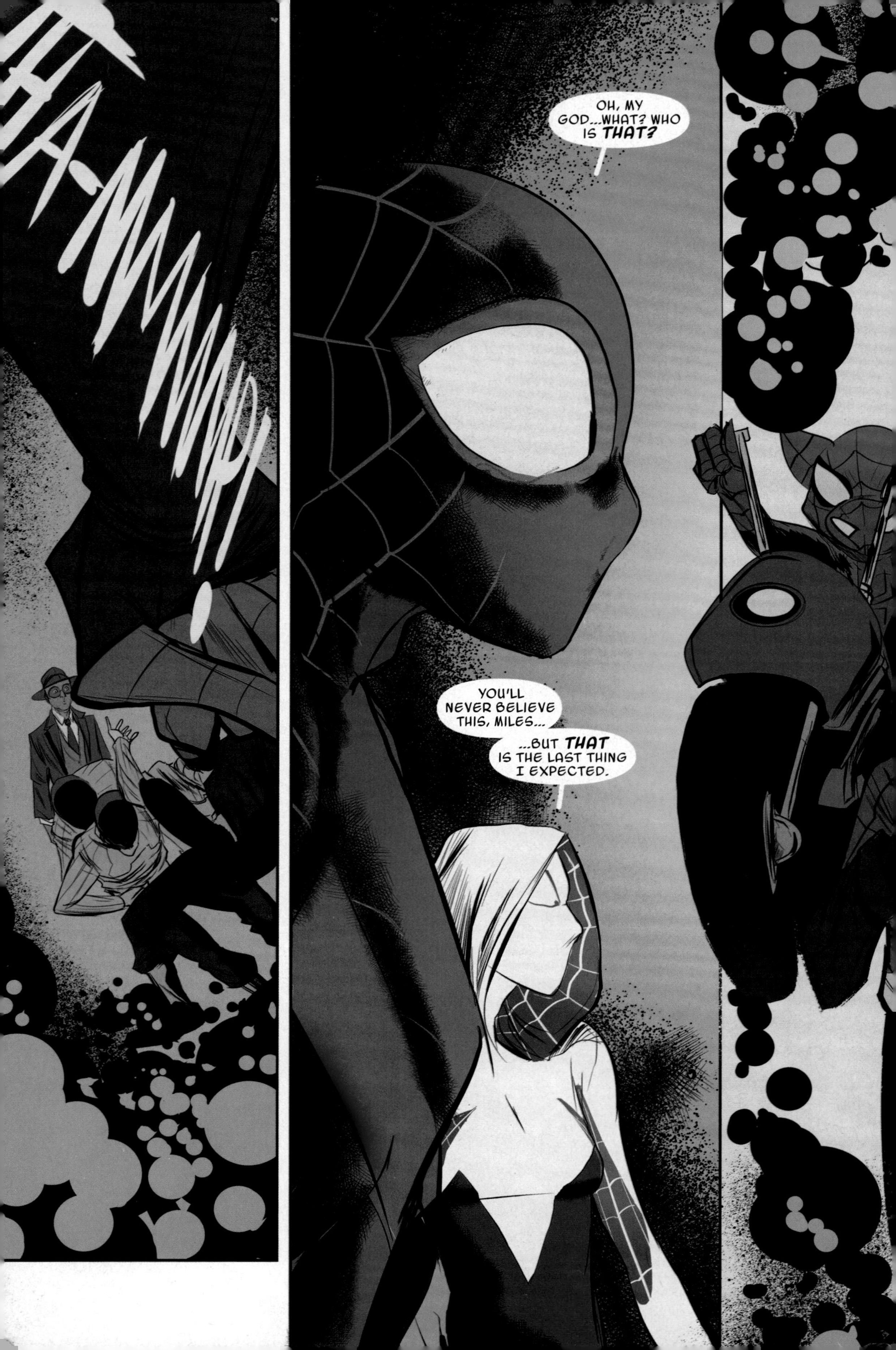
THA-WMMP!
OH, MY GOD...WHAT? WHO IS THAT?
YOU'LL NEVER BELIEVE THIS, MILES...
...BUT THAT IS THE LAST THING I EXPECTED.

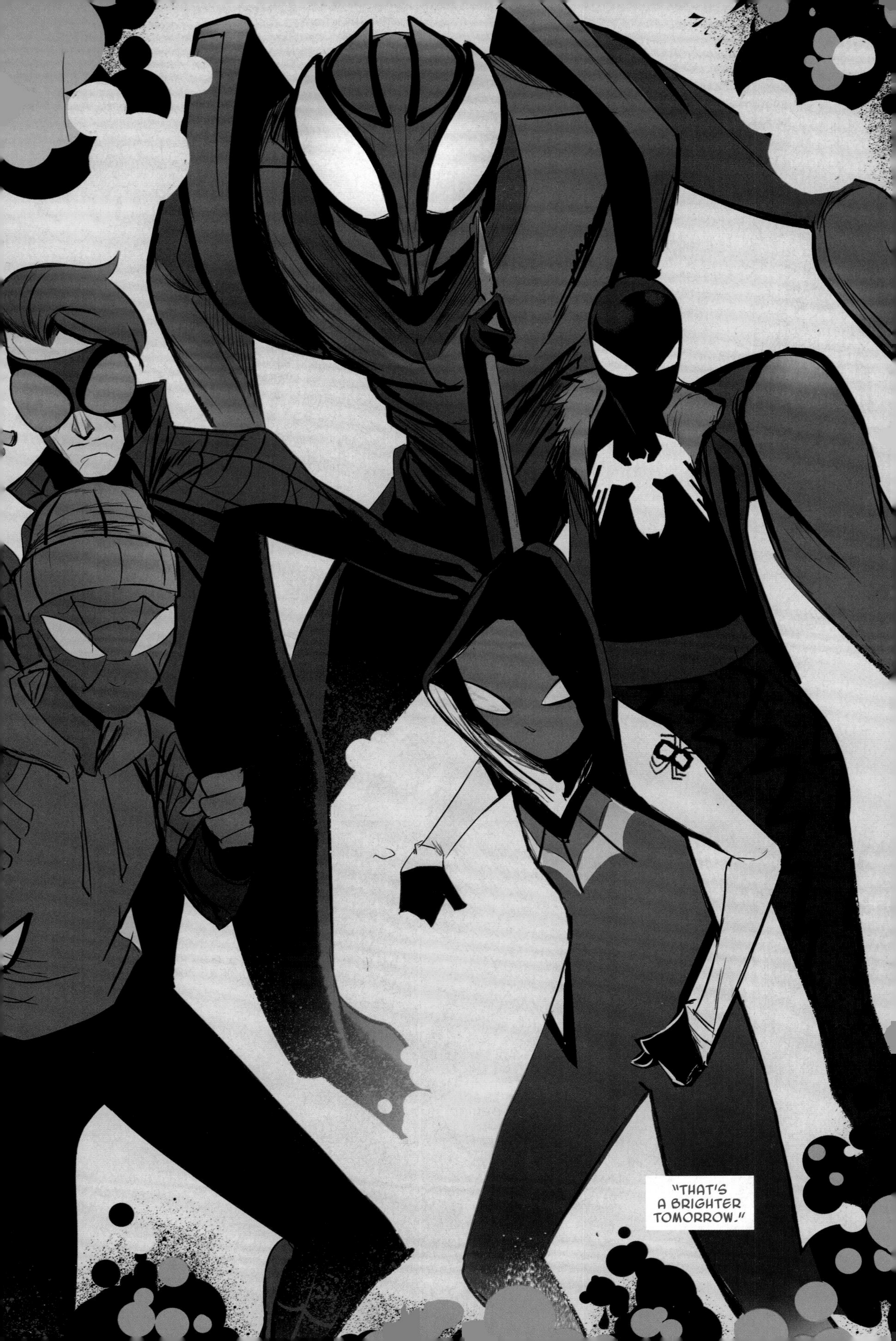
"THAT'S A BRIGHTER TOMORROW."

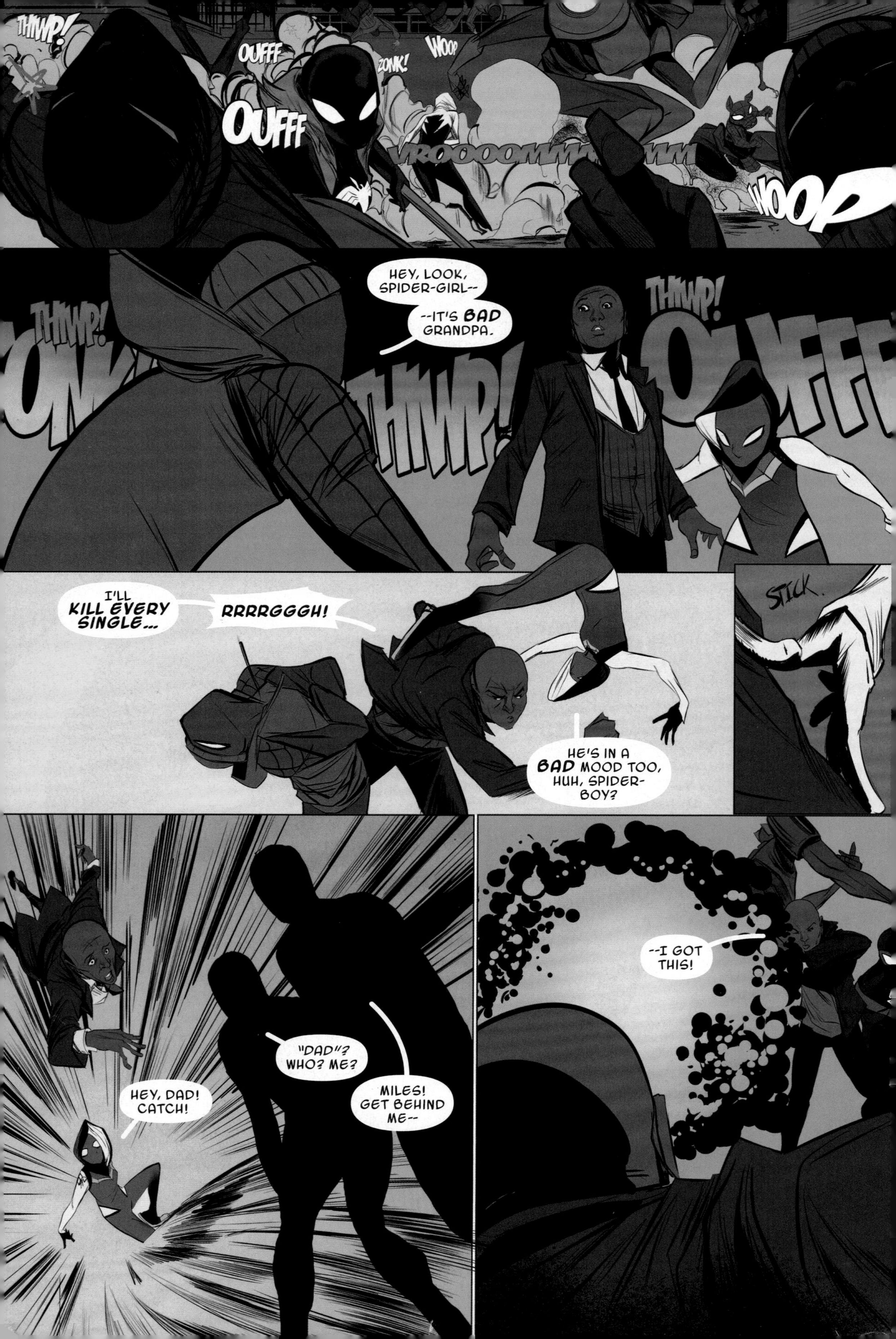
THWP!
OUFFF
ZONK!
WOOP
OUFFF
VROOOOMMMMMM
WOOP
HEY, LOOK, SPIDER-GIRL--
--IT'S BAD GRANDPA.
THWP!
THWP!
OUFFF
I'LL KILL EVERY SINGLE...
RRRRGGGH!
STICK.
HE'S IN A BAD MOOD TOO, HUH, SPIDER-BOY?
HEY, DAD! CATCH!
"DAD"? WHO? ME?
MILES! GET BEHIND ME--
--I GOT THIS!

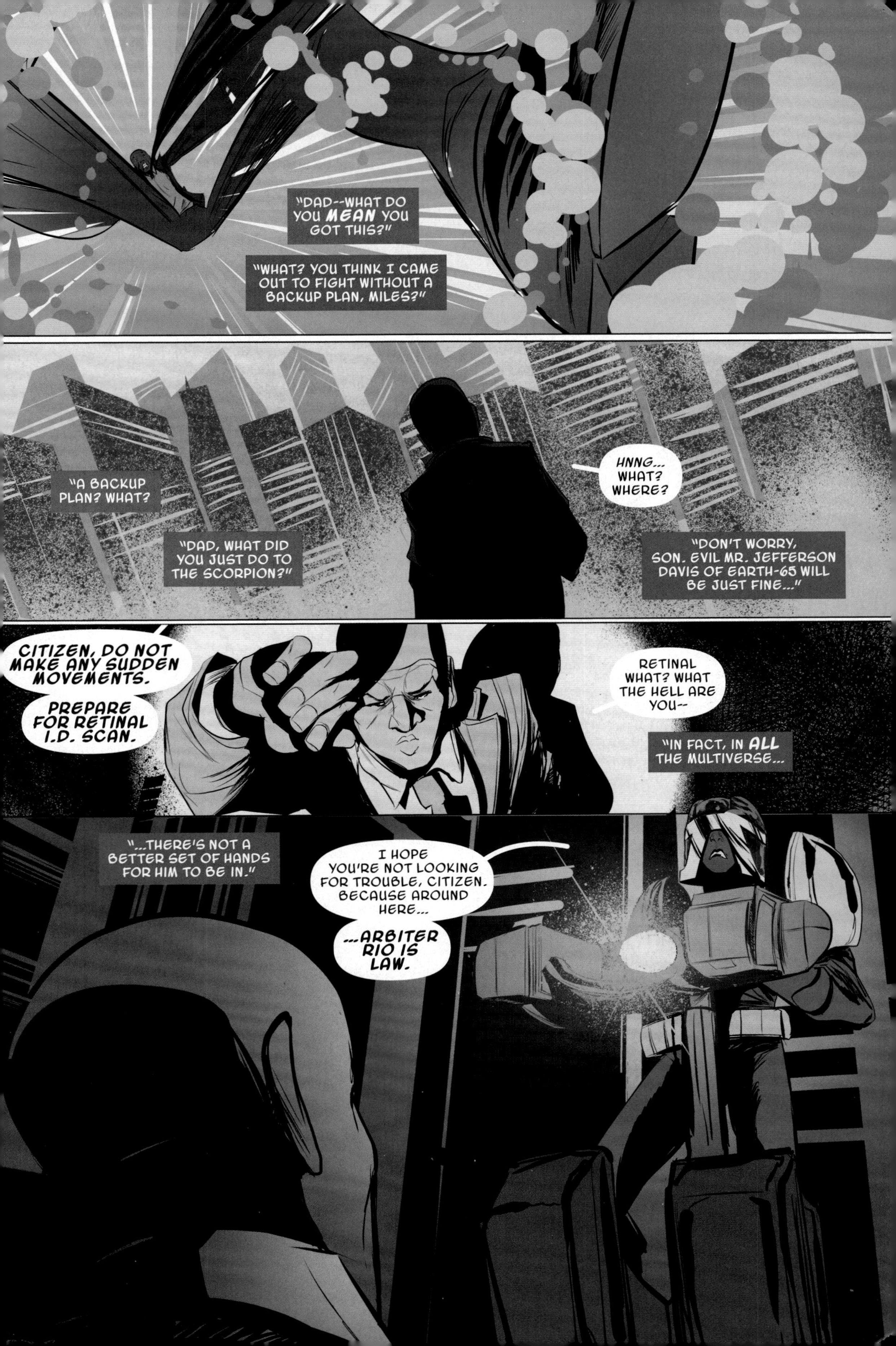
"DAD--WHAT DO YOU MEAN YOU GOT THIS?"
"WHAT? YOU THINK I CAME OUT TO FIGHT WITHOUT A BACKUP PLAN, MILES?"
"A BACKUP PLAN? WHAT?
HNNG... WHAT? WHERE?
"DAD, WHAT DID YOU JUST DO TO THE SCORPION?"
"DON'T WORRY, SON. EVIL MR. JEFFERSON DAVIS OF EARTH-65 WILL BE JUST FINE...
CITIZEN, DO NOT MAKE ANY SUDDEN MOVEMENTS.
PREPARE FOR RETINAL I.D. SCAN.
RETINAL WHAT? WHAT THE HELL ARE YOU--
"IN FACT, IN ALL THE MULTIVERSE...
"...THERE'S NOT A BETTER SET OF HANDS FOR HIM TO BE IN."
I HOPE YOU'RE NOT LOOKING FOR TROUBLE, CITIZEN. BECAUSE AROUND HERE...
...ARBITER RIO IS LAW.

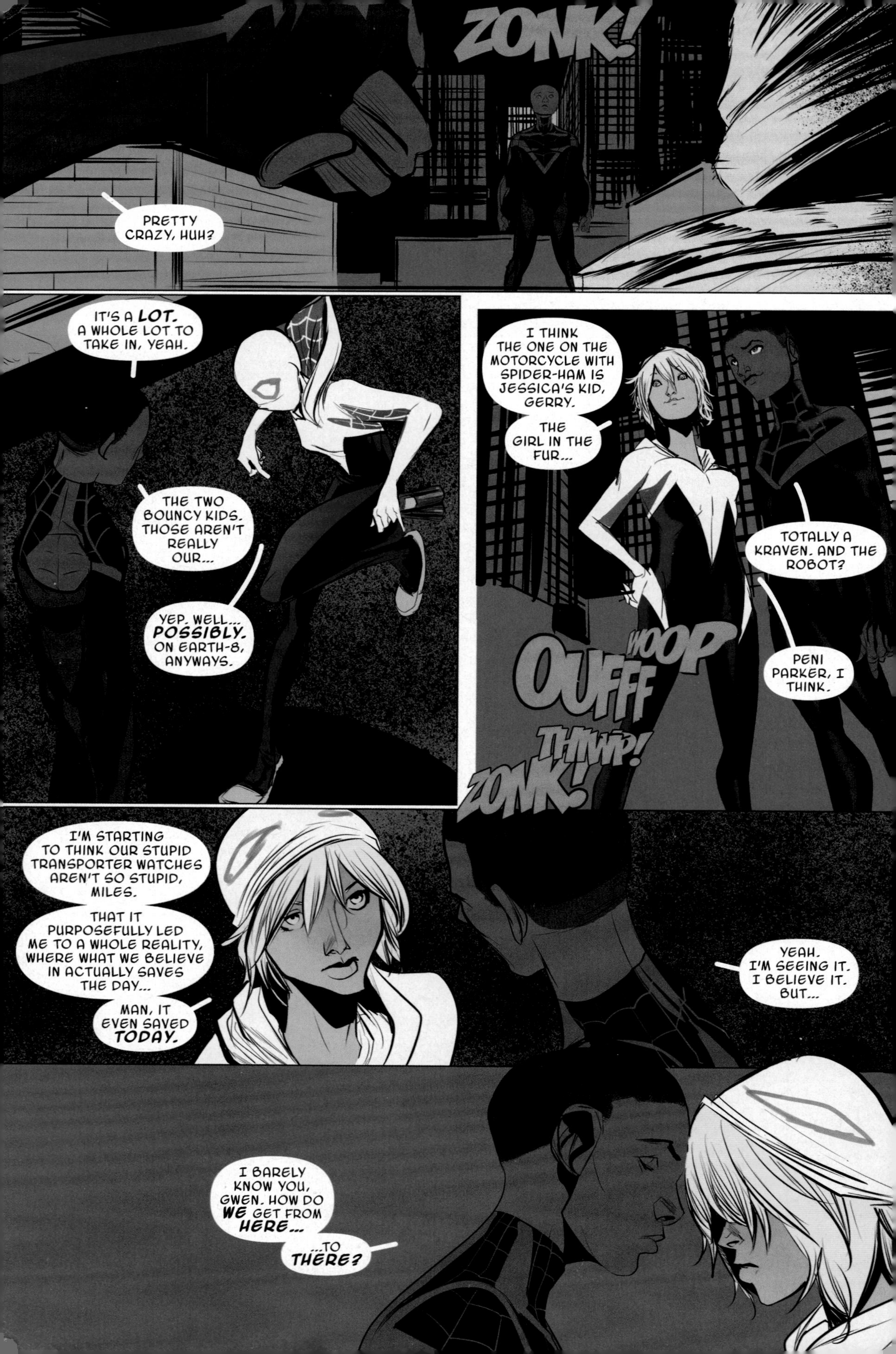
ZONK!
PRETTY CRAZY, HUH?
IT'S A LOT. A WHOLE LOT TO TAKE IN, YEAH.
THE TWO BOUNCY KIDS. THOSE AREN'T REALLY OUR...
YEP. WELL... POSSIBLY. ON EARTH-8, ANYWAYS.
I THINK THE ONE ON THE MOTORCYCLE WITH SPIDER-HAM IS JESSICA'S KID, GERRY.
THE GIRL IN THE FUR...
TOTALLY A KRAVEN. AND THE ROBOT?
PENI PARKER, I THINK.
WOOP
OUFFF
THWIP!
ZONK!
I'M STARTING TO THINK OUR STUPID TRANSPORTER WATCHES AREN'T SO STUPID, MILES.
THAT IT PURPOSEFULLY LED ME TO A WHOLE REALITY, WHERE WHAT WE BELIEVE IN ACTUALLY SAVES THE DAY...
MAN, IT EVEN SAVED TODAY.
YEAH. I'M SEEING IT. I BELIEVE IT. BUT...
I BARELY KNOW YOU, GWEN. HOW DO WE GET FROM HERE...
...TO THERE?

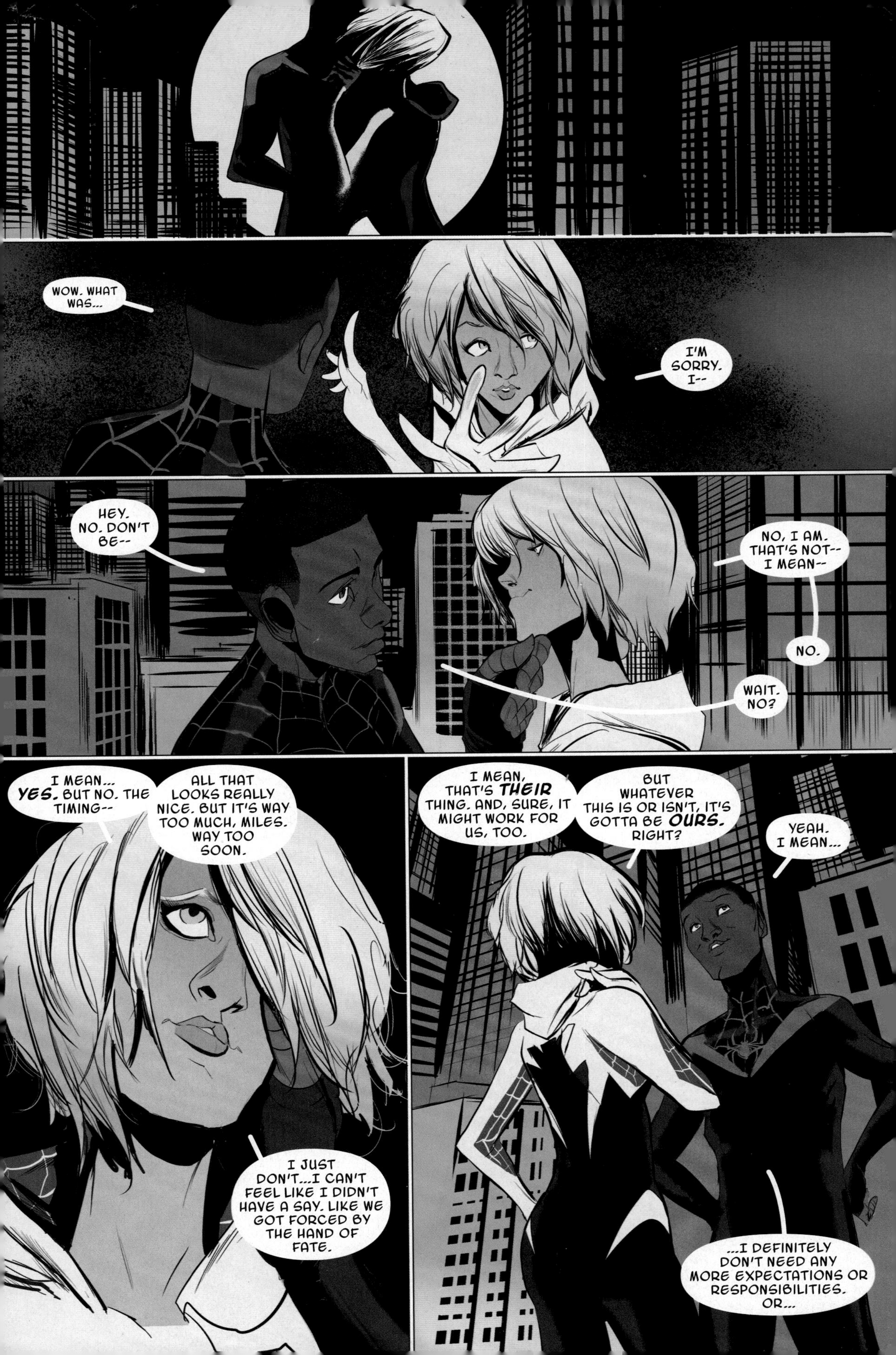
WOW. WHAT WAS...
I'M SORRY. I--
HEY. NO. DON'T BE--
NO, I AM. THAT'S NOT-- I MEAN--
NO.
WAIT. NO?
I MEAN... YES. BUT NO. THE TIMING--
ALL THAT LOOKS REALLY NICE. BUT IT'S WAY TOO MUCH, MILES. WAY TOO SOON.
I JUST DON'T...I CAN'T FEEL LIKE I DIDN'T HAVE A SAY. LIKE WE GOT FORCED BY THE HAND OF FATE.
I MEAN, THAT'S THEIR THING. AND, SURE, IT MIGHT WORK FOR US, TOO.
BUT WHATEVER THIS IS OR ISN'T, IT'S GOTTA BE OURS. RIGHT?
YEAH. I MEAN...
...I DEFINITELY DON'T NEED ANY MORE EXPECTATIONS OR RESPONSIBILITIES. OR...

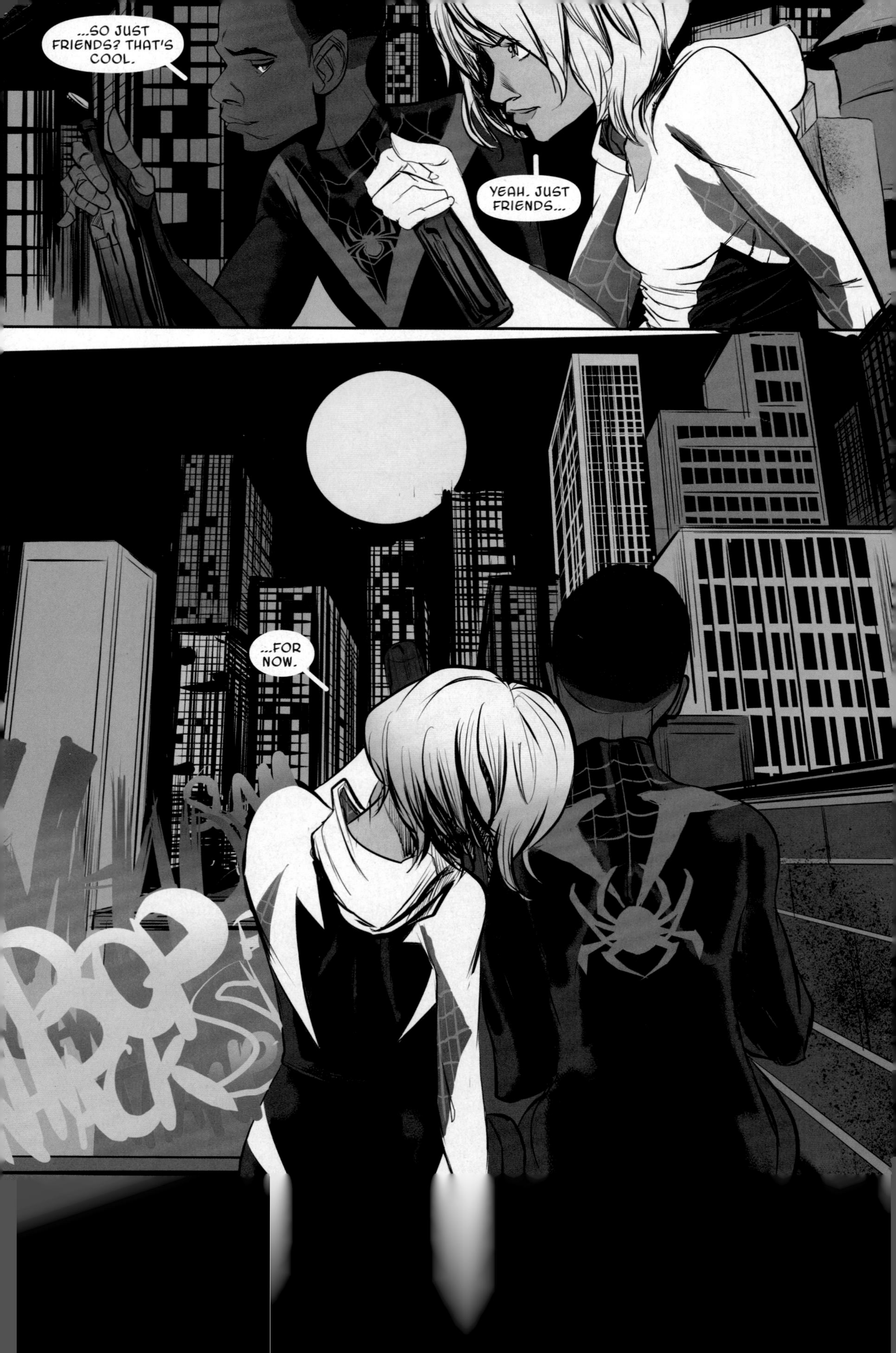
...SO JUST FRIENDS? THAT'S COOL.
YEAH. JUST FRIENDS...
...FOR NOW.

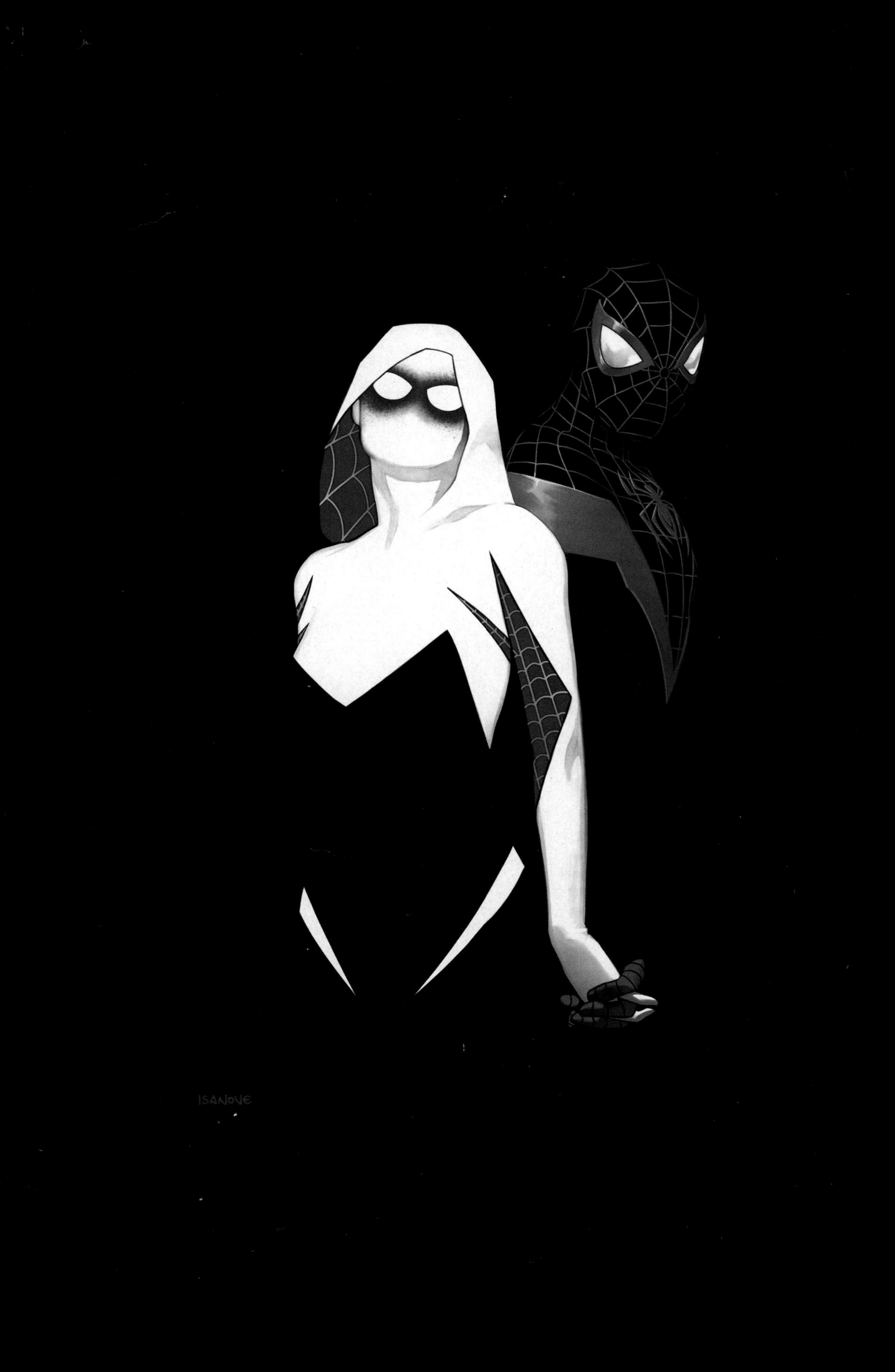
ISANOVE

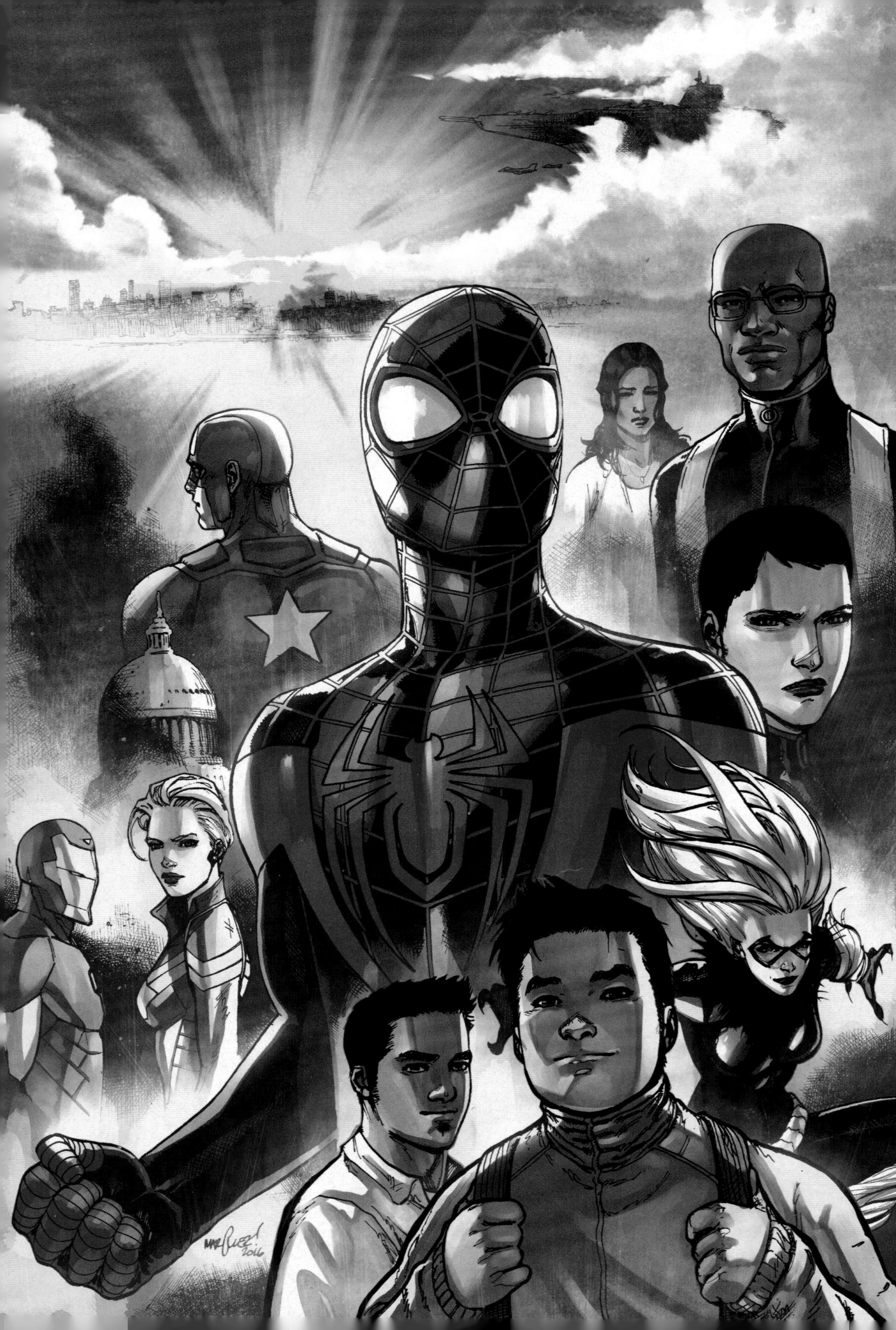

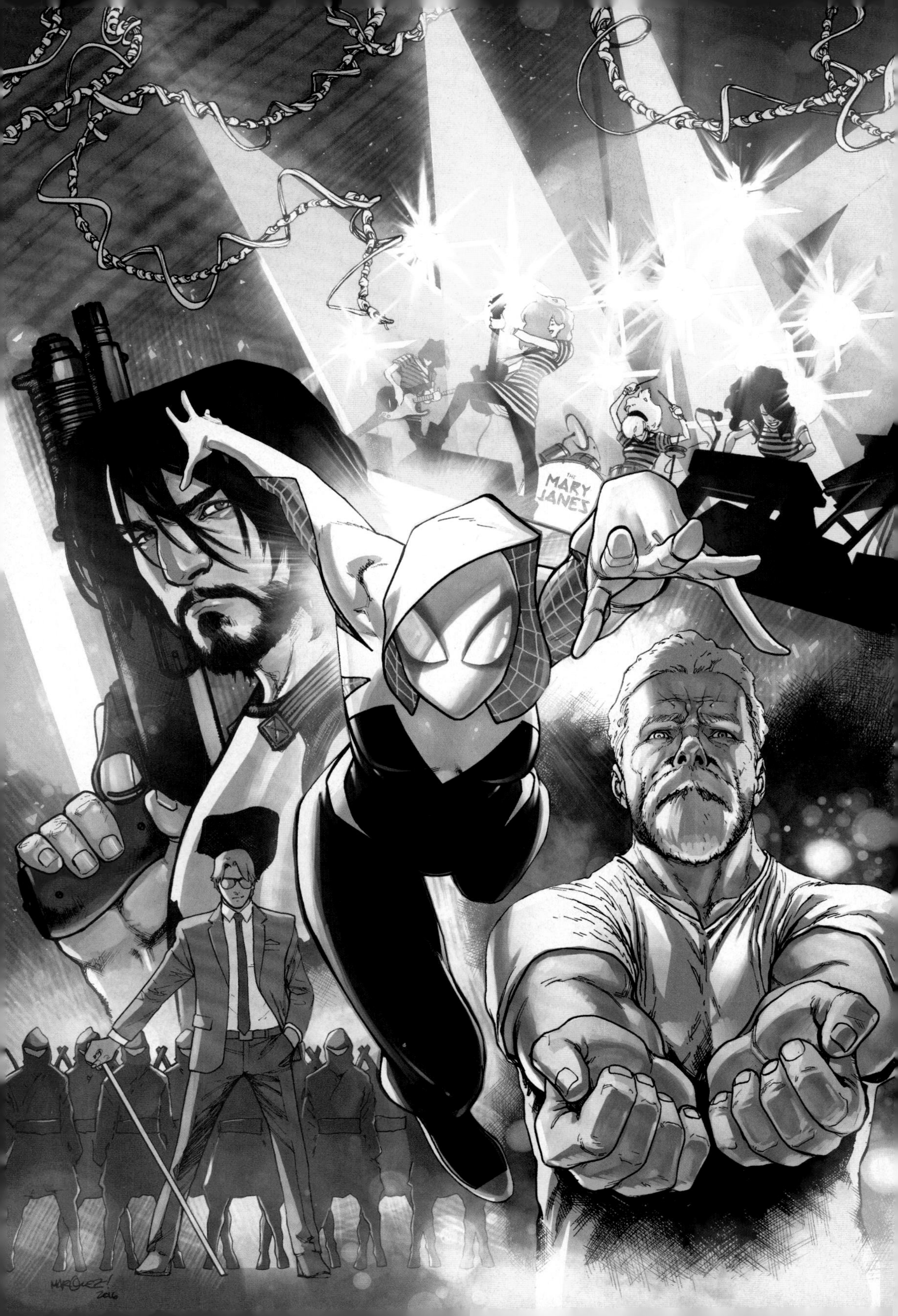
THE MARY JANES
MARQUEZ! 2016

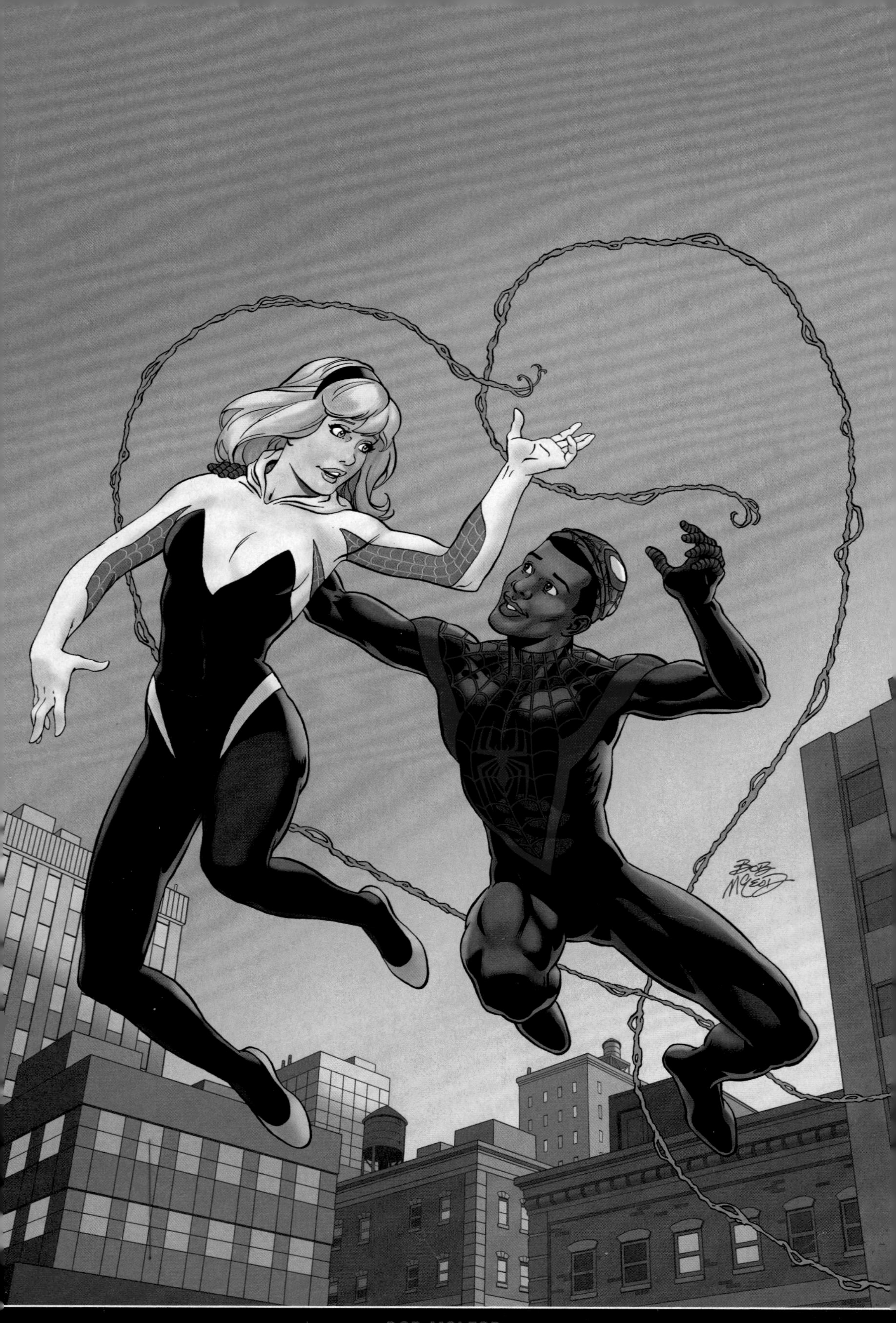
BOB McLEOD

BOB MCLEOD
SPIDER-MAN 12 CLASSIC VARIANT

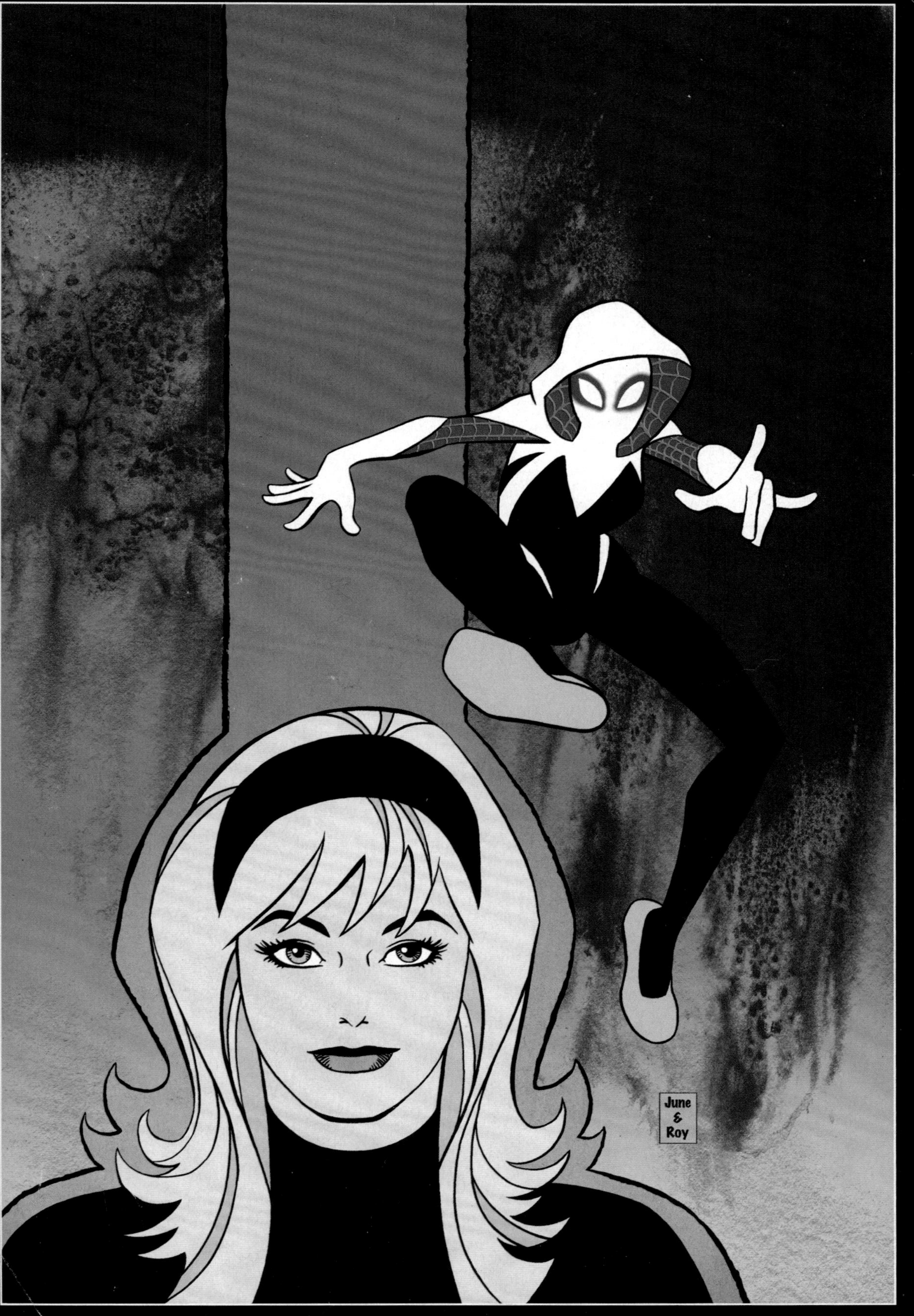
June & Roy

JUNE BRIGMAN & ROY RICHARDSON
SPIDER-GWEN 16 CLASSIC VARIANT

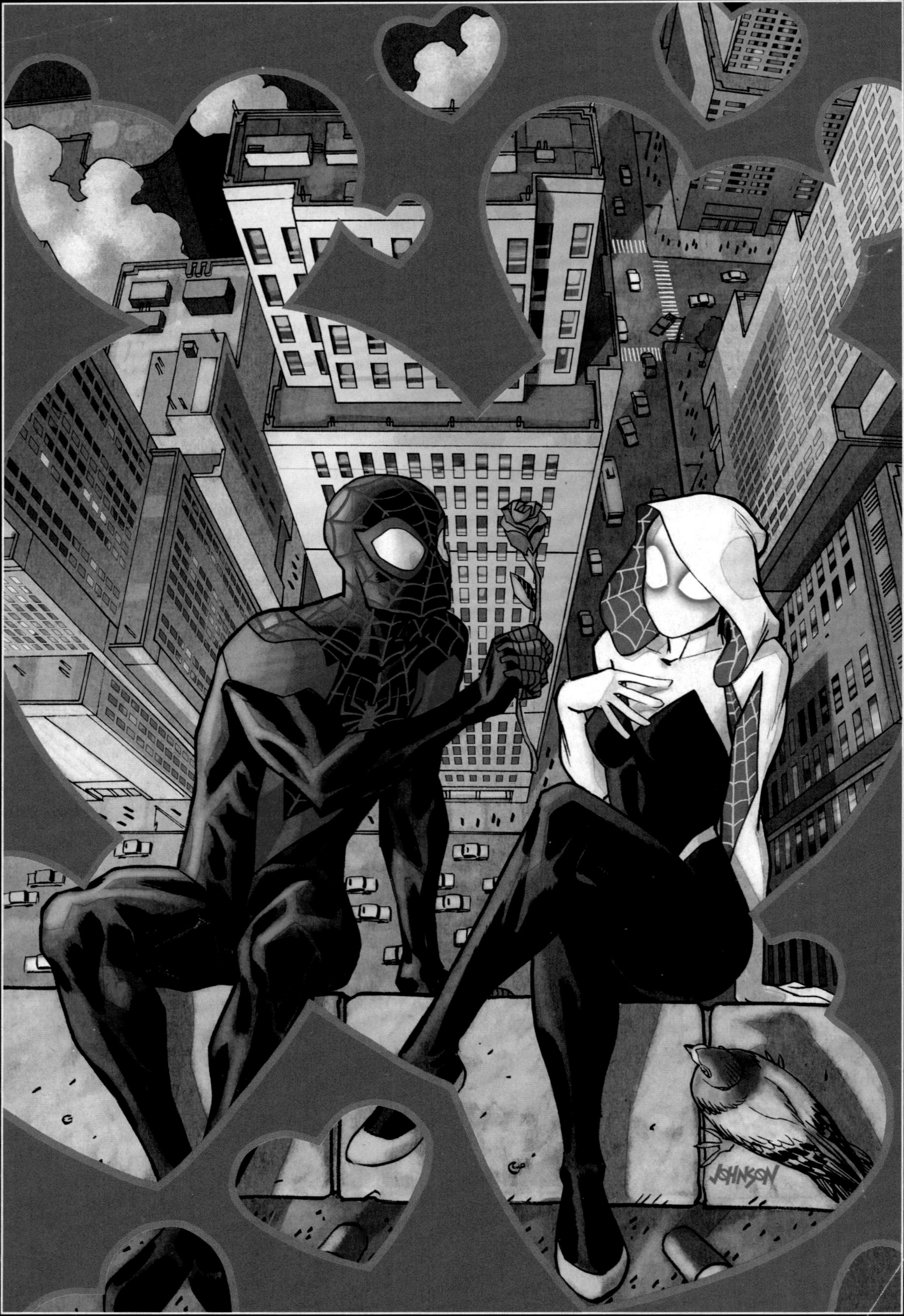
JOHNSON

DAVE JOHNSON
SPIDER-GWEN 16 VARIANT

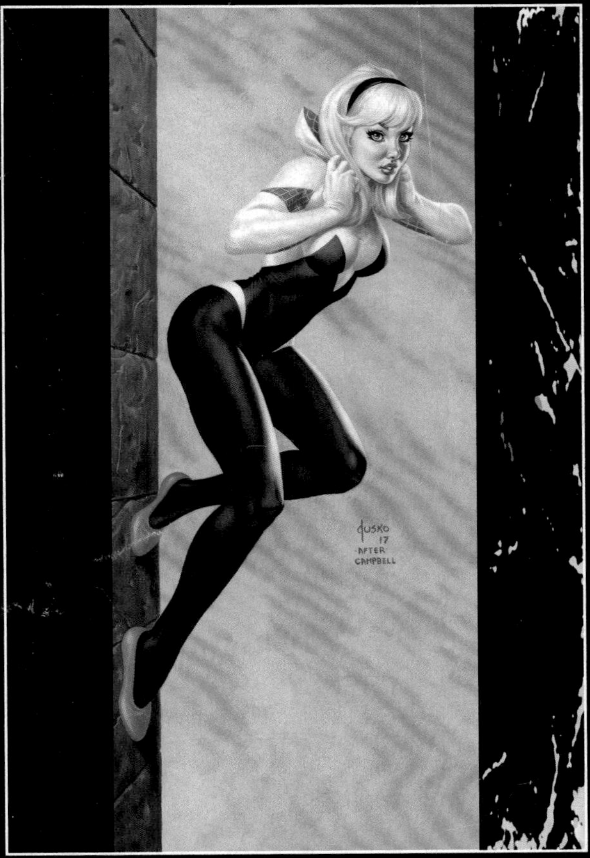
JUSKO
17
AFTER
CAMPBELL

JOE JUSKO
SPIDER-GWEN 17 CORNER BOX VARIANT

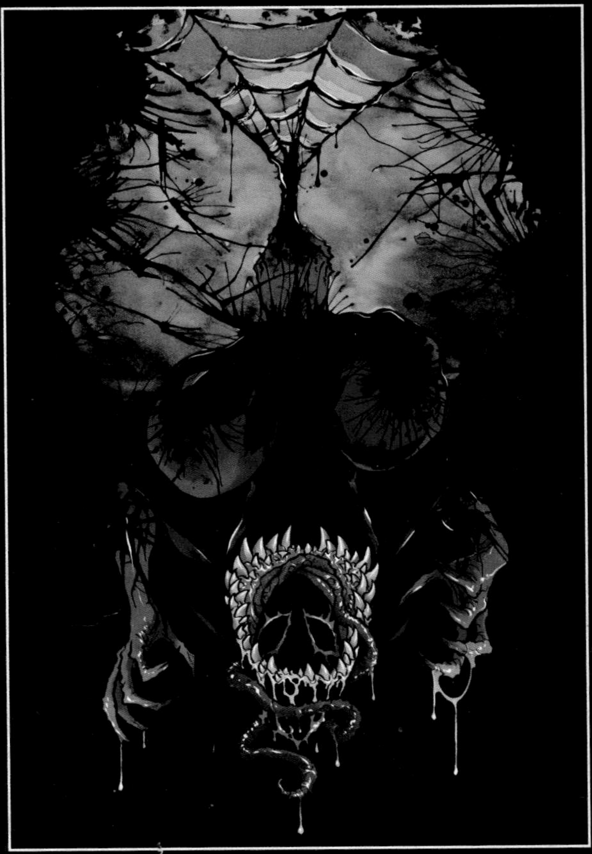

SOPHIE CAMPBELL
SPIDER-GWEN 18 VENOMIZED VARIANT

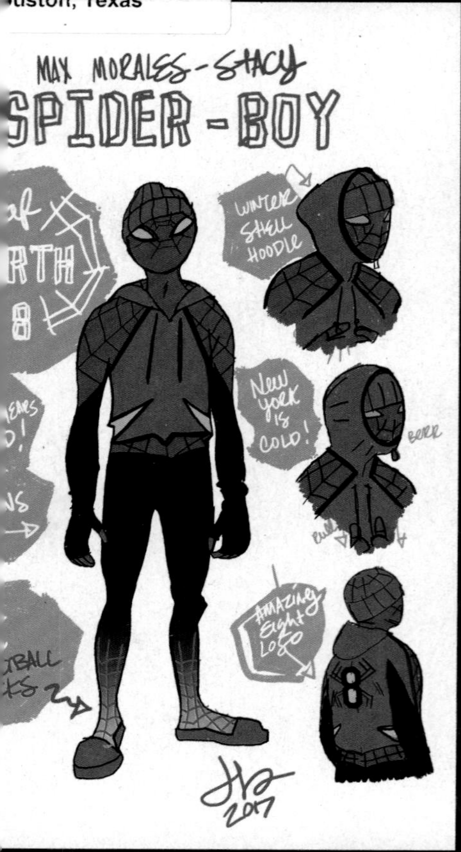
MAX MORALES-STACY
SPIDER-BOY
WINTER SHELL HOODIE
NEW YORK IS COLD!
BRRR
AMAZING EIGHT LOGO
2017

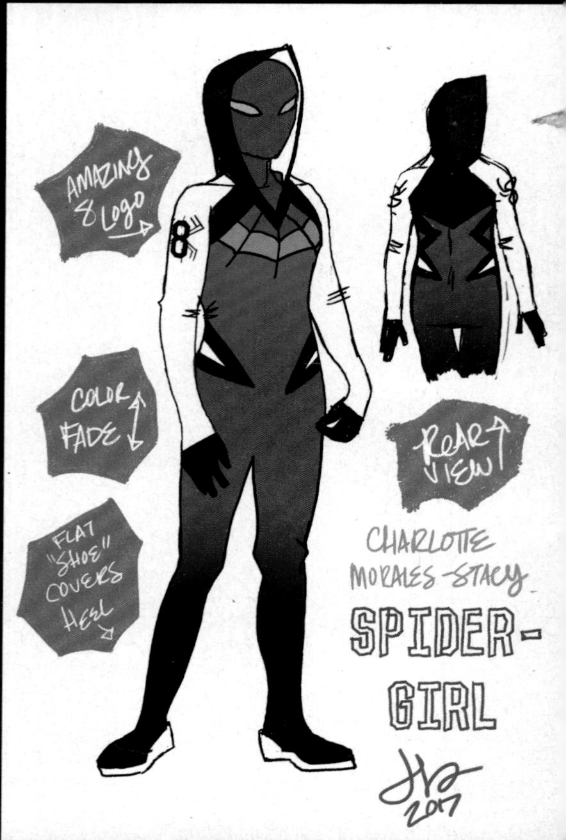
AMAZING 8 LOGO
COLOR FADE
FLAT "SHOE" COVERS HEEL
REAR VIEW
CHARLOTTE MORALES-STACY
SPIDER-GIRL
2017

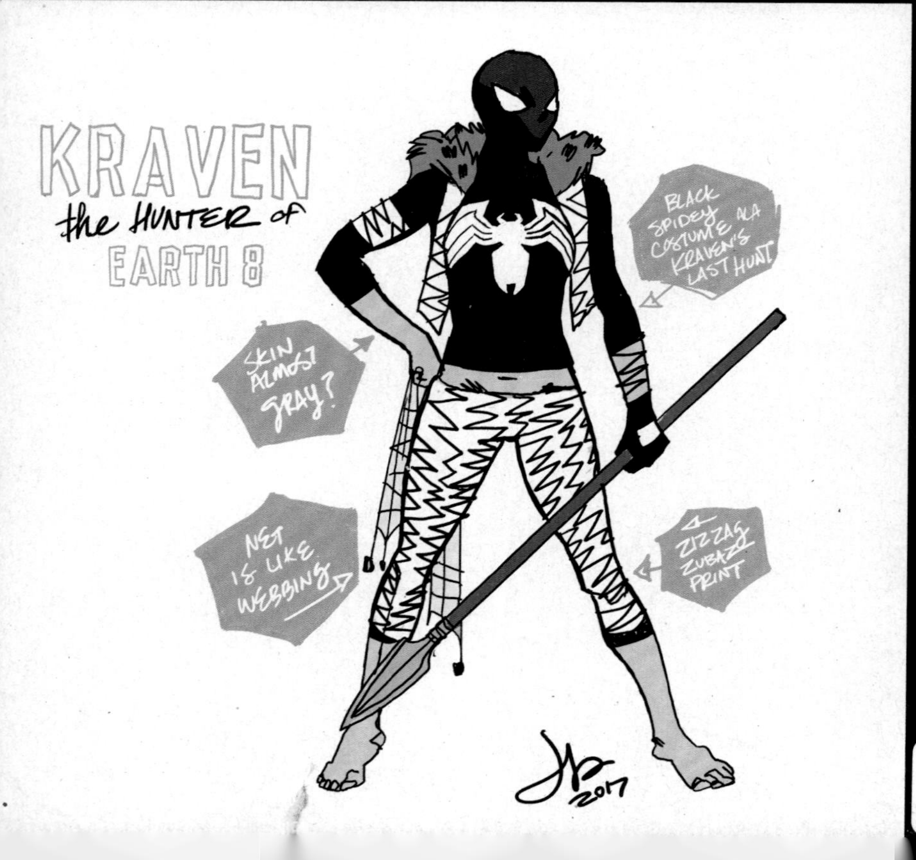
KRAVEN
the HUNTER of
EARTH 8
BLACK SPIDEY COSTUME ALA KRAVEN'S LAST HUNT
SKIN ALMOST GRAY?
NET IS LIKE WEBBING
ZIGZAG ZUBAZ PRINT
2017